The Invisible Constitution of Politics

As social practices now frequently extend beyond national boundaries, experiences and expectations about fair and legitimate politics have become increasingly fragmented. Our ability to understand and interpret others and to tolerate difference, rather than overcome diversity, is therefore at risk. This book focuses on the contested meanings of norms in a world of increasing international encounters. The author argues that cultural practices are less visible than organisational practices, but are constitutive for politics and need to be understood and empirically 'accounted' for. Comparing four elite groups in Europe, Antje Wiener shows how this invisible constitution of politics matters. By comparing individual interpretations of norms such as democracy and human rights, she shows how they can mean different things, even to frequently travelling elite groups.

ANTJE WIENER is Professor of Politics and International Relations in the Department of European Studies and Modern Languages at the University of Bath.

The Invisible Constitution of Politics

Contested Norms and International Encounters

ANTJE WIENER
University of Bath

CAMBRIDGE UNIVERSITY PRESS
Cambridge, New York, Melbourne, Madrid, Cape Town, Singapore, São Paulo, Delhi

Cambridge University Press
The Edinburgh Building, Cambridge CB2 8RU, UK

Published in the United States of America by Cambridge University Press, New York

www.cambridge.org
Information on this title: www.cambridge.org/9780521895965

First published 2008

Printed in the United Kingdom at the University Press, Cambridge

A catalogue record for this publication is available from the British Library

ISBN 978-0-521-89596-5 hardback

Contents

Tables and graphs

Tables

Graphs

Preface

This book's focus on meanings of norms, frictions between interpretations and subsequent conflicts among *inter*national actors reflects a sign of the times of extending social practices beyond the boundaries of modern nation-states. It is likely to be lost on those who are not part of the process. In turn, those who participate in global travel and discussion usually neither move in large stable groups, nor spend much time thinking about those left 'at home'. As a result, experiences and expectations about fair, just and legitimate politics become increasingly fragmented. With more movement yet less time to ponder and probe, the potential for understanding the interpretation of others and the ability to tolerate difference is at risk. In fact, cultural differences often either remain unnoticed or turn into the invisible yet influential elephant in the room. This book's research on contested interpretations of fundamental norms addresses the phenomenon of a gap between shared perceptions of what is just and fair, on the one hand, and individual experience, on the other. It proposes to overcome the gap by focusing on cultural validation as the way in which meaning-in-use is enacted.

The desire to explore this gap's impact on politics emerged through travels across the Atlantic and across the Channel. In the light of a growing web of contracts, agreements and treaties in the global realm which appear to develop more constitutional quality than ever before, on the one hand, and the interrelated process of contesting that very constitutional quality in international encounters, on the other, finding out what lies underneath and beyond the formal validity of norms and the multiple reactions it inspires appears a worthwhile project. The first conceptual discussions with a view towards carrying out empirical research on this matter occurred during a walk up to Santa Brigida on a sunny morning in Tuscany with Thomas Risse and Tanja Börzel, seven years back. At the time, we were not only struggling with the invisibility of it all but fell victims to a higher force when our deliberations were abruptly put to an end by a fierce swarm of bees. The idea of tackling the 'invisible constitution' stuck despite the circumstances. At one workshop, one of so many occasions where the research was discussed, Detlef Sprinz commented, 'why not call it the invisible constitution?' The title prevailed and here it is, *The Invisible Constitution of Politics*.

The book's adoption of a bifocal analysis that elaborates on the link between empirical and normative research inevitably brought its author to the limits of what an education in political science, albeit multicultural, had to offer. The inspiration for a critical approach to international politics goes way back to my first encounter with political science as a student of Volker Finke at high school in Nienburg/Weser. I faced a seemingly overwhelming amount of empirical data but was sustained in my endeavours by the support and expertise of many colleagues and friends, especially Jens Schneider, Anne Huffschmid, Thomas Diez and Raingard Esser, and I would like to thank them all. The discussions with Jim Tully played no small part in fuelling my stamina to complete the manuscript and place it within the larger frame of things. It is to him that I owe special thanks. Last but not least, neighbours in Killyleagh repeatedly confronted me with the hard choice between going sailing or sticking to my writing routine. By leaving the excitement of races to others, from time to time, it is now possible to answer the question repeatedly posed over the garden fence – 'Is your book done yet?' – in the affirmative.

A project requiring as much empirical research as this is impossible to carry out without manifold support. I especially thank all interviewees for sparing the time for the interviews. In addition I would like to thank Henning Dahl-Arnold and Daniel Curran for transcriptions; Uwe Puetter for research assistance; Armin von Bogdandy, Jo Shaw and Joe Weiler for facilitating most interesting exchanges on constitutionalism in the different academic cultures of Germany, the UK and the USA; Dorothee Wiegand for patient and repeated advice on the quantitative aspects of the evaluation; and Ellen Immergut for discussions about 'soft institutions' when we were neighbours at the Hanse Institute of Advanced Studies (and Michael Zürn for bringing me there). For reading and commenting on either the entire manuscript or parts of it, I would like to thank Mathias Albert, Martin Binder, Jutta Brunnée, Nicole Deitelhoff, Raingard Esser, Benjamin Herborth, Anne Huffschmid, Andrea Lenschow, Aidan McGarry, Heinrich Mintrop,

Uwe Puetter, Jens Schneider, Guido Schwellnus, Jo Shaw and Jim Tully. Last but by no means least, I am very grateful for the helpful comments of two anonymous referees, which were crucial for arriving at the final version of the book. For many discussions on norms, I would like to thank my graduate students in Belfast, Bath and Trento as well as the uncountable workshop and conference participants over the years (many probably still wondering whether the 'constitution' might ever become 'visible'). For language editing and formatting, my thanks go to Kathleen Claussen. For excellent advice with regard to the interview evaluation, I am very thankful to Jan Kruse and for guidance and support in the publishing process, my warm thanks go to John Haslam as well as Carrie Cheek, Jo Breeze and Jacqueline French at Cambridge. For financial and logistic support, I would like to thank the British Academy, the Hanse Institute for Advanced Studies, the Social and Legal Studies Association, the University Association for Contemporary European Studies, the Science Center for Social Research in Berlin, the 6th Framework Programme's Network of Excellence CONNEX, the Economic and Social Research Council, the Institute of European Studies and the School of Politics, International Studies and Philosophy at the Queen's University of Belfast, and the Department of ESML at the University of Bath for providing the opportunity to finalise the project following the move over from Northern Ireland. The book would not have been completed without emotional support. I thank my friends, especially Bernd Bittermann, Raingard Esser, Heinrich Mintrop, Martina Rüllmann, Carsten Tiedeken and Dorothee Wiegand, and dedicate the book to my parents Winfriede and Christian Wiener.

Berkeley, 23 March 2008

1 | *Introduction*

Understanding is always against a background of what is taken for granted, just relied on. ... Our understanding resides first of all in our practices.

(Taylor 1993: 47, 50)

This book seeks to make a contribution to *inter*national politics.[1] Following the literatures on economic and societal globalisation, transnationalisation, constitutionalisation, civilisation and bureaucratic institutionalisation, a new constitutional quality can be observed in the international realm. This quality is constituted by processes of international interaction. It is special since its organisational roots and normative substance cannot be derived from either the modern nation-state or an international organisation. This particular constitutional quality thus lies 'in between' (Curtin 1996) different conceptions of a political entity. It entails norms, rules and principles that guide politics and law and that are constituted through social practices. However, with the growing influence of this constitutional quality through a web of treaties within the United Nations (UN), European Union (EU), Mercosur[2] and North American Free Trade Agreement (NAFTA) contexts, and in the light of political and social change on a global scale, the quality is increasingly contested (Koskenniemi 2007). Thus, the reform of the UN system involves a debate that addresses not only the UN institutions but the very future of international law. And, the EU treaties' periodical

---

[1] Note that the italics indicate the consideration of relations between different national entities and/or their representatives. This literal application of the term indicates the constitutive role of nations in the United Nations system of civilised nations; see, e.g., Habermas 2004: 117. It stands in contrast to the term '*trans*national' indicating a situation in which national boundaries are blurred.

[2] Mercosur represents an agreement on economic collaboration between South American countries. It is a regional trade agreement signed in 1991 between Brazil, Argentina, Uruguay and Paraguay as full members, and Bolivia, Chile, Columbia, Ecuador and Peru as associate members, while Venezuela is awaiting the ratification of its membership agreement.

update and revisions have, for the first time in five decades, triggered an intensive constitutional debate. Both processes sustain the notion of contested norms, rules and principles in the international realm.

While contestation is routine in both politics and law, albeit to varying degrees, the scope and impact of these debates have changed in a way that justifies speaking of a critical juncture in international politics.[3] In the European context this critical juncture is exemplified by a discourse which addresses a radical turn away from the routinised step-by-step approach to treaty reform that used to set the pace over roughly the past five decades. This discourse includes such terms as 'failure' and 'obsolescence' with regard to the EU constitutional treaty referendums in 2004 (Daase 2005). In the UN context, it is exemplified by a discourse of 'broken' system (Ikenberry and Slaughter 2006; Zürn, Binder, Ecker-Ehrhardt and Radtke 2007) and 'paradigmatic change' following the UN reform in 2005 (Wolf 2007). International Relations scholars have raised the question of whether reform of the UN system is possible at all, and, if so, what is at stake. In turn, European integration scholars have asked whether integration theory might be obsolete, while the public discourse represents a heated debate over the very constitutional quality that remains in the 'Reform Treaty'[4] which replaced the 'Constitutional Treaty'[5] in June 2007.

Research questions

While it could be argued that the conflict over how to interpret treaties and the impact of their reforms should be readily resolvable with reference to the respective written documents themselves, the on-going

---

[3] On the definition of 'critical juncture', see Bulmer and Burch 2001.

[4] The Reform Treaty titled 'Draft Treaty Amending the Treaty of European Union and the Treaty Establishing the European Community' was agreed at the European Council Meeting on 23 June 2007; CIG 10/7, Brussels 23 July 2007. For the document, see: www.fco.gov.uk/servlet/Front?pagename=OpenMarket/Xcelerate/ShowPage&c=Page&cid=1139992024177 (accessed on 25 September 2007).

[5] The document is titled *Draft Treaty Establishing a Constitution for Europe* and will henceforth be referred to as 'Constitutional Treaty' in distinction from the 'Reform Treaty'; since both documents are draft treaties, this distinction appears most appropriate. The text produced by the European Convention is titled *Draft Treaty Establishing a Constitution for Europe*, see CONV 850/03, Brussels, 18 July 2003. For the final document, see *Treaty Establishing a Constitution for Europe*, Rome, 29 October 2004.

contestation in academic writings, politics and public debate casts doubt on such a suggestion. It could be argued, therefore, that the internationalisation of the global realm[6] is likely to develop into a deeper problem for international politics and law, since international interaction stands to increase rather than decline in the future. The first question of this book takes these developments into account and asks the general question of how to understand international interaction in relation to global norms?

Take, for example, the current dispute about whether the EU's so-called Reform Treaty is actually a constitutional document, hence requiring a referendum, or whether it is a treaty, hence appropriately dealt with by parliament only and not requiring a referendum. As the continuing debates in the Netherlands and the United Kingdom suggest, reading the documents so that their detailed and distinct quality can be identified apparently does not suffice. Yet, the consequence of how the document is read and how much constitutional quality it is interpreted to entail will be indicative for distinct political procedures, i.e. either a referendum or ratification in parliament will be the consequence. It is therefore important to establish a better way of understanding diverse interpretations and their impact on politics. Two research perspectives matter for this task. *Empirical* research maps and compares interpretations of norms. And *normative* discussion seeks to approach ways of making sure that the normative substance reflects standards of legitimacy so as to ensure that the expectations of those governed by it are respected.

The second question raised in this book is more specific. It asks whether, given the increasing internationalisation of politics and law, it is sufficient for research to point to interaction and identity formation within international organisations. After all, decisions are often not taken within a specific institutional environment but with reference to a document that had been drafted elsewhere, or, 'out of context', so to speak. With respect to the European Union's constitutional quality and with a view to identifying the appropriate procedure of ratifying the revised treaty, one could therefore ask: who is the ultimate interpreter of the EU's constitutional quality? Alternatively, and in the absence of

---

[6] Note that I use the term 'internationalisation' purposefully so as to express increasing international interaction without precluding type, shape, scope or result of this activity.

an ultimate interpreter whose universal authority is uncontested, the book asks which interpretations can be accounted for (Garfinkel 1967), so that they can be fruitfully acknowledged in politics and policy-making?

The assumption is that while norms are always meaningful, their meaning is constituted through an interactive process. *Interpretation is thus derived from the social practice of enacting meaning that is used in a specific context.* Research therefore needs to explore and compare interpretations of the norms, rules and principles laid down in, say, the EU's treaties and ask whether they are likely to differ to the point of divergence, overlap to the point of convergence or demonstrate a different pattern all together, when asking actors in different contexts. The final question focuses on the research findings, asking whether distinct general patterns can be identified.

Three dimensions of norms

The book suggests a distinction between three dimensions that matter for research on norms and their impact on international politics. While following the distinction between formal validity and social recognition according to the literatures of International Law/Relations and European institutional law, I propose adding the third dimension of cultural valida-tion. Accordingly, *formal validity*, defined as the details written down on paper in the form of treaties, conventions, agreements, decisions or other documents, i.e. what international lawyers call 'treaty language' (Chayes and Chayes 1993), provides an inconclusive reference for sub-sequent action. As Curtin and Dekker have specified, 'a reduction of a legal system to duty-imposing norms is both theoretically and empiri-cally untenable' (1999: 87). Drawing on Weinberger, they conclude therefore that, 'as complexes of norms the legal institutions are linked to an actual whole on the strength of their connection with an existing factual sphere or one being constituted by these norms and they are institutionalized as social practices' (Curtin and Dekker 1999: 91, citing Weinberger 1991: 21–2).

That is, formal validity requires the additional dimension of *social recognition*. This social reference frame provides guidance for the implementation and interpretation of norms, rules and principles. Social recognition thus enhances the conditions for informed action on formal documents such as agreements, treaties or conventions.

This reference also applies to common practices, norms and rules which have evolved in relation to these documents and which are specified to an even lesser extent. The encompassing International Relations literature on norms has built upon this insight and found that social recognition provides a framework of reference for the implementation of norms, rules and principles in international negotiations. This literature has drawn predominantly on organisational sociology and pointed to the effects of learning and socialisation within the environment of international organisations, epistemic communities or regimes. It pointed out the importance of repeated interaction and shared identity which are developed by members of international communities (Wendt 1987; Klotz 1995; Finnemore 1996; Katzenstein 1996; Adler 1997; Zürn and Checkel 2005).

Leading assumptions that inform the case study tackle the impact of national background (national identity options), belonging to a specific community (liberal community hypothesis), social group (layer-cake assumption) or context of interaction (rule-in-practice assumption) and identify which factor matters in which way for the interpretation of norms.[7] Accordingly, the case study seeks to reconstruct and compare the normative structure of meaning-in-use in different contexts. It is argued that the concept of the structure of meaning-in-use allows for empirical access to and thus a better understanding of the constitutive dimension of norms. Their meaning can be brought to the fore by reconstructing and mapping the *cultural validation* of norms as an interactive process. As Habermas notes, 'Values – including those which can count on global recognition – are no pie in the sky, but obtain validity exclusively within normative orders and practices of particular cultural life-styles.'[8] Both represent the structural and the individual dimension of interactive international politics.

The argument which will be developed in the following chapters holds that quite the contrary is the case. It contends that searching for explanations of the negative outcome in the Constitutional Treaty's text proves as helpful as searching for keys under the proverbial lampshade.

---

[7] For a detailed development and discussion of four research assumptions, see chapter 3.
[8] Habermas, *Frankfurter Allgemeine Zeitung*, 17 April 2003, 23.

For an understanding of the outcome of the respective Dutch and French referenda, the Constitutional Treaty's formal contents will provide fewer cues than its social recognition based on the 'ways of life' in different contexts.[9] That is, the sociocultural context in which the individual voter is situated and forms his/her opinion provides access points for assessing particular voting behaviour. This observation indicates a relationship between three dimensions which determine the invisible constitution of politics. In this case, they reflect, for example, the perception of 'things constitutional'. The three dimensions become empirically accessible based on the methodological distinction between formal content, generally accepted substance and cultural validation of a norm. The formal validity is the result of treaty negotiation; social recognition is a structural component that provides a reference frame and guides behaviour; and cultural validation is the active component that reflects and constitutes the meaning that is actually in use. They allow for an empirical assessment with reference to their interactive constitution through structures of meaning-in-use and individually enacted connotations, thus reflecting and reconstituting meanings within a specific context.

In sum, these three dimensions of interpretation are proposed as indicators to study the meaning of norms. They allow for the desegregation of the unit of analysis from the 'national' towards group- or individual-based assessments which reveal variation in the interpretation of the meanings. They shift the perspective from analysing treaty *texts* towards understanding the input of social practices that form expectations of treaty *substance*.[10] That is, the approach is inductive and focuses on gathering information about normative meanings. In addition, it involves the normative discussion about how constitutional

---

[9] Note that 'recognition' is used as a derivative of 'practice' rather than a normative principle of justice. For the latter, see the literature on 'cultural recognition' and 'struggle for recognition' in, e.g., Taylor 1994 or Fraser 2005. Chapter 3 elaborates the terminology of 'validity' and 'facticity' with reference to Habermas 1992 rather than Weber 1978: 31, cited in Schluchter 2003: 544.

[10] Compare Skinner's approach to studying the meaning of historical texts here. While this book agrees with Skinner's critical rejection of universal approaches that expect meaning to be evident within a text, this book's investigation focuses on meanings assigned to norms that remain invisible to the speaker. It thus departs from Skinner's assumption that since every utterance entails a particular intention, the range of intentions – all possible language games – can be assessed theoretically (1988: 55).

norms, rules and principles may be revised in order to accommodate diversity. The latter would include, for example, the citizenship right to difference and access to participation and its institutional presence in beyond-the-state contexts that claim democratic legitimacy.[11] In addition to the two more familiar dimensions of norms research which include formal validity and social recognition, cultural validation adds a third interactive dimension. The innovative aspect of this dimension allows for shedding light on the more specific questions about divergence and convergence of individually perceived normative meanings under conditions of internationalisation. It investigates meaning associated with norms out of context. The empirical research therefore seeks to identify meanings that are associated with norms under conditions of moving social practices outside the familiar contexts, e.g. outside a nation-state or an international organisation as limited contexts that guide formal validity or social recognition. The book therefore compares the familiar setting in which formal validity and social recognition overlap and unfamiliar settings in which this overlap is not granted are compared.

Three theoretical moves

The book distinguishes between visible and invisible factors. The visible factors establish formal validity. They are defined as formal constitutional functions such as community-creating or power-limiting as well as ordering functions. The invisible factors entail expectations of norms and the interpretation of their respective meanings derived from the historical and cultural contingency of the respective constitutional function (Peters 2001). The reference to the invisible factors that constitute expectations towards meanings draws on Tully's observation of the 'hidden constitutions of contemporary societies' (Tully 1995: 99). While Tully proceeds to reconstruct possible, yet historically missed, constitutional arrangements based on multicultural dialogues over time in Canada to bring the hidden to light, this book is interested in reconstructing interpretations of meanings of which often not

---

[11] For a similar twofold approach that is based on two types of questions, 'the more normative or theoretical questions of justice and recognition on one side and the more institutional or empirical questions of accommodation and stability on the other' (Tully 2001: 2), see, e.g., the contributions to Gagnon and Tully 2001.

even the speakers are aware. It seeks to reconstruct ways of being in the world based on connotations of commonly acknowledged norms and politics.

To identify these invisible factors and discuss their impact on politics, the book takes a 'bifocal form of critical analysis' (Tully 2000: 471) which links both empirical and normative research. The intention is to develop a methodological approach that can account for a relatively high degree of complexity while not losing analytical clout. *Three theoretical moves* prepare the grounds for a comparative case study. They provide a reference frame for the qualitative and quantitative evaluations of the empirical research and for the discussion of the normative implications. The investigation is concerned with the emerging constitutional quality in the global environment. It asks whether that quality is matched by processes of *trans*nationalisation. To that end, an activity-oriented rather than an actor-oriented definition of 'transnational' is applied. That is, instead of the key reference to the *type of actor*, which holds that once at least one non-state actor is involved in addition to states, it is suggested that we speak of transnational actors, networks and so on (Risse-Kappen 1995), this book uses the term to indicate a *type of activity* such as frequent and repeated international interaction that is conducive to blurring national boundaries. As the outcome of a process of interaction among actors of different (national) socialisation, transnationalisation is thus not taken for granted qua theoretical assumption but needs to be identified empirically.

The three theoretical moves build on this interdisciplinary background with a view to developing approaches to norms in international relations further. The *first move* includes a discussion of constitutionalism as a framework for the analysis of the social practices that are constitutive for constitutional quality. These social practices involve both organisational and cultural practices, thus taking into account the more visible political and public dimension of constitutional politics, on the one hand, and the more invisible day-to-day practices which often escape the public or official documentation of constitutional quality, on the other (chapter 2). The *second move* includes a discussion of norms in international relations and international law. It establishes a generic distinction between three types of norms and seeks to establish conditions under which norms are particularly contested (chapter 3). The *third move* turns to conceptualise a methodological approach to the study of norms based on discourse analysis. To that end, it develops a case study design that includes conducting and evaluating interviews based on qualitative analysis (chapter 4).

The case study maps, evaluates and compares interpretations of meaning systematically and comparatively (chapters 5 to 7). It centrally applies the concept of 'structures of meaning-in-use' (Weldes and Saco 1996; Weldes 1998: 218; Milliken 1999). This concept allows for examining and comparing different ways of enacting meaning. Surely meanings are never developed outside relationality with others and within a specific context. However, individuals do move between contexts, and such moves will necessarily lead to crossing the boundaries of 'webs of meaning' (Adler 2005: 11, cited in Brunnée and Toope 2008, ch. 2: 3) and interacting with different structures of meaning-in-use. Considering the increasing international interaction on the one hand, and a growing and contested constitutional quality outside national state boundaries on the other, it is therefore important to identify how the 'normative baggage' an individual gathered through experience and in interaction with a specific context (Puetter and Wiener 2007: 1067) and its structure of meaning-in-use compares to another individual's normative baggage.

The project

Routinised references to norms include, for example, the structural adjustment policies of the World Bank and the International Monetary Fund (IMF) as well as the European Union enlargement process. The World Bank and IMF made the provision of development aid conditional on adherence to the norm of democracy or, more recently, gender mainstreaming. These norms became important conditionalities for so-called developing countries in the 1980s and 1990s. Similarly, the EU's most recent and most massive enlargement process involved reference to the norm of minority rights as a new conditionality for central and eastern European candidate countries.[12] These processes made

---

[12] This particular enlargement process began with the 1993 Copenhagen Accession Agreements and brought ten new member states into the EU in 2004. For the first time, member states established the minority rights conditionality, in addition to the generally accepted enlargement *acquis*. For critical assessments of this process, see Fierke and Wiener 1999; Williamson 2000; Witte 2000; Wiener 2003a; Wiener and Schwellnus 2004.

routine the reference to modern constitutional norms as conditions for membership in *inter*nationally constituted communities. Once the 'stick' of modernising constitutional arrangements had been accepted, and the 'carrot' of membership was obtained, the international communities expected the new members to adhere to their norms, rules and regulations.

Questions about the specific meaning of such norms usually do not ensue until a later point in time. Two cases of norm contestation are typical: one involves the specific action required to transpose and implement norms from one context to another; the other involves protest or challenges that are raised with regard to the legitimacy of the norm-setter/norm-follower relationship. For example, in the case of the EU enlargement, the politics of conditionality with regard to the minority rights norm were contested by the designated norm-followers.[13] Upon signing the EU treaties, accession agreements and all other agreements that have resulted from international negotiations, member states are expected to implement and respect their content; however, divergence with regard to the interpretation of the norms adhered to in these agreements, such as those regarding the meaning of minority rights, democracy, gender mainstreaming, sovereignty or non-intervention, questions assumptions about the shared interpretation of the content of the agreements. While the carrot of membership in a community presents a powerful incentive to comply with its fundamental norms, this incentive works for a limited period of time only. Once implementation on a day-to-day basis for regular members of a community comes into play, and especially under conditions of crisis, a more in-depth understanding is required of how internationally established norms work.[14]

International agreements such as treaties, documents and conventions are outcomes of negotiations among individual government representatives with different cultural origins. The government representative will sign the agreement once the participating negotiators are satisfied

---

[13] Minority rights had been contested as a new conditionality that had been added to the EU's enlargement *acquis* (Schwellnus 2005, 2007).

[14] In the light of routinised practice of norm recognition, it is puzzling to see a new divide emerging within EU member states' interpretations of global norms revealed, for example, through UN Security Council debates over Resolution 1441 and related political interaction among the member states (Wiener 2004; Puetter and Wiener 2007).

with the text. The text entails 'what is agreed to'; it is therefore considered to have formal validity. Subsequently, it is expected that the contracting parties will comply with the agreement. That is, implementation is an implicit outcome of the agreement. Compliance is motivated by appropriateness and social recognition. Often, however, agreements are not successful, so that the question may be raised as to how it is possible that despite documented formal validity and social recognition, agreements are contested.

Two explanations for norm contestation are offered by two bodies of literature, respectively. The first explanation is 'more universalistic', following the modern tradition of the Enlightenment and universal values established by and with the emerging authority of the institutions of the modern nation-state (Tilly 1975; Tully 2000). It holds that in cases of non-compliance with international treaties, if social learning will not enhance compliant behaviour, the designated norm-followers will eventually be pressured into norm-following based on 'naming' and 'shaming'. If sanctions do not apply, this process is expected to be pushed by non-state actors such as non-governmental organisations or transnational action networks. Usually, a certain amount of 'coercion' is involved in making less powerful actors, such as 'southerners' or 'outsiders of a community', comply based on the 'carrot' of membership. In any case, the outcome of compliance is less one of social recognition than one of coercion. The second type of explanation follows a 'more contextualised approach' (Tully 2000) that seeks to understand why and how the situation of contested normative meaning has come about and how it could be improved with respect to democratic legitimacy.[15] Following this tradition, the understanding of contested interpretations of international agreements can be substantially enhanced by critically appreciating the interplay between social practices and the construction of the structures of meaning.

This book seeks to tackle that issue. Therefore the research is based on the reconstruction of discursive interventions regarding core constitutional norms in three different nationally constituted contexts: a British context in London, a German context in Berlin, and a transnational context in Brussels. The empirical research encompasses such discursive interventions generated by fifty-three interviews with elite

---

[15] For a discussion of participatory democracy, see especially Pateman 1970.

groups in London, Berlin and Brussels (here, both British and German Brusselites were interviewed). The questions raised in these interviews targeted three new European policy fields: 'Schengen', 'Enlargement', and 'Constitutional Politics'.

Substantively, the interviews involve conversations about firstly, the Schengen field and the policy which led to the abolition of internal borders among a number of European countries;[16] secondly, the Enlargement field which has been developing through the on-going process of negotiating and accepting new members into the European Communities/Community and now Union;[17] and, thirdly, the field of Constitutional Politics as a new area of supranational policy-making, referring to treaty-making and treaty revision with a view to regulating EU policy and politics and enhancing the treaties' constitutional quality.[18] As issue areas, the policy fields are linked to keywords indicating individually transported associative connotations with three sets of core constitutional norms. They include 'citizenship rights', 'democracy and the rule of law', and 'human rights and fundamental freedoms'. The case findings are summarised in chapter 8. Finally, chapter 9 picks up the theme of diversity, discusses its impact and possibilities for democratic governance in beyond-the-state contexts and derives a working hypothesis. The book's research is considered as a pilot study that seeks to generate a working hypothesis for research on norms. The aim of the project is to understand the impact of agreements that are negotiated among international parties, and which are expected to be implemented in contexts other than the negotiation environment, assuming that the political arenas of negotiation and implementation do not usually overlap.

---

[16] The implementing Schengen countries include Austria, Belgium, Denmark, Finland, France, Germany, Iceland, Italy, Greece, Luxembourg, Netherlands, Norway, Portugal, Spain and Sweden. All these countries except Norway and Iceland are EU members. For details on the agreement, see www.eurovisa.info/BackgroundInfo.htm as well as http://en.wikipedia.org/wiki/Schengen_Agreement (accessed 4 October 2007).

[17] For a summary of various enlargement rounds and different policy areas and political rationales generated by the process, see, e.g., Schimmelfennig and Sedelmeier 2005.

[18] For summaries on the policy field of constitutional politics and the emerging policy rationales, see, e.g., Neunreither and Wiener 2000; Beaumont, Lyons and Walker 2002; De Burca and Scott 2003; Weiler and Wind 2003.

Constitutional quality beyond the state

Legal systems which are bound by a constitutional agreement provide a triadic framework for conflict resolution in modern communities. Law and politics are intertwined by a concept of law that links positive law with a legitimating mode of law-making (Habermas 1994: 84). This relation between politics and law is challenged, however, when politics transgresses state boundaries.[19] The crossing of state borders highlights the lack of conceptual fit between the constitutionally organised context of modern (nation-) states, on the one hand, and the anarchic context of international relations, on the other. While this conceptual split reveals conflicting interpretations of rules, procedures and principles of governance, the constitutional institutions as well as the interplay between law and politics as facilitators of good governance not only raise issues for students of International Relations, but, as Friedrich Kratochwil notes, also remain to be addressed in more detail by comparativists.

> By making social order dependent upon law and law, in turn, upon the existence of certain institutions – be they the existence of a sovereign or central sanctioning mechanism – we understand the international arena largely negatively, *i.e.*, in terms of the 'lack' of binding legal norms, of central institutions, of a sovereign will, etc. As inappropriate as this 'domestic analogy' may be for understanding international relations, *the conceptual links between order, law, and special institutions remain largely unexamined even for domestic affairs.* (Kratochwil 1989: 2; my emphasis)

Following the problematic relation between politics and law both outside and inside modern state boundaries, it comes as no surprise that the draft text for a European constitution instantly became the subject of academic and political debate. For example, one question which has been raised in the aftermath of the negative referenda is whether the 'no' of the Dutch and French voters accounts for a rejection of the European project writ large, for a failure of European integration theories, even.[20]

---

[19] Note the emphasis on 'state' rather than 'national' boundaries. In a beyond-the-state context, governance may still be influenced by national identity options. Yet, it is moved away, albeit partially, from the sovereign jurisdictional territory that underlies the control of the political organs of the modern state.

[20] Some academic discussion raised, for example, the question of whether academics are to conclude that European integration theory has become obsolete considering the respective referendum outcomes. See, among numerous academic

Yet, regardless of extensive and continuing debates,[21] the question of why the Constitutional Treaty failed to generate recognition and support, despite some substantial improvements for citizens with regard to fundamental freedoms as well as an improved political role for the European Parliament and the enhanced involvement of member state parliaments, raises deeper questions about the emergence and substance of constitutional quality beyond the state.

While constitutionalisation has been an on-going process throughout the almost five decades of European integration (Witte 2002: 39), the language shift from calling the document a 'treaty' to calling it a 'constitution' has captured the attention of the European public. In the process, it activated both hopes and fears pending on individual experience with and expectations of 'things constitutional'. Given the dramatic shift in language, and, in the absence of a clear understanding of the substance brought about by the Constitutional Treaty, questions were raised regarding whether this document was functional to the political organisation of a 'consortium' such as the European Union (Schmitter 2000), and whether it was actually appreciated by the European citizens.

Yet, while the debate about whether European integration was to be considered a 'failure' after the French and Dutch negative referenda had played out in the media, academic research has pointed to another, perhaps deeper yet invisible layer of constitutionalisation in Europe. That is, in addition to and apart from the specific drafting procedures of the Constitutional Treaty, over the past five decades the process of constitutionalisation in Europe has generated an emerging constitutional layer (Craig 2001; Stone Sweet 2002; Rosamond and Wincott 2006). This layer entails evolving constitutional quality beyond the state (Weiler and Wind 2003; Wiener and Shaw 2003), which often refers to the constitutional norms of modern constitutionalism, i.e. the rule of law, democracy, human and fundamental rights and equal citizenship, while consistently and progressively challenging the 'stable certainties of the constitutional settlement derived from the peace of Westphalia' (Everson 2004: 125).

discussions, for example, a 2005 symposium in the German journal of International Relations which discusses the issue of whether integration theory has to be considered obsolete in the light of the referenda (*Zeitschrift für Internationale Beziehungen* 12(2), 2005).

[21] As Rosamond and Wincott note, 'the Constitutional Treaty had provoked a flurry of domestic debate ... such a public debate was long overdue' (2006: 1).

The bifocal approach taken by this book is expected to generate two insights. Following the observation that the transnationalisation of politics in many ways bears a resemblance to an Aristotelian understanding of the constitution as an immanent organising principle of a specific political order,[22] the book firstly seeks to make the invisible yet constitutive elements of politics accountable based on empirical research; and, secondly, it discusses the inclusion of these elements in approaches to democratic constitutionalism. To that end it develops a framework to study the contested meaning of norms in international politics. The goal is not one of 'testing' or 'verifying' theories.[23] Instead, observations are formulated to facilitate plausible assumptions and an appropriate research design for the empirical case study. Research assumptions and hypotheses are considered tools for providing the rationale for the selection of case studies and the research focus.

The specific interest of this project lies in identifying invisible elements that have an impact on the constitution of politics. The potentially contested interpretation of meanings of norms provides the starting point for the enquiry. It observes that the invisible cultural dimension of a community's constitution has been largely omitted by the particular version of modern constitutionalism with its lack of appreciation for cultural practices. Despite the knowledge that 'the "rule" lies essentially *in* the practice' (Taylor 1993: 58; emphasis in original), the impact of cultural practices has received less analytical attention than organisational practices in modern constitutionalism. If cultural practices shape experience and expectations, they need to be identified and made accountable based on empirical research. As Habermas notes, it is

the cultural patterns of interpretation, evaluation and expression [which] serve as *resources* for the efforts in understanding those participating in

---

[22] 'Aristotle defines "constitution" as "a certain ordering of the inhabitants of the city-state". ... The constitution is not a written document, but an immanent organising principle, analogous to the soul of an organism. Hence, *the constitution is also "the way of life" of the citizens*.' See Aristotle (III.1.1274b32-41 and IV.11.1295a40-b1, VII.8.1328b1-2, respectively; cited in Miller 2002); my emphasis.

[23] 'Empirical research goes far beyond the passive role of verifying and testing theory; it does more than confirm or refute hypotheses. Research plays an active role: it performs at least four major functions which help shape the development of theory. It *initiates*, it *reformulates*, it *deflects* and *clarifies* theory' (Merton 1948: 506; emphasis in original).

the process of interaction and negotiate a shared definition of the situation and within this framework seek to reach a consensus on something in a world. (Habermas 1988b: 203; emphasis in original)

The political importance of these resources comes to the fore in moments of friction, i.e. in situations which reflect divergence in interpreting the meaning of norms. That is: 'Culture and language develop a peculiar resistance in those rare moments when they fail as *resources* which we experience in situations of disturbed communication' (*ibid.*: 204; emphasis in original). While these elements remain invisible to the untrained eye of researchers and politicians alike, they are nonetheless constitutive for politics. They are ultimately decisive for compliance with international agreements and will often hold the explanation as to why some actors opt in favour of military interventions and others do not. This book contends that while we know that these invisible resources matter, we need to know more about how they matter. In order to establish the latter, they need to be made 'accountable' (Garfinkel 1967: 1).

Conclusion

Assuming that a constitution is also 'the way of life' implies that it entails an informal dimension in addition to a formal one. In the literature, these dimensions are distinguished as 'what is agreed to' and 'what is customary' (Tully 1995: 50).[24] Both are social practices – the former organisational, the latter cultural – with an impact on the regulation of politics. The latter remains institutionally invisible by definition. The constitution's role of 'organising the political' (Preuss 1994) has evolved over centuries in interrelation with different types and shapes of polities, ranging from city-states to non-states such as the European Union. More recently this interrelation has been influenced by the enhanced movement of social practices across modern constitutional boundaries. This movement is generally captured under the label of globalisation including an, albeit partial, transnationalisation of politics. Thus, the social practices of constitution building are increasingly placed within a context that is best defined as 'beyond the state', i.e. it cannot be understood by the criteria of either modern

---

[24] For details on this distinction, see chapter 2.

statehood or international organisations. This raises the question of how the interpretation of invisible constitutional elements will have an impact on politics in light of the changing relation between organisational and customary practices. These questions are particularly salient considering the partial transnationalisation of politics.

While individual actors are moving and engaging within emerging transnational spaces, structures change more slowly; however, normative meaning is located in both the individual and the structural elements of politics. It follows that any effort to assess normative meaning empirically would need to begin from the theoretical knowledge that individually transported meanings move relatively quickly while structures change slowly. If we now assume that interpretations of normative meanings are constitutive for politics, albeit invisibly so, the question of how normative meanings can be identified empirically arises. Searching for an appropriate way to answer this empirical question is the first purpose of the book. The second purpose is to engage the findings obtained from empirical research based on a normative theoretical perspective. To target both purposes, a bifocal approach is applied. Despite the expanding literatures on constitutionalism and norms, respectively,[25] transdisciplinary research on norms still has some way to go. This book seeks to bring various literatures to bear with a view to developing such a perspective. The main research interest lies in intangible – emotional, cultural, interpretive or associative – aspects and their influence on political decisions in a world of politics that stretches beyond the boundaries of modern nation-states. The object of inquiry can thus be called the *invisible constitution of politics*.[26]

This book argues that a major analytical challenge for students of constitutional quality beyond the state lies in assessing the potential for converging interpretations of norms in transnational contexts. In

---

[25] For contributions that cross disciplinary boundaries and offer potential for creating a transdisciplinary framework to study the role norms in world politics, see Preuss 1994; Tully 1995, 2000, 2002a; Reus-Smit 1997, 2001b; Weiler 1999; Abbott, Keohane, Moravcsik, Slaughter and Snidal 2000; Cass 2001; Brunnée and Toope 2001; Finnemore and Toope 2001; Shaw 2001, 2007; Koskenniemi 2002, 2007; Walker 2002; Slaughter and Burke-White 2002; Weiler and Wind 2003, forthcoming.

[26] Note András Sajó's finding of an invisible constitution in the realm of legal practice as a 'coherent system which serves as a secure standard of constitutionality, *as an invisible constitution* above the Constitution in force which is still subject to modifications dictated by daily political interest' (1995: 258; my emphasis).

accordance with the project of seeking to make different meanings of
norms accountable so that their impact on politics can be understood,
the book distinguishes 'meanings of norms' that are in use, i.e. which
can be derived from specific discursive interventions. It is here where a
lack of commonality in the interpretation of core constitutional norms
is likely to lead to misunderstandings with potentially wide-ranging
political consequences. The focus on cultural practices seeks to assess
the degree of difference in the interpretation of core constitutional
norms based on day-to-day interactions by making meaning accountable. The outcome of the case study will therefore critically matter for
discussions about the reconstitution of modern constitutionalist institutions beyond the state.[27]

---

[27] For such an endeavour, see, for example, RECON/Reconstituting Democracy in
Europe, a European Union 6th Framework Integrated Project that 'seeks to
clarify whether democracy is possible under conditions of pluralism, diversity
and complex multilevel governance'; see: www.reconproject.eu/projectweb/
portalproject/ProjectSummary.html (accessed on 24 September 2007).

PART I

Three theoretical moves

2 | *Constitutionalism beyond modernity*

Constitutionalism is, ... but a prism through which one can observe a landscape in a certain way, *an academic artefact* with which one can organize the milestones and landmarks within the landscape ..., an intellectual construct by which one can assign meaning to, or even constitute, that which is observed.

(Weiler 1999: 223; my emphasis)

Introduction: emerging constitutional quality in a global context

When speaking of a constitution, we mean a set of norms, principles and provisions and the mandate to organise the political (Snyder 1990; Preuss 1994; Rosenfeld 1994). In distinction from other agreements such as conventions or treaties, constitutions are expected to offer a 'civilised' and 'embedded' approach to settling conflicts while respecting the constituents' wishes and ways of life. Constitutions relate to a set of cultural and social conditions within specific contexts, and they represent an agreement (written or not) among representatives of the governed within a community to make sure that the governors proceed according to the wishes of the former (Tully 1995; Walker 2002; Maduro 2003). While this type of agreement has had a long-standing role in domestic politics in Europe starting with the Greek city-states, a similar constitutional quality has emerged only much more recently in international politics. Thus, the creation of international organisations that attempt to move ahead with arrangements of an increasingly binding constitutional quality[1] such as the United Nations, the European

---

[1] Thus, the debate about the EU's erstwhile rejected and now 'reformed' constitutional treaty is still on, scrutinising the changes of the treaties after the German EU Presidency under Chancellor Angela Merkel's leadership. See, e.g., the assessments by Giuliano Amato and Giscard d'Estaing, *euobserver.com*

Union (and its predecessors), Mercosur, the Association of South East Asian Nations (ASEAN)[2] and the African Union (AU),[3] dates back to the past century only.

Nonetheless, as Koskenniemi (2007) observes, a 'global enthusiasm' about the possibilities of the rule of law had emerged with the beginning of the post-Cold War era. Subsequently, and taking the stable normative structure in world politics at the time into account, many spoke of a process of 'constitutionalisation' in beyond-the-state contexts. While communities that were part of quasi-constitutional arrangements such as the European Union by means of its various treaties, or the United Nations by means of its Charter, were much less defined by the boundaries of a Hegelian state than by international agreements negotiated among government representatives, the language of 'civilisation', 'constitutionalisation' or 'the rule of law' did create an overarching framework of reference for practising international law as well as global politics. The addressees of this framework were the 'civilised nations' that had signed the UN Charter (Article 38(1)c ICJ (International Court of Justice)) and/or the Treaty on European Union (Article 6 TEU, Article 11 TEU), respectively.[4]

The expanding literature on 'things constitutional'[5] notes an emergent constitutional quality of international agreements in real-world political contexts in the early twenty-first century.[6] That quality constitutes an

16 July 2007, at http://euobserver.com/9/24481 and 18 July 2007, at http://euobserver.com/9/24498, respectively (accessed 19 July 2007).

[2] ASEAN was founded on 8 August 1967 in Bangkok by the five original member countries, namely, Indonesia, Malaysia, Philippines, Singapore and Thailand. Brunei Darussalam joined on 8 January 1984, Vietnam on 28 July 1995, Lao PDR and Myanmar on 23 July 1997, and Cambodia on 30 April 1999; see www.aseansec.org/64.htm (accessed 20 July 2007).

[3] The AU was founded in 2001; it consists of fifty-three African states and brings together the former Organisation of African Unity and the African Economic Community. Like Mercosur, the AU's progress is inspired by the European integration process. See www.africa-union.org/root/au/AboutAu/au_in_a_nutshell_en.htm (accessed 21 July 2007).

[4] See http://europa.eu.int/eur-lex/en/treaties/selected/livre106.html (accessed 4 August 2007).

[5] The term 'things constitutional' is used for the time being so as to indicate the often unspecific and unsystematic application of various terms on the constitutional issues and processes, such as 'constitutionalisation', 'constitution' and 'constitutionalism'. The terms will be detailed in the following sections of this chapter.

[6] For an expanding literature, see Slaughter and Burke-White 2002; De Burca and Scott 2003; Jackson 2005; Fischer-Lescano 2005; Koskenniemi 2007.

additional – often invisible – layer of international and regional organisations as well as a wide-ranging network of international organisations within and related to the UN such as the World Trade Organisation (WTO) and the International Criminal Court. In sum, and despite their formal differences, both types of institutions – regional and international – share the issue of *contested constitutional quality*. The norms, principles and rules that guide politics within these contexts provide the substance of this quality. It is their input, i.e. the way they 'work', which establishes the invisible constitution of politics. Given the necessity of social recognition for the interpretation of any kind of legal document, this *invisible constitution of politics* is crucial for the interpretation of norms. The following four sections offer a summary of the literature on constitutionalism with a view to setting a frame of reference for studies that seek to grapple with this invisible layer of politics. The next section distinguishes between modern and contextualised constitutionalism. A section then elaborates on contextualised constitutionalism with special reference to its empirical focus on social practices and the normative standard set by the principle of social recognition. The following section raises research questions regarding the European Union's specific case of contemporary constitutionalism. And the final section concludes with insights gained from a contextual approach to constitutionalism.

Constitutionalism: modern and contextualised

While the understanding of a constitution and its assigned role as the guardian of the political process is commonly associated with modern constitutionalism[7] and builds on institutionalised and mythical links with statehood that had been forged over centuries (Cassirer 1946; Anderson 1983), it still merely reflects the contingent quality derived from the way constitutionalism has been working throughout a particular period of time and at a particular place. Nonetheless, this particular type of constitutionalism has been and continues to be powerful. This has significant implications for current theories and politics of

---

[7] See also Sartori who distinguishes between 'the constitution as any "State order," and constitutionalism as a specific "content" of guarantees' (1962: 856). Drawing on the 'terminology of the Constitution of Pennsylvania of 28 September 1776, a constitution contains two basic elements: a "plan (or frame) of government," and a "bill of rights"' (*ibid.*).

constitutionalism. So much so, that students studying 'contemporary' constitutionalism (Tully 1995) as a distinct type of constitutionalism, which unfolds *beyond* the boundaries of modern states, face the 'problem of translation' of constitutional norms from statist to non-state contexts (Weiler 1999; Walker 2002: 322). This observation renders the fact that 'many would regard modern constitutionalism as the continuation, in the philosophy of the state, of the social contract' (Di Fabio 2001: 1) problematic. The following elaborates on approaches which distinguish between different types of constitutionalism by situating specific constitutional qualities in their respective contexts of emergence and practice.

There 'appears to be no accepted definition of constitutionalism but, in the broadest terms, modern constitutionalism requires imposing limits on the powers of government, adherence to the rule of law, and the protection of fundamental rights. ... However, the relationship between constitution and constitutionalism and the very boundaries of the concept of constitutionalism tend to become increasingly blurred' (Rosenfeld 1994: 3). Most basically, modern constitutionalism 'does impose certain definite broad requirements – such as limited government, adherence to the rule of law, protection of fundamental interests, and compliance with the demands of abstract equality' (*ibid*.: 14). More specifically, it builds on two types of identities which are related to the central rights entailed in a constitution. The first type of identity is derived from the shared recognition of the type of rights that stand to be defended and protected by the constitution among the framers and the subjects of a constitutional order; the second identity builds, more directly, on the notion of 'each member of a society as a bearer of the same constitutional rights' (*ibid*.: 6).

Core norms of modern constitutionalism include the 'commitment to limited but effective government, adherence to the rule of law, and adequate protection of fundamental rights' (Rosenfeld 1997: 215). These norms and their protection by modern nation-states have achieved such a degree of familiarity that often, even for learned scholars, a constitution is unthinkable without a state.[8] Notably, however, contemporary constitutionalism evolves under conditions of inter- and

---

[8] For this assumption of an axiomatic link between 'constitution' and an unqualified general concept of 'the state' in current political philosophy and International Relations theory, see Morgan 2006.

transnationalisation.[9] It therefore challenges the conceptual 'tool kit' of modernity, especially the founding relationship between constitutions and states.[10] The process facilitates new insights into evolving norms of constitutionalism with a view to examine the origin, role and function of norms in world politics (Nettl 1968; Ruggie 1998a; Weiler and Wind 2003). Work engaging on this prospect focuses on 'soft institutions'.[11] Ranging from organisational theory towards Kantian visions of global politics, this work does not, however, necessarily cover common normative ground. Its potential input into the definition of constitutionalism is contested as 'an academic artefact' (Weiler 1999: 223), now enhanced by contributions from International Relations and International Law. It remains to be assessed empirically in some more detail.

Following the law-in-context tradition (e.g. Snyder 1990), constitutionalism entails a framework of rules, norms, principles and practices that reflects the constitutional quality of treaties, conventions and agreements and is constituted through social practices i.e. in jurisprudence and/or academia. Given the contingency of this quality, constitutionalism differs according to time and place. At issue for students who seek to examine constitutional quality is therefore an understanding of the diversity and commonality in the application and recognition of the respective interplay between rules, norms, principles and practices at a particular place and time. Based on this understanding, it is possible to carry out a bifocal analysis to assess both – the stability and effectiveness of such agreements in the eyes of the agreements' addressees, as well as the normative substance and durability of an agreement according to the normative standard of democratic legitimacy.

In other words, *constitutionalism* is a product made and re-made through on-going debates, reflecting the contested quality of its own

---

[9] For a detailed definition of the term, see chapter 3.

[10] On the use of tool kits, see Wittgenstein's comparison of actual tools such as a hammer, saw and nails and the use of words that express rules. As Wittgenstein notes, while the 'sameness' in appearance might prevail, the difference in application in different contexts reflects a difference in use and meaning, depending on the practices through which they are used (2003: 18).

[11] Soft institutions include practices, rules, procedures and principles. The definition draws on the new institutionalist debates in the social sciences which took place in the 1980s and 1990s. For seminal contributions to this literature, see Skocpol 1986; March and Olsen 1989, 1998; Hall and Taylor 1996; Finnemore and Sikkink 1998; and, more recently, Barnett and Finnemore 2004; Wiener 2006: 419.

very norms, rules and principles (Gallie 1956; Lessig 1996; Kahn 1999). As a heuristic theoretical framework, it entails meta-theoretical debates about questions such as why a constitution is legitimate, why it is authoritative and how should it be interpreted, on the one hand, and a more descriptive approach that establishes whether particular features of a constitution are in place or not, including the assessment of constitutionalisation as the process which leads to the establishment of such specific constitutional features, on the other (Craig 2001: 127; Maduro 2003). While constitutionalism has been considered hard to define, a foggy concept on which little academic agreement exists (Kommers and Thompson 1995: 23),[12] it is precisely its quality as an academic artefact which makes it such a helpful tool. The reflection of the practice of jurisprudence and academic discussion about the law sustain the contextuality of constitutionalism. In turn, *constitutionalisation* is an exclusively descriptive concept. It indicates the recollection of constitutional norms, rules and decisions as outcomes of a process (e.g. Rittberger and Schimmelfennig 2007). In this process, particular institutions and routine procedures adopt a legally binding quality which underlies the triadic practice of constitutional scrutiny (Stone Sweet 2002). For analytical purposes I therefore propose to distinguish between constitutionalisation as a social process and constitutionalism as an analytical framework.

The social construction of the *nomos*

Any political order depends on social recognition by its citizens, i.e. those who agreed, in principle, to be governed by the specific rules, norms and principles of a particular community (Tully 1995: 131). For modern nation-states, this principle meant that core constitutional norms had to be considered valid by the constituents of a constitutional agreement.[13] For constitutional arrangements established under conditions

---

[12] As Kommers and Thompson write, 'Walter Murphy has suggested, and we agree, that, without a clear definition, the term "constitutionalism" is an invitation to debate about ghosts or, to shift the metaphor, to enter a trackless verbal swamp' (1995: 23, cited in Murphy 1993, no page provided).

[13] This detail is often under-appreciated in empirical terms. Subsequently 'constituents' are always in danger of being considered as mere 'norm-followers'. This is of particular importance for studies of compliance with 'basic procedural norms' which are the substance of international treaties (Jackson 2005).

of transnationalisation, these conditions differ, however, as the boundaries of a community are not permanent but in flux. Subsequently, the addressees of the constitutional arrangement cannot be assumed to be stable. Their identities vary. Subsequently, social practices that are constitutive for the meaning of such a constitutional arrangement differ according to type of actor and the context in which the constitution is enacted. In regional organisations such as the European Union, they may be inferred, for example, from citizens, social groups, organisations, or member state governments. The constitutional text will mean different things to each of these constituents.

For empirical research that examines the normative quality produced by the interplay between formal validity and social recognition of norms, three social science perspectives on democratic legitimacy have been influential. They include firstly, the Weberian concept of 'domination by virtue of legality';[14] secondly, and in critical reference to the first, the Habermasian understanding of legitimacy as resulting from the interplay between culturally and universally derived value perceptions;[15] and thirdly, with critical reference to the second, the concept of cultural recognition based on the institutions that facilitate on-going dialogue (Taylor 1994; Tully 1995, esp. ch. 4). The major distinction between the first two conceptions of legitimacy as opposed to the last one lies in the appreciation of universality. Unlike Weber and Habermas, Tully cautions against a universalistic approach to constitutionalism (1995: 131),[16] yet crucially the shared reference frame for

---

[14] According to Weber 'there is a general obedience by "virtue of 'legality', by virtue of belief in the validity of legal statute and functional 'competence' based on rationally created rules"' (1972: 79). For Weber, the imagination ('Vorstellung') of a legitimate order, on the one hand, and its actual implementation which confirms the validity ('Geltung') of this order, on the other, are linked by social action (1984 [1921]: 54).

[15] As Habermas notes, 'Weber has not sufficiently distinguished between particular value contents of cultural traditions and those universal value standards which allow for the formation of increasingly independent cognitive, normative and expressive components of a culture and form obstinate complexes of rationality' (1988b: 340).

[16] This distinction reflects two broad traditions of critical philosophy: one is a 'more universalistic approach', the other a 'more contextual approach' (Tully 2000: 481). Tully associates Chambers, Habermas, Held and Honneth with the more universalistic approach and Benhabib, Foucault, Fraser, Rawls, Taylor and Young with the more contextual approach.

all three approaches is the bounded community of the modern state. They differ, substantially and profoundly, however, in the role they assign to the organisation of the state and the elements which influence the legitimacy of the rules and norms that organise governance in this conflict.

While to Weber, the modern state's *'monopoly of the legitimate use of physical force* within a given territory' (1946: 78; emphasis in original) is the centre point of legitimate governance, both Habermas and Tully bring in an interactive dimension, focusing on 'communicative action' and 'dialogue', respectively. While Habermas and Weber work with modern nation-states as their community of reference, Tully criticises the *modern* influence on constitutionalism and proposes to replace it with a contemporary version of constitutionalism. To this end, he activates insights from *ancient* constitutionalism to reconstruct the emergence of cultural diversity as a process of becoming. He points out that the social dimension which expressed the 'customary' in ancient constitutions has been eliminated with arguable success from modern constitutions (Tully 1995: 59, citing McIlwain 1947: 3).

The Greek term for constitutional law, *nomos*, means both what is agreed to by the people and what is customary. When Cicero translated *politeia* as *constitutio* he used it to mean both the fundamental laws that are established or laid down by the mythical lawgiver and the fitting or appropriate arrangement in accord with the preceding customary ways of the people. (Tully 1995: 60; see also Maddox 1982: 808, citing Loewenstein 1965: 129)

For the purpose of an empirical research frame, we can therefore conclude that constitutional law entails two sets of practices: organisational practices and cultural practices. Organisational practices entail the process of reaching an agreement about the definition of the core principles, norms and procedures which guide and regulate behaviour in the public realm of a polity. In turn, cultural practices refer to day-to-day interaction about what is 'customary' in multiple spaces of a community. In the absence of 'modern' boundaries of a community, these spaces may be termed 'cultural fields' (Bourdieu 1993). Both types of practices are interactive and by definition social. As such they are constitutive for the 'fundamental laws, institutions and customs' recognised by a community (Tully 1995: 60). In the following, I will refer to the former as 'organisational' and to the latter as 'cultural' practices.

The contextual approach allows for empirical openness when studying the diversity of meanings in contexts other than modern nation-states. Contextualising constitutional quality is a first step towards understanding social recognition as a process that is more 'practical and "permanent" rather than theoretical and end-state oriented' (Tully 2000: 477).[17] Thus the development of different types of constitutionalism over time can be distinguished. For example, ancient constitutionalism puts a stronger emphasis on the social construction of the *nomos*, while modern constitutionalism focuses on constitutional design to provide guidelines for the organisation of a polity. In order to recover the social construction of constitutional substance, Tully proposes to reconstruct multicultural dialogues by 'looking back to an already constituted order under one aspect and looking forward to an imposed order under the other' (1995: 60–1). This approach to constitutionalism respects the 'Janus-faced' constitutional quality and diverse expectations towards and interpretations of constitutional substance in multicultural societies.[18] It raises the general question of how to incorporate cultural and organisational practices of the past while establishing equal access to participation in a constitutional dialogue in the present and the future.

To accommodate diversity based on cultural validation, the customary dimension needs to be brought back in. Following this line of argument, this book's case study highlights the impact of the societal underpinning of evolving constitutional law beyond the state. It differs, however, from Tully's focus on accommodating cultural diversity within the constitutional framework of a *one-state* context (Canada), by addressing recognition in a constitutional framework within a *beyond-the-state* context (European Union). That is, in addition to the vertical time axis in Tully's reconstruction of constitutional dialogues, a

---

[17] While Tully has made this distinction with regard to research on struggles over social recognition, this book is less interested in this actual struggle than in the fact that meaning is constituted through processes of interaction that are 'permanent' in their impact on the constitution of meaning.

[18] For a different perspective on the constitution as a 'Janus-faced concept', see Sartori's critical discussion of the assumption that the constitution had been about political order and political freedom since Aristotle, or of, whether this Janus-faced aspect had been introduced much more recently with the Pennsylvanian constitution in 1776, as he holds (1962: 860). This position is refuted, however, by Maddox who maintains that constitutionalism 'arose in ancient society' (1982: 808).

horizontal space axis requires analytical attention. Once constitutional norms are dealt with outside their sociocultural context of origin, a potentially conflictive situation emerges. The conflict is based on unlinking the two sets of social practices that form the agreed-upon political aspect, on the one hand, and the evolving customary aspect of a constitution, on the other.

Unlike modern constitutionalism's firmly centred focus on organisational practices, ancient constitutionalism includes both cultural and organisational elements as two interrelated aspects of the social constitution of the *nomo*s. According to McIlwain, the Aristotelian definition of a constitution can be summarised as 'a term which comprises all the innumerable characteristics which determine that state's peculiar nature, and these include its whole economic and social texture as well as matters governmental in our narrower modern sense' (1958 [1947]: 24, cited in Maddox 1982: 807). In turn, modern constitutionalism with its focus on the state as its central concept has contributed to an increasing detachment of the constitution from its context of emergence. So much so, that, as Ernst-Wolfgang Böckenförde notes, 'Usually, talk about the "constitution" implies a reference to the constitution of a *state* as the basic order and organisation of *state*-political life' (1992: 29; my emphasis).

If 'a free and democratic society will be legitimate even though its rules of recognition harbour elements of injustice and non-consensus if the citizens are always free to enter into processes of contestation and negotiation of the rules of recognition' (Tully 2000: 477), then the interplay between past, present and future social practices must be considered as a key to approaches that reflect the persistence of inequality and the normative goal of achieving democratic legitimacy. This perspective stresses the importance of the customary element present in ancient constitutionalism as opposed to the regulative element of modern constitutionalism, holding that: '*Constitutions are* not fixed and unchangeable agreements reached at some foundational moment, but *chains of continual intercultural negotiations and agreements* in accord with, and violation of the conventions of mutual recognition, continuity and consent' (Tully 1995: 183–4; my emphasis). It makes a strong case for bringing the customary dimension back in, in order to understand and subsequently accommodate diversity that evolves from different social practices – expressed as diverging interpretations of normative meaning.

Constitutional quality in Europe: towards a case study

This chapter focuses on the analytical aspect of constitutionalism. The task at hand is neither to engage with the justification of particular constitutional norms, rules and procedures for any particular polity,[19] nor to contribute to the constitutionalisation literature with further descriptive details.[20] Instead, the purpose is to lay out a framework for empirical research that is able to grapple with the perception, recognition and validation of modern constitutional norms under conditions of transnationalisation. I return to the normative issue in the conclusive chapter 9 for a critical discussion of democratic constitutionalism and its potential for survival in a context of governance beyond the state.

According to Jon Elster, constitutionalism 'stands for the rare moments in a nation's history when deep, principled discussion transcends the logrolling and horse-trading of everyday majority politics' (1993: 6). The European experience with 'things constitutional' in the early twenty-first century had almost the diametrically opposed effect. Rather than moving away from logrolling, it started logrolling. Rather than engaging in deep and principled discussion about fundamental norms, it focused on organising principles and standardised procedures to clear the mess left by the negative referenda. But how bad a mess was this? Instead of a failure, critical constitutional awareness and contestation may turn out to be a possibility rather than a constraint for democratic politics in Europe.

While it is considered as 'highly unlikely that specific constitutional structures and provisions could successfully survive wholesale transplantation from one country to another' (Rosenfeld 1994: 14), the European Union's supranational treaty nonetheless echoes these central requirements of modern constitutionalism. Thus, Article 6 of the TEU stipulates that, 'The Union is founded on the principles of liberty, democracy, respect for human rights and fundamental freedoms, and the rule of law, principles which are common to the member states.'[21]

---

[19] For such endeavours focusing on the Europolity, see, e.g., Hix 1999; De Burca and Scott 2000; Craig 2001; Beaumont, Lyons and Walker 2002; Walker 2002; Bellamy and Castiglione 2003; and Bogdandy and Bast 2006.

[20] See, e.g., Craig 2001; Stone Sweet 2002; or Rittberger and Schimmelfennig 2007.

[21] See Article 6, Consolidated Version on the *Treaty of European Union*, http://europa.eu.int/eur-lex/en/treaties/dat/C_2002325EN.000501.html (accessed 20 July 2007).

These 'core constitutional norms' (Rosenfeld 1997: 216) are common within all member states of the EU, in so far as their validity has been formally acknowledged by all heads of state and government by the act of signing the treaties. Based on each member state's individual constitution, these norms are also socially recognised within each domestic constitutional realm.

Does this move of core constitutional norms from the familiar modern nation-state context into the context of a regional organisation imply that the latter obtains state qualities? Approaches that are based on modern constitutionalism would suggest that, as the following sections discuss in some more detail. However, if constitutionalism is defined as an academic artefact which evolves through social practices – both in and outside academia – over time, the characteristics of the European Union's constitutional quality are expected to differ from that of modern nation-states. Two insights from constitutional research sustain this expectation. Firstly, while the term 'constitution' implies the formal text defining the key principles, norms and procedures that are agreed as having formal validity for a selected and limited group of addressees, i.e. citizens of a community or members of an organisation (Snyder 1990), a constitution is not merely an instrument to organise politics (Elster 1993). It also refers to a way of being in the world (Kahn 1999). Secondly, while the role of constitutions as a framework for organisational practices has been decisively forged during the formative stages of modern statehood, constitutions are not exclusively linked to 'the state' (Sartori 1962; Böckenförde 1992; Morgan 2006). Instead, the specific constitutional quality of each constitution, or treaty, is contingent upon the social practices which are constitutive for its emergence and on-going recognition.

To analyse how norms work in contexts beyond the state, empirical research would raise the question of whether, in the light of the presence of such constitutional norms, the meanings of treaty language and constitutional discourse and the practices that were constitutive of them as well as guided by them can be expected to converge. As an academic artefact, constitutional*ism* offers an analytical reference frame for such an assessment. It provides different perspectives on the process of constitutionalisation, distinguishing between a meta-theoretical perspective on possibilities and purposes of a constitution, and a descriptive perspective to establish whether or not particular features of a constitution are actually in place (Harlow 2002). The latter perspective details constitutionali*sation* as the actual process leading to the establishment of such specific constitutional features (Craig 2001: 127; Stone Sweet 2002: 96).[22]

A key question for research that seeks to assess the constitutional quality of agreements which have been established in beyond-the-state contexts lies in assessing compliance with these agreements (Chayes and Chayes 1993, 1995). On a general level, and notwithstanding the conceptual roots of this approach, the successful implementation of any documents of constitutional quality depends on the degree of social recognition it is able to generate among its addressees. These addressees are usually distinct from the signatories of the document, especially when the document is an internationally agreed treaty (Curtin and Dekker 1999; Finnemore and Toope 2001). That is, in addition to the formal validity of that document expressed by the norms, principles and rules derived through negotiations by the signatories, its substance must be socially recognised in order to be respected, accepted and implemented.[23]

To summarise, the potential for conflict caused by moving constitutional norms outside the bounded territory of states, i.e. outside the domestic polity and away from the inevitable link with methodological nationalism, lies in decoupling the customary from the organisational. It is through this transfer between contexts, that the meaning of norms becomes contested, as differently socialised actors such as politicians, civil servants, parliamentarians or lawyers trained in different legal traditions seek to interpret them. In other words, while in supranational contexts actors might well agree on the importance of a particular norm, such as the proposition that human rights matter, the agreement about a specific norm based on a formal agreement (formal validity) does not allow for conclusions about the meaning of norms. As in different domestic contexts that meaning is likely to differ according to experience with 'norm-use' (Kratochwil 1989: 18; see also Dworkin 1978), it is important to recover the crucial interrelation between both types of social practices, i.e. the cultural practices that generate the

---

[22] For the constitutionalisation of political order in Europe, see Diez and Wiener 2003, ch. 1.

[23] While reference to the citizens of a community as a constitution's *pouvoir constituant* is always assumed, in practice, this remains an idealist assumption, or as Donald Galloway (1998) has argued, it is a 'jurisprudential paradox'.

Table 2.1 *Types of constitutionalism*

Modern	Contemporary
Civilised nations	*Beyond the state*
Examples:	Examples:
UN, Article 38(1) ICJ	UN, EU, WTO
EU, Article 17 TEC[*]	
Nation-state	*One-state (many nations)*
Example:	Examples:
Westphalian Peace	Canada, USA, Mexico

[*] Treaty Establishing the European Community.

customary, on the one hand, and organisational practices facilitated by public performance that interprets the norm for political and legal use, on the other. Both contribute to the interpretation of meanings that are entailed in constitutional norms.

Awareness of the multiplicity in meaning matters, therefore, for constitutional norms in beyond-the-state contexts such as, for example, the European Union. For norms to 'work' in the way intended by the treaties' signatories, mechanisms which allow for on-going exchange about the multiple meanings of norms are important. This awareness needs to be sustained by academic research. It depends on the proper analytical tools to capture how the complex interplay between the customary and the organisational is linked. As a heuristic theoretical framework, constitutionalism allows for the reconstruction of the quality of contemporary constitutionalism. This approach leads beyond the confines of methodological nationalism by making a main distinction between a focus on modern features of democratic representation both in the domestic and in the international context, on the one hand, and contemporary features of democratic representation that emerge from a multiverse of social practices and hence constitutional possibilities worldwide, on the other. Table 2.1 summarises this major distinction with reference to current examples.

Whether or not current beyond-the-state contexts are likely to offer the context for matching normative meanings remains an open question. I propose exploring this question from a political science perspective. To that end, I examine the sociocultural underpinning of evolving constitutional law in a beyond-the-state context empirically. Once the empirical research has established the conditions of divergence,

Table 2.2 *Research propositions*

No.	Proposition
1	Converging interpretation of the meaning of constitutional norms is more likely within one single political arena than in many different arenas.
2	Converging interpretations of the meaning of constitutional norms in different political arenas are likely to increase with repeated interaction across community boundaries.
3	Interaction across community boundaries is more likely to involve elites than other social groups. Elites are therefore most likely to enhance cultural harmonisation.

convergence or diffusion of interpretation of constitutional norms, the results are discussed from a normative perspective. This perspective assesses the possibilities of democratic constitutionalism in a constitutional multiverse that reflects cultural diversity. Three research propositions can be derived from this particular constellation of community formation, diversity and nationality (see Table 2.2).

Conclusion

By taking up Tully's call for bringing culture back into constitutionalism, this book seeks to highlight empirically the influence of cultural practice. While organisational practices might be fully reflected in a single constitutional frame such as the European treaties, it is the cultural practices of the treaties' addressees that will have a decisive impact on how core constitutional norms are interpreted individually. This situation is relevant for the interpretation of constitutional norms in any context including, for example, the respective Canadian or US one-states as well as the European or United Nations beyond-the-state contexts. Comparative case studies are therefore important to reveal the contingent impact of culture on interpreting the meaning of constitutional norms.

Ultimately, the book seeks to generate a working hypothesis for future empirical research based on the theoretical distinction between international negotiations and transnational arenas. It does so by sustaining this distinction not only theoretically but also with findings derived from empirical research. As Rosenfeld points out,

In particular, focus on Europe affords a privileged vantage point for examining the nature and function of contemporary constitutions, assessing *the
extent to which core constitutional norms may be deemed universal*, and
*evaluating the potential transplantations of constitutional arrangements
from one country to another and for their successful spread beyond the
nation-state*. (Rosenfeld 1997: 215–16; my emphasis)

It is here, where the book seeks to make a contribution. The goal is
to bring the empirical advantage of the European case to bear without assuming a particular 'European' dimension as axiomatic. As this
chapter has demonstrated, reference to constitutionalism as a heuristic
framework allows for a definition of modern constitutionalism as but
one specific representation of constitutionalism from *a range of possible* –
and actually existing – *constitutional representations*.[24]

'European constitutionalism beyond the state' (Weiler and Wind
2003) is not an isolated phenomenon, nor is it restricted to one particular place. This book chooses to focus on the European Union for its
case study since the Europolity represents an exceptionally advanced
stage of constitutionalism beyond the state. It involves a community
of member states whose day-to-day politics and policy are governed by
a set of shared values, principles and norms that resemble the core
constitutional norms of modern nation-states. Most member states
share additional memberships in various other international communities and would therefore sustain an expectation of shared recognition
of these norms based on the logic of appropriateness. That is, much of
the literature on compliance with international norms would expect
members of a community to share not only respect but also a sense of
appropriateness for the same rules, norms and beliefs. According to this
literature, a situation of contestedness rather than recognition of norms
among members of a densely constitutionalised polity such as the EU's
would come as a surprise, especially when considering the degree of
transnationalisation of this polity. The book will scrutinise this expectation in due course.

---

[24] For the analytical distinction between 'possible' and 'actual' constitutional
   representations, I thank Jim Tully (email exchange May 2006, on file with
   author).

3 | *The dual quality of norms*

It is hard to imagine any social scientist, even the most ardent methodological individualists among us, arguing with Searle's general claim that social facts *are* facts. Yet *this* fact tells us nothing about intentions as such, much less about their collective form or other properties.

(Onuf 2002: 227; my emphasis)

Introduction

This chapter moves from the general framework of constitutionalism to the specific conceptualisation of norms. It takes the project of bringing in the customary dimension of the *nomos* with a view to examining the impact of the 'hidden' aspects of contemporary constitutionalism one step further. To that end, it recalls the main contributions to the literature on norms advanced by constructivist work in International Relations theory, including insights from conventional, consistent and critical constructivist strands.[1] The following assessment of the role of norms and their hidden meanings – which add a degree of contestedness to international politics – builds on the juxtaposition of two fundamentally distinctive conceptualisations of 'interaction' in International

---

[1] For the different strands of constructivism, see, e.g., Karin Fierke's distinction between two strands. She argues 'that the second constructivism is more consistent than "conventional" constructivism. I use the label "consistent constructivism" to highlight that its assumptions correct the inconsistency at the core of conventional constructivism. This contrasts with the more common distinction between conventional and critical constructivism. The latter term often includes post-structuralism, while the idea of consistent constructivism presented here does not' (Fierke 2006: 12). See also Price and Reus-Smit 1998. In turn, I would hold that distinguishing among conventional, consistent *and* critical constructivism (defined as an approach that engages in the critical enterprise of 'rethinking conceptual foundations') highlights an important difference between normative and non-normative approaches (Weldes 1998: 217). See also Reus-Smit 2003 and Wiener 2006.

Relations theory.[2] The first approach evolves from a behaviourist understanding of strategic interaction. It holds that, as the dependent variable,
government behaviour demonstrates a reaction to particular types of
norms. Accordingly, interaction is both regulated and constituted by
norms; norms are conceptualised as 'social facts' which structure behaviour (Ruggie 1998b); and the concept of a norm is used 'to describe
collective expectations for the proper behavior of actors with a given
identity' (Katzenstein 1996: 5). The second approach works with a
reflexive understanding of interaction. It focuses on the meaning of
norms[3] that is embedded in social practice. It stresses the dual quality
of norms as structuring and constructed, arguing that the 'structural
properties of social systems are both the medium and the outcome of
the practices that constitute those systems' (Giddens 1979: 69).[4] The
crucial difference between the two approaches is that the behaviourist
approach operates with stable norms, while the reflexive approach works
with the assumption of norm flexibility.

   That norms matter for politics is a widely shared observation. There
is less agreement on how they matter. The following argues that despite
a widely shared agreement on the social ontology of norms, conceptual
differences on how norms 'work' prevail.[5] The differences arise with
regard to the quality assigned to norms. For example, one perspective
studies behaviour *in reaction to* norms, thus stressing the structural
quality, the other considers interventions *in relation* to norms. The
conceptualisation of norms as either stable or entailing a dual quality

---

[2] A more extensive earlier version of this chapter has been published as Wiener
   2007a.
[3] See also Florini 1996: 363 for turning norms rather than behaviour into the
   dependent variable; note, however, that here the *explanans* is the 'meaning of
   norms' whereas Florini seeks to explain the change of norm type.
[4] See also Bourdieu 1982, 1993 as well as Schluchter's observation that also 'for
   Weber, action is related to meaning and meaning is incorporated into structures
   which restrict and at the same time render possible social action, while themselves
   being produced and reproduced only through action' (2003: 543).
[5] See Kratochwil's point that 'material factors such as the changes in the technology
   of destruction have to be noted, as have changes in our ideas concerning issues of
   legitimacy, sovereignty, governmental powers, etc. Recovering the original is,
   therefore, not an idle undertaking. But understanding the "original" is only a first,
   although indispensable, step. The second step entails going beyond the conventional
   conceptual divisions and their constitutive assumptions, and casting a fresh and
   unobstructed look at *how ... norms and rules "work"*, i.e., what role they play in
   molding decisions' (Kratochwil 1989: 4; my emphasis).

marks a rather significant conceptual difference with potentially interesting consequences for politics and policy towards legitimate governance beyond the state. By illuminating the conceptual differences, I highlight the distinct impact of norms on international politics, more generally. To that end, I address the question of how normative meanings that have been generated in transnational arenas, say during treaty negotiations, change during the transfer from the transnational to the domestic political arena. While most approaches would agree on the key input of 'interaction in context' as the intervening variable that offers an additional explanatory dimension to explain action or understand how different interpretations have become possible, their respective concepts of interaction differ considerably. For example, some conceptualise interaction as behavioural (Morris 1956), others as deliberative (Müller 2004; Ulbert and Risse 2005; Deitelhoff 2007), or as intersubjective (Kratochwil and Ruggie 1986; Koslowski and Kratochwil 1994; Weldes and Saco 1996; Niesen and Herborth 2007).[6] In the following I argue that, if and when contested, norms are likely to spark conflict. Yet, at the same time contestation is a key condition for democratic governance since it is the basis for revealing and demonstrating meaning, agreement and, ultimately, understanding (Taylor 1993). Thus, while contestation is a process which creates conflict and coordination problems for behaviourist scholars, it is a necessary condition for establishing legitimacy from the perspective of democratic constitutionalism.[7]

I therefore argue that the challenge for research on compliance with norms consists of how to assess contestation as both a conflictive process and hence a potential problem, on the one hand, and as a possibility to enhance social recognition and ultimately the legitimacy of an international agreement, on the other. Both aspects come to the fore once norms are contested. The remainder of this chapter is organised in three further sections. The next section focuses on 'appropriateness' and 'arguing' as two logics of interaction. These logics allow for an

---

[6] The respective conceptualisations include, for example, interaction based on behavioural sociology (Morris 1956), communicative interaction based on deliberation (see Müller 2004; Ulbert and Risse 2005; and Deitelhoff 2007), or 'contestation' as an indicator of democratic governance (Dahl 1971).

[7] Compare, for example, the debate among neoliberal and critical International Relations scholars on the politicisation of international institutions in the German International Relations journal *Zeitschrift für internationale Beziehungen* 14(1), 2007.

empirical assessment of the relation between the social environment and interaction as key factors for research on norms. In the subsequent section, a normative dimension of interaction takes this contextualised approach to interaction further with a view to establishing the principle of contestedness as a *Grundnorm* for democratic politics in beyond-the-state contexts (Kelsen 1968).[8] The final section critically assesses Habermas's distinction between facticity and validity and summarises four main research propositions with a view to the case study.

Two logics of action

Norms as *facts: the logic of appropriateness*

Peter Katzenstein and his collaborators coined an influential definition of norms as 'collective expectations for the proper behaviour of actors with a given identity'. Norms are considered as 'spontaneously evolving, as social practice; consciously promoted, as political strategies to further specific interests; deliberately negotiated, as a mechanism for conflict management; or as a combination, mixing these three types' (Katzenstein 1996: 5, 21). This approach considers domestic institutional trajectories, learning capabilities of elites, and framing activities of non-state actors as key variables for the analysis of norm implementation (Sikkink 1993; Keck and Sikkink 1998; Finnemore and Sikkink 1998; Risse, Ropp and Sikkink 1999; Checkel 2001a). It brought insights from organisational sociology to bear in International Relations theory (Finnemore 1996). It is important to note that it made a conscious decision to eliminate the uncertainties of culture and cognition evoked by the notion of morality. As Katzenstein points out, 'One of the main difficulties in making the sociological approach … attractive for scholars of international security lies in the intuitive equation of the concept of norm with morality.' He therefore prefers to focus 'primarily on the analysis of *regulatory norms* (defining standards of appropriate behaviour) and *constitutive norms* (defining actor identities)'; touching 'less directly on *evaluative norms* (stressing questions of morality) or *practical norms* (focusing on commonly accepted

---

[8] A *Grundnorm* 'denotes a body of meta-norms, rules that specify how legal norms are to be produced, applied and interpreted' (Stone 1994: 447). See also Jackson's definition of 'basic procedural norms' in world politics (2005: 16–17).

notions of "best solutions"' (Katzenstein 1996: 5). This conceptualisation leads to an emphasis on the constitutive role of norms in world politics (Haas 1992; Adler 1997; Risse 2000: 5). This perspective reflects the sociological distinction between norms and values, holding that 'values are individual or commonly shared conceptions of the desirable, i.e. what I and/or others feel we justifiably want – what it is felt proper to want. On the other hand, norms are generally accepted, sanctioned prescriptions for, or prohibitions against, others' behaviour, belief, or feeling – or else. *Values can be held by a single individual, norms cannot*' (Morris 1956: 610; my emphasis). It attaches a structural role to norms as prescriptive standards that can be widely understood, emphasising that: 'Norms must be shared prescriptions and apply to others, by definition' (*ibid.*). Unlike values which are individually transported, norms operate within a social environment. They are defined by norm-setters for norm-followers to be obeying them. 'Values have only a subject – the believer – while norms have both subjects and objects – those who set the prescription, and those to whom it applies' (*ibid.*). This analytical separation of norm-setters and norm-followers has been adopted by students of International Relations, who thereby set a preference for conceptualising norm-following as habitual rather than reasoned (compare Table 3.1).

This behaviourist perspective focuses on the 'logic of appropriateness' (March and Olsen 1989: 23). It considers the impact of norms as predominantly structural and less as relational. The stability assumption of the behaviourist perspective manifests itself in three key observations. Firstly, it implies that norms entail recognisable and hence enforceable prescriptions for behaviour (Checkel 2001b: 180, 182). Subsequently, and secondly, it recognises no significant difference in the impact of legal and social norms on human behaviour. Martha Finnemore stresses the issue of similarity rather than difference between social and legal norms, stating, 'What distinguishes legal norms from other norms is simply not clear' (2000: 701, 703). Thirdly, it means that while the kind of norm, say human rights, environmental standards or minority rights, is arguable, contestation of a norm's meaning, say between norm-setter and designated norm-follower, between different groups of norm-followers or over time, remains analytically bracketed.

It follows that norm implementation is likely to be successful in contexts such as the 'OECD [Organisation for Economic Cooperation and Development] world' (Zürn 2000) or the group of 'civilized

Table 3.1 *The logic of appropriateness*

Basic assumption	Norms are considered as stable and studied as social facts.
Observation	Formal validity is unproblematic; social recognition, once established, is taken as equally stable.
Proposition	The social recognition of norms structures behaviour; actors follow the *logic of appropriateness*.

nations' which share universally held values (Risse 2000). Outside community environments, strategic action is required to enforce norm implementation. Studies on human rights policy, strategic action of 'norm entrepreneurs' and diffusion through elite learning sustain the point (Finnemore and Sikkink 1998: 893, 895; Risse, Ropp and Sikkink 1999; Liese 2001; Locher 2002). While socialisation is considered as a key factor for compliance with norms,[9] the prevailing reading of socialisation works with the behaviourist assumption that actors are socialised to fit a given identity. Analytically, 'creating membership in a society where the intersubjective understandings of the society become taken for granted' (Johnston 2001: 494) follows a top-down concept of socialisation. Based on this concept, both policy analyses and diplomatic strategies will inevitably fail to appreciate the interactive dimension of norms. For example, 'the goal of diplomacy is often the *socialization of others* to accept *in an axiomatic way* novel understandings about world politics' (*ibid.*: 489; my emphasis).

To overcome this impasse, the origins of identities and other normative factors need to be better theorised (Kowert and Legro 1996: 468; Finnemore and Sikkink 1998: 896). If the assumption that norms are conceptualised as both stable and flexible holds, and they hence entail historically contingent meanings, identifying their origin will disclose important information. While at a particular point in time norms may, for example, be defined as stable, they do 'evolve over time' (Klotz 2001: 229). They are subject to change. In the absence of social

---

[9] As Risse and Ropp point out, for example, 'norm compliance becomes a habitualized practice'. Accordingly, domestic institutionalisation is perceived as threefold, including 'processes of bargaining and adaptation, of arguing and moral consciousness-raising, and of institutionalization and habitualization'. Social interaction is thus seen as a key component of 'an overall *socialization process* by which domestic actors increasingly internalize international human rights norms' (Risse and Ropp 1999: 237; my emphasis).

process, norms – by definition – do not exist. The behaviourist perspective circumvents intersubjectivity as a practice which produces change in all participating actors (and institutions) by assuming that the new 'others' will be persuaded to share the dominant validity. Yet, as Dallmayr stresses,

> genuine dialogue or consensus requires a reciprocity of understanding, in the sense that it is not only up to others ('them') to understand 'our' perspective, but it is equally up to 'us' to grasp things from 'their' perspective. Seen in this light, the so-called 'fusion of horizons' postulated by Gadamer does not signify the assimilation of others to 'us', but rather the growing 'convergence of our and their perspectives through a process of reciprocal learning'. (Dallmayr 2001: 341)

In sum, exploring the construction and change of norms within their sociocultural contexts conveys one part of the story; the role of norms as causing rule-following behaviour conveys the other. Together, both perspectives shed light on the dual quality of norms as stable and structuring *as well as* flexible and constructed.

Norms *as* disputed *facts: the logic of arguing*

More recent constructivist literature has added the process of norm validation. By problematising the assumption of normative stability, this approach adds the assumption that validity cannot be taken for granted but must be established through deliberation among norm-*setters*. It is important to note here that the assumption of deliberation does not, however, extend towards including the designated norm-*followers*. Nonetheless, by drawing on Habermas's theory of communicative action, it brings shared understandings about truth, moral virtues and ethical concerns into processes of negotiation, thus stressing the input of agency over mere behaviour, on the one hand, and the analysis of justification over that of causation, on the other (Brandom 1998: 8, 11). In effect, arguing thus extends beyond approaches that study norms with reference to the logics of appropriateness or the logic of consequences, respectively. It is proposed to turn to arguing as a rational process.[10] In forwarding a 'triadic' instead of a 'dyadic'

---

[10] For contributors to this approach, see especially Risse 2000; Müller 2001, 2004; Ulbert and Risse 2005; Deitelhoff and Müller 2005; Deitelhoff 2007; as well as the majority of contributions in Niesen and Herborth 2007.

approach to bargaining, this approach stresses the role of shared external reference frames as a 'mutually accepted external authority' for
the negotiating actors (Ulbert and Risse 2005: 343). These reference
frames are assumed to function as guideposts in the process of deliberation over norm validity. Notably, this approach works with the problematic assumption of the negotiators' shared life-world experiences
(Müller 2004).

The conceptual opening towards norm contestation conveyed by
the arguing approach thus represents an important first step towards
incorporating the 'contestedness' of norms in contexts of international
negotiation.[11] Empirical research studies deliberation in order to probe
how a preferred norm came to have an impact within a specific international context. This approach agrees with the key question of the
behaviourist perspective, namely, why do actors comply; however,
it emphasises the additional dimension of norm validation through deliberation in negotiation situations. Nonetheless, the logic of arguing fails to
apply beyond the conversations among norm-setters. That is, norm-
following is still explained according to either the logic of appropriateness, i.e. as a habitual reaction to norms, or the logic of consequences
when strategic action to persuade designated norm-followers kicks in.

This approach facilitates a partial opening towards a societal
dimension. The innovative step involves a focus on the contestedness
of norm types. That is, normative meaning is considered to evolve from
different cultural backgrounds; arguing about norms hence brings
different and potentially conflicting preferences of the norm-setting
negotiators to light. The arguing approach thus successfully extends
the behaviourist perspective towards the dimension of the contested

---

[11] 'Contestedness' (Lessig 1996), 'contestation' (Dahl 1971) or 'contestability'
(Pettit 1999: 63) are concepts that are considered as necessary dimensions of
legitimate proceedings in law and/or politics. As a process, contestation qualifies
politics as open-ended and subject to change despite being firmly rooted in the
rules of procedure of a particular political order (Rawls 1971). Contestedness is
considered as important for deliberation in the courtroom where the concept is
'relevant to a court not because it identifies the subjective, but because it marks
out that space where, in the present interpretive context, there is no clear link
between a) an authoritarian legal context and b) one or another view of a
contested matter' (Lessig 1996: 1449). In turn, contestation has been identified as
a criterion for assessing the democratic quality of governance. For example, Dahl
suggested to consider the 'right to access to public contestation' as an indicator
for comparative studies on democratic governance (1971: 4).

Table 3.2 *The logic of arguing*

Basic assumption	Norms are stable; yet types of norms are contested.
Observation	Internationally the social recognition of norms is established through arguing. Once established, it is stable and structures behaviour.
	Norm-setting follows the logic of arguing; norm-following occurs according to the logic of appropriateness.
Proposition	The hierarchy of norm types is contested; it therefore requires assessment based on the *principle of communicative action*.

normative legitimacy (see Table 3.2). The assumption is that, in order to be powerful, norms must acquire a degree of shared legitimacy for a significant group of negotiating actors. The shared validity of norms is established through communicative action during which different socioculturally determined preferences are adapted and changed based on the willingness to be persuaded by the better argument. Norm validation, then, is a result of deliberation in transnational or supranational negotiations. The stronger the shared frame of reference, the more likely is the successful implementation of the norm. Whether or not, and if so to which degree, the validated norm is recognised, implemented and accepted in domestic political arenas remains to be established, however.

The limits of arguing

While constructivists have established the regulative impact and the constitutive role of norms for actors' identity and interests, we still know little about the construction and impact of normative meaning. More than two decades ago, Kratochwil noted that social scientists should 'inquire into the conditions and types of rule-governed behaviour and investigate the *emergence, development, and decay of norms* and the incentives for compliance and non-compliance' (1984: 690; my emphasis). By bringing in sociology, the behaviourist perspective has introduced two action-theoretic logics, i.e. the logics of appropriateness and arguing. Both do, however, ultimately consider the stable quality of norms or the facticity dimension as the make-or-break point for the power of norms, establishing whether norms are followed by a group of actors who consider them as either appropriate or legitimate. The majority of compliance studies referred to the logic of appropriateness. Drawing on Habermas, normative legal theories were later incorporated by including the logic of arguing. Overall, the separation between norms and values came at the cost of eliminating agency from the process of norm origin and change. While norms may appear as stable over a prolonged, albeit limited, period of time, drawing the analytical conclusion of norms as stable social facts implies ontologising norms. That is, norm types are considered as ontologically primitive units of analysis which entail no distinct elements other than those ascribed to that type. The analytical shift from the phenomenological to the conceptual level has occurred almost unnoticed. It entails the risk of extending the much criticised billiard ball metaphor – which has, at one time, informed a Hobbesian concept of the state in International Relations theory – to norms.[12] This development raises questions for further studies. Two insights stand out. As observable units, norms not only cause or structure behaviour but also evolve in relation to social interaction. Both processes need to be considered if norm implementation and norm resonance are at stake. The causal impact reflects the facticity of norms as an observable and arguable disputed social fact, such as the rising number of human rights claims in global politics (Soysal 1994; Jacobson 1996). In turn, the relational impact sheds light on the perceived validity of norms, for example why the death penalty is considered as legitimate in some democracies but not in others.

Depending on whether compliance is understood as implementing rules or as accepting rules as legitimate, the extent to which norms work is defined differently by various strands of constructivism. While some stress the mutual recognition of a norm's validity as a sine qua non for normative legitimacy, others would include the possibility of applying coercion to achieve compliance. In the latter case, compliance is thus more correctly defined as an instrument of smooth governance rather than a matter of good governance. The preference for research that seeks to pursue the organisational rather than the substantive impact of norms may turn out as particularly problematic in transnational

---

[12] This view builds on the observation of the ontologisation of social phenomena elsewhere. For example, Alberto Melucci had warned against the ontologisation of social movements. See Melucci 1988: 330; 1989: 26; see also Wendt 1987 for a similar critique of the ontologisation of the state.

political arenas. It is in these arenas where the assumption that all involved actors share perceptions of norm validity is most likely to produce misleading conclusions. The trap is twofold. Firstly, the validity perception is likely to vary among actors according to their context of origin as the root location of individually transported 'normative baggage' (Puetter and Wiener 2007: 8), i.e. the respective domestic arenas in which notions of appropriateness are constituted through social practices on a day-to-day basis (Garfinkel 1967: 35). Secondly, assumptions about normative legitimacy (which is derived through deliberation in limited negotiation settings where the process of arguing is situated) do not hold if the resort to coercion when implementing the norm is not excluded in principle.

Between *facts and norms: the principle of contestedness*

Other – consistent and critical – constructivist approaches that follow the linguistic turn in the social sciences more generally understood have emphasised the emergence, change and decay of norms and their meaning (Kratochwil 1984). They stressed a dialectical perspective on norms as evolving through practice and in context, applying discourse analysis, Wittgensteinian language game theory and Habermas's communicative action theory, respectively.[13] These scholars argue that while norms may be considered as valid and just under conditions of interaction in one cultural context, the assumption cannot be generalised. After all, normative validity cannot be assumed as stable in different political arenas without providing empirical evidence. This perspective draws on the critical juxtaposition of Kantian 'regulism' which holds rules as explicit, on the one hand, and Wittgensteinian 'pragmatism', on the other. It moves on from the assumption of 'norms explicit in rules to norms as implicit in practices' (Brandom 1998: 18). This move offers an important conceptual platform from which to elaborate on the dual quality of norms in two ways. Firstly, by expanding the process of norm validation, it elaborates on the contestation of norms. Secondly, by raising the issue of legitimacy, it places norm construction and contestation within a wider societal context. While the first aspect has been raised by the arguing approach, the second aspect stands to be appreciated

[13] For the three approaches, see Weldes and Saco 1996; Bohman and Rehg 1997; Fierke 1998; Barnett 1999; Milliken 1999; and Crawford 2004: 22–5.

more fully by students of International Relations. It requires a perception of the contexts in which norms work and the social practices that
are constitutive for their meanings (Reus-Smit 2001a: 538).

To elaborate on this perspective, this section focuses on the distinction between normative facticity and validity.[14] I propose working with
the tension that derives from a dialectical relationship between norm
facticity and norm validity. This assumption follows from Habermas's
observation 'that the tension between facticity and validity, which is
embedded in the use of speech and language, and returns in the ways in
which societalised – or, for that matter, communicatively societalised –
individuals are integrated, needs to be worked out by the participants.
Social integration which is realised through positive law stabilises this
tension ... in a particular way' (1992: 33). The facticity–validity tension
thus provides a working link between law and politics. It is hence considered as the basis for a legitimate and radically democratic state of law
which in turn provides a framework for performing social integration
based on discursive processes towards the application of positive law.
Individual action must therefore be based on a set of organising principles
such as equal access to participation and mutual recognition in an on-
going dialogue (Tully 1995; Gagnon and Tully 2001; Taylor 2001).

To that end, Tully proposes the two principles of constitutionalism
and democracy. The principle of constitutionalism implies that the
discussion of successful norm implementation needs to consider the
fact that 'reasonable disagreement and thus dissent are inevitable and
go all the way down in theory and practice' must be appreciated, since
there 'will be democratic agreement and disagreement not only *within*
the rules of law but also *over* the rules of law' (Tully 2002a: 207;
emphasis in original). It follows that deliberation over norms in bargaining situations in transnational arenas is unlikely to cover the whole
story when considered as a 'snap-shot' situation in which interaction is
limited according to time and context. In turn, and following the

---

[14] The literal translation of Habermas's *Faktizität und Geltung* (1992) should read
'facticity and validity'. The English translation of the book title as 'between facts
and norms' appears to obscure the literal emphasis on validity suggested by the
German original title. In the following I develop the facticity–validity tension
from the relation between formal validity (*Geltung*) and social facticity
(*Faktizität*). In turn, Weber's definition of 'validity' is a structural concept based
on the following observation: 'the probability of action will be called the
"validity" of the order in question' (1978: 31, cited in Schluchter 2003: 544).

democratic constitutionalist perspective, deliberation is not reduced to mere – sociologically observable – performance. Instead, it bears the potential of having an impact on normative substance at the same time. The principle of democracy

> requires that, although the people or peoples who comprise a political asso-
> ciation are subject to the constitutional system, they, or their entrusted repre-
> sentatives, must also impose the general system on themselves in order to be
> sovereign and free, and thus for the association to be democratically legit-
> imate. ... These democratic practices of deliberation are themselves rule
> governed (to be constitutionally legitimate), but *the rules must also be open
> to democratic amendment* (to be democratically legitimate). (Tully 2002a:
> 205; my emphasis)

It follows that, in principle, democratic procedures are a precondition for establishing the validity of norms (Joerges 2002: 146). This premise brings the evaluative dimension of norms, which had been left out by the modern constructivist research programme, squarely back in (see Table 3.3).

If norms are inexorably linked with a larger societal context from which they accumulate and transport meaning for strategic actors, then negotiation and bargaining situations are by definition not limited to the strategic or 'rhetorical' reference to stable norms, even though bargaining situations may suggest just that (Schimmelfennig 2001). Instead, the assumption that discursive interaction transcends institutional boundaries implies a conceptual link between social practices which create meaning, on the one hand, and strategic action which mobilises this meaning as a political resource, on the other. As an intersubjective process, discursive interaction draws on resources which have been created prior to the negotiating and/or bargaining situation. Communicative action thus not only contributes to the social construction of norms but also reconstructs sociocultural patterns of the life-world. As such, it has a constructive impact both within modern societies and beyond them. If communicative action is conceptualised as intersubjective, it potentially produces 'new values' in the process of deliberation (Müller 2001: 173). These new values need to be transferred into the respective elite negotiators' root communities. Studying the meaning of norms in a comparative perspective, then, would generate a better understanding about how out-of-context norm interpretation (and conflict) works. In other words, it is suggested that the transfer of normative meanings casts light on the link between

Table 3.3 *The principle of contestedness*

Basic assumption	The dual quality of norms implies that they are both stable and flexible.
Observation	While norm validity is in principle contested, norm recognition does structure behaviour. In turn, as a social practice, behaviour has an effect on type and meaning of a norm.
Proposition	The role of norms in politics is based on the *principle of contestedness*.

the negotiating actors and their communities of origin. In contexts of norm negotiation in transnational arenas, the absence of the life-world has been studied more at length than the issue of contested meanings of norms and their translation into different contexts. The latter remains difficult to conceptualise and requires empirically complex and interdisciplinary exploration. After all, political struggles or strategic arguing always 'bring very different and often conflicting traditions of interpretation, conceptions and weightings of constitutional and democratic considerations to bear on a case at hand' (Tully 2002a: 206).

Normative change is then not exclusively observable as an outcome of a negotiation situation in transnational political arenas. It will invariably occur in domestic arenas as well. To capture the missing link between transnational and domestic arenas, 'analysis should proceed beyond the agreement because the agreement and the normative models of its assessment will always be less than perfect, partial, subject to reasonable disagreement, and dissent will likely break out in practice and theory, reigniting the process' (*ibid.*: 227). Any assessment of norms within an analytical framework that underestimates this link runs the risk of shaky predictions. After all, as Tully rightly stresses, 'the traditional end-point of normative analysis, even when it is related to practical case studies, leaves the entire field of implementation and review to empirical social sciences, often under the false assumption that implementation is different in kind from justification, simply a technical question of applying rigid rules correctly' (*ibid.*). If norm validity is considered beyond the point of acceptance among elites in bargaining situations, a closer focus on the embeddedness of normative meaning in the life-world is invaluable. After all, if the meaning of norms stems from day-to-day practices (Habermas 1985: 237), their social dimension is inexorably linked with that context.

Conclusion: four research assumptions

The following summarises four research assumptions and hypotheses from the literature on norms. These assumptions will guide the selection of indicators for the empirical research project in chapter 4, and provide a reference point for evaluating the research findings. While three of the following research propositions, i.e. the liberal community hypothesis, layer-cake assumption and national identity-options assumption, are firmly grounded in a universalistic approach to norms, the fourth, i.e. the rule-in-practice assumption, follows from a contextual approach. That is, only the rule-in-practice assumption is, in principle, conceptually prepared to deal with the necessary flexibility that would allow for identifying non-modern constitutionalist elements. Each assumption or hypothesis expects a typical outcome with regard to the interpretation of norms that have been moved outside modern constitutional boundaries. They also suggest a selection of indicators for research that seeks to make meaning accountable. The following summarises these respective expectations and then details each approach.

The *liberal community* hypothesis would expect convergence among elites from member states that hold memberships in a number of international communities including the UN, the EU, the North Atlantic Treaty Organization (NATO), the WTO and others. Divergence in the interpretation of normative meaning would present a puzzle for this approach. The *layer-cake* assumption would expect cultural harmonisation among elites before any other social group. If we were to find cultural harmonisation, then a study of elite groups in different contexts and with regard to different topics should demonstrate it. The *national identity-options* assumption would expect elites to behave differently according to their respective national origin, rather than context of interaction. Convergence among different nation-based elite groups would hence be a puzzle to this approach. The *rule-in-practice* assumption expects interpretations of meaning to differ according to interaction in context. The more interaction in context, the more likely is convergence. Divergent interpretations of the meaning of norms within transnational contexts of high-frequency elite interaction would be puzzling for this approach.

The 'liberal community hypothesis' (Schimmelfennig 2003: 89) is derived from the compliance literature. Typically, compliance research builds on assumptions about state behaviour (see Table 3.4). These

Table 3.4 *Liberal community hypothesis*

Members of a community with a given identity share norms, values and principles.
▪ Socialisation establishes appropriateness.

▪ Expectation:
Membership in a supranational community enhances norm convergence.

assumptions are based on the impact of state interest in collaboration among states, which is enhanced by processes of socialisation that provide the glue of international communities. In addition to socialisation, the input of advocacy group action such as naming and shaming are considered as intervening variables, as both influence behaviour. They create a situation which enhances compliant behaviour by (state) actors that wish to be accepted by a larger community. Socialisation is considered a key factor to explain the compliant behaviour of designated norm-followers who are usually conceptualised as outsiders of and potential newcomers to a particular liberal community.[15] 'Community', 'identity' and 'norm types' are thus considered as *stable factors* by this approach. Accordingly, *change* is expected to occur exclusively with the norm-following actor who aspires to become a good member in a community.[16] Obtaining membership in a community is likely to enhance norm convergence. That is, following the bracketing of community, identity and norms, the appreciation of intersubjectivity remains limited to a partial application to the two processes of negotiating norm types and to the process of shaming outsiders into compliance.

The *layer-cake assumption* follows Karl Deutsch's research, more than five decades ago. At the time, he listed two research questions which address the analytical relation between social groups and cultural change in the process of European integration.

[15] See Schimmelfennig 2001 and Johnston 2001.
[16] Studies on European enlargement, especially considering the round of massive enlargement that was completed with the entry of ten new member states in May 2004, offer a typical view on such expectations towards norm-followers. In these cases the conditions for new members provide the stick and the achievement of membership will offer the carrot. See, e.g., Fierke and Wiener 1999 and Schimmelfennig and Sedelmeier 2005.

What are the cultural and social prospects of integration? Can there evolve a single people ... How *compatible* are the cultures and the social and economic [as well as the legal, AW] institutions of the participating peoples?

Are there *leaders, leading groups,* and *symbols* to give expression to the actually existing facts and trends? (Deutsch 1953: 194–5; emphasis in original)

Following the interplay of language and cultural assimilation over the centuries, a recurring 'layer-cake pattern' was observed (*ibid.*: 170). This pattern entailed

a high degree of cultural assimilation and participation in extended social communication among the top layers of society; a lesser degree on the intermediate levels; and little or no assimilation or participation among the mass of the population at the bottom. (*ibid.*)

According to Deutsch, this pattern was part of a cycle from 'local isolation to "universal" empire and back' (*ibid.*). While the layer-cake pattern displayed a 'variation' in assimilation to common standards by the upper classes, the difference in influence on elites and masses was found to be distinct, with the former being involved and developing various shades of assimilation,[17] while the latter characteristically displayed 'continued passivity and lack of direct participation in affairs of wider import' (*ibid.*: 171). At the time, Deutsch found that 'only when this relatively passive population was mobilized in the process of economic growth and political organization, did its cultural and social characteristic acquire ... a new and crucial importance in the process of nation-building' (*ibid.*: 172).[18] Subsequently, he stresses four aspects as outcomes of processes of interaction over time. They include, firstly, the enhanced potential for effective communication; secondly, accumulation of economic resources and social mobilisation to allow for the

---

[17] As Deutsch notes, 'From the point of view of nationality, all these were variations of the common layer-cake pattern. Assimilation to a common standard among the upper classes might be feeble, as during the "dark ages" in western Europe; it might be somewhat more strongly developed, as among the European nobility at the time of the Crusades; or it might be almost complete, as in a universal state, as it had been in that of Imperial Rome' (1953: 71).

[18] Note that, when talking about nation-building here, Deutsch refers to the examples of the Czech and German populations, respectively, in Bohemia, on the one hand, and the Malay and Chinese populations, respectively, in Malaya, on the other.

Table 3.5 *Layer-cake assumption*

High degree of cultural assimilation and participation follows social interaction.

▪ Extended social communication is expected among the top layers of society.

▪ Expectation:

In international processes of integration, harmonisation most likely occurs among elites.

social division of labour; thirdly, social accumulation and integration of memories and symbols; and fourthly, a 'social learning capacity is developed invisible in the minds of individuals; some of it can be observed in the habits and patterns of culture prevailing among them; some of it finally is embodied in tangible facilities and specific institutions' (*ibid.*: 190).

From these insights into the generation of shared, albeit often invisible, patterns of social learning, social mobility and access to participation, it follows that, in general, convergence of meanings is most likely to occur in relation with elite interaction (see Table 3.5). This expectation has largely been sustained by the more recent Europeanisation literature.[19] While it is now common – especially among constructivists of all convictions – to view the perception of and compliance with supranational norms as an interactive process, it still remains firmly situated within an international society of sovereign states. That is, the differentiation between types and degrees of statehood, for example, expressed by the distinction of one-state, modern state or beyond-the-state contexts, leaves some margin for improvement. While the thrust of these studies point to an eventual diffusion of – in this case, 'European' – norms that sooner or later leads to convergence (Checkel 2001b), some have cautioned against generalising too quickly. As Eder has argued, for example, a more likely scenario might be one of 'two faces of Europeanization' (2004). This more sceptical view of the harmonising

---

[19] For summaries, see, among others, Radaelli 2000; Cowles, Caporaso and Risse-Kappen 2001; and Olsen 2004.

potential in Europe suggests that differentiated cultural representation plays a key role in processes of regional integration. The case study elaborates on this thought. To that end, the impact of cultural practices on the interpretation of constitutional norms in a selection of domestic and transnational political arenas will be examined.

The *national identity-options assumption* follows research by Marcussen, Risse, Engelmann-Martin *et al.* who found that elites carry a 'nation-state identity' in addition to a set of other identities (1999: 616). Accordingly, various national identity options are available according to national descent. In Europe, for example, these involve firstly, 'liberal nationalist identity' constructions where the 'we' is confined to one's own nation-state; secondly, the perception of 'Europe as a community of values'; thirdly, the perception of 'Europe as a "third force"'; fourthly, a 'modern Europe as part of the western community'; and finally, the perception of a 'Christian Europe' (*ibid.*: 618). The choice of national identity options is displayed nationwide by elites of one nation-state during a particular period of time. Importantly, this research found that '*nation state identities* which have become consensual in a given polity *remain rather stable over time*' (Marcussen, Risse, Engelmann-Martin *et al.* 1999: 614; my emphasis). This research works with the assumption that for identities to change, they require elite manipulation. Since the chance for such manipulation is reduced over time, identities are assumed to be relatively stable (see Table 3.6). While both German and French elites have settled for 'Europeanised' identities, the British have not. The nation-state identities once adopted are considered as '*sticky rather than subject to frequent change*' (*ibid.*: 616, citing Fiske and Taylor 1991: 150–1; my emphasis).

Note that unlike the cognitive abilities of individuals addressed by this research, studies on institutional adaptation and change found that the likelihood for 'Europeanisation' was enhanced by difference rather than commonality between member state and European Union institutional settings.[20] For the purposes of the research project at hand, the assumptions about individual behaviour are of major relevance, since the research focus is interested in the impact of transnationalisation as a social activity and hence concentrates on individuals who move between domestic and transnational political arenas.

[20] See, e.g., Lenschow 1997; Knill and Lenschow 2000; and Börzel and Risse 2000. For overview articles, see especially Bulmer and Burch 2001 and Olsen 2004.

Table 3.6 *National identity options*

National identities held by elites are stable.
- Enduring national identity options

- Expectation:
Interests diverge based on national identity patterns.

Sociologists have raised the issue of (non-)synchronicity in this regard, pointing out that the challenge of European integration is how to make 'a democratic culture of synchronicity in a social space of increasing non-synchronicity among those moving in this space' (Eder 2004: 97). Here it is important to notice the issue of non-movement as well. After all, in addition to non-synchronicity generated by individual cross-arena movements, the *lack* of movement also creates divergence based on the lack of institutional adaptation and stable national identity options in the respective domestic political arena. As Eder maintains, while legal and social integration present the first face of Europeanisation, 'cultural representations of this space, such as the European house, the internally bounded space or the variable geometry' create the second face (*ibid.*: 90, 97). Hence empirical research would need to capture subject positions embedded in 'cultural representations which can be seen as elements of an emerging new culture of synchronicity' (*ibid.*: 97) in order to examine the social recognition of fundamental norms. Conceptually, this observation sustains the analytical shift from structural- or system-level research on norms towards studying *individual* impact proposed by this book.

Subsequently, and in distinction from more universalistic approaches, a more contextual approach to norms cautions against a causal relation between norms and (state) behaviour. Instead, it stresses the dual quality of norms. That is, normative interpretation is not exclusively based on social recognition and formal validity but also on cultural validation derived through day-to-day practices. In the absence of a constitutional consensus which provides the institutional framework of reference for *inter*national negotiations, intersubjectivity is therefore expected to enhance contestation. This would imply that the political success of internationally negotiated treaties, conventions or agreements depends on the variation of meanings that are influential for the interpretation of the respective fundamental norms. In the absence of more detailed knowledge about the origin of such variation, conditions of consensus will be hard to grasp analytically. Subsequently, a compromise which might look like a full agreement on paper is likely to turn into a source of conflict, for example, when submitted to voters' scrutiny in domestic referenda.

The *rule-in-practice assumption* conceptualises rules inextricably related to social practices which, in turn, are constitutive for the environment in which they occur (see Table 3.7). This conceptualisation of

Table 3.7 *Rule-in-practice assumption*

Normative meaning is constituted by social practice in context.
▪ *Interaction* is constitutive for and draws on meanings.
▼
▪ Expectation:
Contestation enhances legitimacy.

social practices is central to the study of meanings. It follows the view that, 'understanding comes, if it comes at all, only by engaging in the volley of practical dialogue' (Tully 1995: 133). This dialogue involves social practices that extend beyond international negotiations. The focus of analysis which follows this approach seeks to understand variation in the meaning of norms based on three assumptions: (i) norms entail a dual quality; (ii) the meaning of norms is embedded in a structure of meaning-in-use; and (iii) meaning evolves through interaction in context – it is embedded in social practice and therefore subject to change. All individuals carry specific normative baggage, and all interpretations of meanings are expected to vary according to their context of emergence. For example, as an interactive process, intergovernmental negotiations over appropriate responses to foreign policy events bring the normative baggage of all individual participants to bear. They are an expression of the 'normative context' (Katzenstein and Okawara 1993: 84) in which governance processes evolve and facilitate input from and change of a particular structure of meaning-in-use. Here, behaviourist approaches are interested in studying variation in state behaviour in relation to norms as intervening variables. Reflexive approaches focus on the meaning of norms.[21]

---

[21] Positivist research designs would therefore identify it as their 'dependent variable'.

Summary

According to the liberal community hypothesis, actors who enjoy membership in a community and hence share a given identity are likely to consider the same rules, norms and principles as appropriate. According to the layer-cake assumption, elites are most likely to produce a pattern of cultural harmonisation. The national identity-options assumption assumes that identities are sticky and therefore relatively stable. Finally, the rule-in-practice assumption expects meanings to change according to interaction in context. Based on these research assumptions, the case study considers elites in two countries which share multiple memberships in various international communities. With regard to the European context, this condition suggests a choice of two long-term member states as opposed to studying new member states who do not share a prolonged period of social interaction during the past three periods of European constitutionalisation spanning about five decades of integration. If a pattern of stable diverging national positions and parallel evolving converging transnational positions can be confirmed, a larger case study should follow with a view to setting up a more comprehensive database. The following chapter takes a step further towards the empirical research by identifying a research methodology and method to study variation in the interpretation of normative meanings and its impact on international politics.

4 | Making normative meaning accountable for international relations

[T]he practice not only fulfils the rule, but also gives it concrete shape in particular situations. Practice is … a continual 'interpretation' and reinterpretation of what the rule really means.

(Taylor 1993: 57)

Introduction: bringing cultural practices back in

The previous chapters have addressed the emergent constitutional quality as a new phenomenon in world politics. It has been suggested that the political impact of this phenomenon should be addressed with reference to the role of norms. In two theoretical moves from constitutionalism to work on norms in international politics and law, these chapters have made the case for a contextualised approach which takes social practices into account. Notably, these practices have been distinguished as organisational practices which are predominant in *modern* constitutionalism and as cultural practices that have had stronger impact on *ancient* constitutionalism. The dual quality of norms' assumption of the contextualised approach holds that social practices are always inextricably linked with norms. Under conditions of transnationalisation, social practices transgress the boundaries of organisational units with an impact on normative meaning that stands to be established empirically.

In a third move, this chapter addresses this empirical aspect. It operationalises the case study based on specific methodological details that are required for the project of making meaning accountable. To that end, it turns to discourse analysis. While much of the available literature in International Relations theory, especially in the area of foreign policy analysis, has conducted empirical research based on discourse analysis, the methodological details require borrowing from the neighbouring disciplines of anthropology, ethno-methodology and sociology. This chapter thus undertakes the innovative step of deriving a methodological framework that is fit to apply discourse analysis to the study of norms in world politics. The framework comprises distinctive norm types, conditions of norm contestation, types of norm divergence and a specific interview evaluation technique. The next section places the three dimensions of normative understanding – formal validity, social recognition and cultural validation – within the context of transnationalisation. It also introduces distinctive conditions of contestation and types of norms. Subsequently, a section details the methodological approach, i.e. the discourse analytical method of conducting and evaluating interviews. It presents the technique of opposition-deriving with a view to reconstructing the structure of meaning-in-use, and then identifies the research indicators. The final section summarises the research design.

Transnationalisation

The process of transnationalisation both in its narrow political definition as *type of actor* including at least one non-state actor, and in the wider social definition as *type of activity* has been characterised as having constitutional effects. Yet, a debate has ensued as to whether the European treaty revisions over the past five decades since the Treaty of Rome was signed were indicative of the founding treaty's transformation from an international treaty towards a constitutional treaty (i.e. the Constitutional Treaty). While being aware of differences in tradition and type of social practices in different domestic contexts, students of constitutionalism have been less concerned with exploring varying interpretations of the meaning of constitutional norms in the transnational realm.[1] Or, when they do, the transnational risks falling prey to implicit generalisations which result from large-scale regional comparisons such as American vs European constitutionalism.[2] Yet, the

---

[1] Legal scholars have, for example, studied norm convergence or divergence with reference to the human rights norm in relation to the European Convention of Human Rights (ECHR) and the jurisprudence at the Strasbourg Court and with reference to national laws and practices. The goal of such studies is to establish 'the degree of conformity with those norms, but also the extent to which such implementation, transposition or absorption of norms might be occurring in ways which are quite distinctive and specific to the various national legal systems' (De Burca 2002: 131).

[2] As Rosenfeld writes, for example, 'Europeans embrace a more teleological conception of constitutionalism owing to their stronger commitment to community and deeper commitment to state-promoted welfare' (1997: 216).

question remains whether a general overlap in how 'Europeans' interpret the meaning of core constitutional norms can actually be observed.
Studying the role of meaning is by no means trivial, as the 'intentionality
of action and assertion' may clash 'with the meaning of speech' (Dunn
1978: 149). Thus, describing a concept in a treaty may trigger different
expectations, even among readers of the same text. To understand the
impact of individual experience, it is therefore necessary to identify the
constitutive input of social practices. How to address this by way of
empirical research is the main concern of this chapter.

As chapter 2 has demonstrated, cultural practices play a key role for
the project of uncovering hidden meanings of norms which deviate from
the texts of legal documents and expected shared recognition stipulated
by modern constitutionalism. This specific perspective on cultural practices involves a 'prospective' as opposed to a 'retrospective' method of
analysis.[3] Methodologically, the focus is set on specific decisions taken at
'major historical choice points' in the past to inquire why they come
about and seeks to show that the outcomes might have been different if
additional information had been available (Tilly 1980: 679). The choice
points that matter to this investigation about the meaning of fundamental norms involve the series of decisions which led to the signing of
the Constitutional Treaty in 2004. It is argued that these decisions,
especially the final step towards signing the blueprint of that treaty,
might have taken a different turn if additional information about the
significant divergence in the interpretation of meaning of fundamental
norms held by elites in various EU member states had been available at
the time.

As the following will demonstrate in more detail, the additional and
heretofore hidden information can be revealed by empirical research on
cultural practices as the dimension which has become increasingly
neglected with the hardening of modern constitutional features and
its reliance on organisational practices only. Tully's studies to recover
hidden constitutional meanings in the context of the Canadian one-state
(Tully 1995) employed a retrospective method, beginning with a particular historical condition (inequality before the constitution according
to cultural identity) and searching back for its causes. In turn, this
prospective analysis works with a view to the European context, beginning with a particular historical condition (conflicting interpretations

---

[3] For details of these two methods, see Tilly 1975: 14 and 1980.

of norms) and searching forward to the alternative outcomes of that condition with a specification of the paths leading to each of the outcomes. This approach follows the assumption that, in addition to reconstructing constitutional dialogues with respect to both sets of practices – organisational and cultural – that are constitutive for the meaning of constitutional norms, understanding norms in contexts beyond the modern state requires a comparison of different – transnational and domestic – arenas, as the places in which international politics take place.

Accordingly, the comparative research is designed to identify patterns of interpretation.[4] Following the rule-in-practice assumption (see Table 3.7) conflictive interpretations of norms are expected as a consequence of decoupling organisational and cultural social practices of the *nomos*. It is hence expected that the transfer between different contexts enhances the contestation of meanings, as differently socialised individuals – politicians, civil servants, parliamentarians or lawyers – who have been trained in different legal traditions and socialised in different day-to-day circumstances seek to interpret them. While the potential for misunderstandings and conflict can be kept at bay by adding a deliberative dimension to facilitate arguing and ultimately persuasion that one meaning should legitimately trump another, it is important to keep in mind that arguing will establish agreement about a particular sort of norm within a limited situation only. After all, once norm interpretation and implementation are to be carried out in the various domestic contexts, the meaning attached to this sort of norm is likely to differ according to the respective domestic experience with norm use. It is therefore important to recover the crucial interrelation between the social practices that generate meaning, on the one hand, and public performance that interprets the norm for political and legal use, on the other (Dworkin 1978; Kratochwil 1989). To fill this gap, which is considered the central aspect of the *invisible constitution of politics*, the case study reconstructs the normative structures of meaning-in-use in three different contexts: London, Berlin and Brussels.[5] To identify the

---

[4] As Reinhard Bendix notes, for example, 'comparative studies illuminate the meaning of sociological universals'. They allow us to question 'usual connotations' which may be adopted into scholarly language from ordinary speech and seek to 'make these connotations explicit' (1963: 535).

[5] Note the distinction between this concept of 'meaning-*in*-use' based on contextualised structures of meaning which come to life only through *interaction*, and the concept of 'meaning *as* use' which implies meaning that 'refers to speaker

more detailed aspect of the research design, the following first defines conditions for norm contestation and then identifies generic norm types.

Enhanced contestation

As the International Relations literature has demonstrated, norms may achieve a degree of appropriateness reflected by changing state behaviour on a global scale. However, in the absence of social recognition, norms are likely to be misinterpreted or simply disregarded. This also holds true for legal norms which require social institutions to enhance understanding and identify meaning, i.e. normative practice.[6] The documented language about norms indicates no more than the formal validity of a norm, while their social recognition stands to be constructed by social interaction. In other words, understanding does not follow from reference to 'objective reality', 'rather it is inherently constructed and sustained by social processes' (Colombo 2003: 1). This link between what is deemed obligatory or right in legal texts and the social context of interpretation facilitates an important empirical access point. It is especially valuable when studying enhanced norm contestation, that is, situations where legal text and social context of interpretation do not overlap (see Table 4.1). Following critical constructivists' work on norms, this can be achieved by examining individual enacting of meaning-in-use. This additional dimension would allow for a way of identifying the cultural validation based on the experience of an individual's day-to-day life. Cultural validation therefore needs to be accounted for in addition to the formal validity and social recognition of norms, bringing cultural practices back in to examine the degree of divergence, convergence or diffusion with regard to the interpretation of norms involves identifying variation with regard to the cultural validation of norms.

Norms – and their meanings – evolve through interaction in context. They are therefore contested by default. This is particularly important in beyond-the-state contexts where no 'categorical imperatives' are in

---

meaning and particularly the *intention* of the speaker or the desired communicative effect of the utterance' in semantics (Mwihaki 2004: 128; my emphasis).

[6] As lawyers have pointed out, for example, legal institutions are not exclusively based on 'black letter law' but are, in the first instance, 'fiction' (Curtin and Dekker 1999: 88, cited in Ruiter 1993: 363).

Table 4.1 *Enhanced contestation of norms: three conditions*

Steps	Type	Condition
1	Contingency	Historical *contingency* means that norm interpretation depends on context.
1 + 2	Social practices	Moving selected *social practices* (i.e. organisational practices only) beyond a given social context reduces the social feedback factor when interpreting norms.
1+2+3	Crisis	A situation of *crisis* raises the stakes for norm interpretation as time constraints enhance the reduced social feedback factor.

practice, and where 'the context, or situation, within which activities take place is extremely important' (Jackson 2005: 19–20). As social constructs, norms may acquire stability over extended periods of time, yet, they remain flexible by definition. We can therefore hypothesise that the contested meaning of norms is enhanced under three conditions. Each condition indicates an increase in contestedness due to the declining social feedback factor. Firstly, the *contingency* of normative meaning indicates a change of constitutive social practices both cultural and organisational, and hence normative meaning over time. Secondly, the extension of *social practices* beyond modern political and societal boundaries changes the social environment and hence the reference frame provided by social institutions. And thirdly, a *situation of crisis* raises stakes for shared understanding as time for deliberation is limited (see Table 4.1).

The case study focuses on the second condition. It seeks to generate a working hypothesis that stands to be substantiated for example by larger research samples or by applying it to the third condition of crisis. More specifically, the empirical research explores the impact of changing governance processes, understood as moving social practices beyond the boundaries set by modern nation-states. Here it is important to note the selective, or out-of-synch, movements of organisational and cultural practices. The research focuses on such moving social practices and the subsequent impact on the meaning of constitutional norms stipulated by the European Union's treaties. If norm interpretation is historically contingent, then moving social practices outside the domestic political arena indicates a transfer of normative meanings outside the familiar context of interpretation. While social feedback is high in the domestic arena where organisational and cultural practices overlap, it is expected to decrease with a lack of overlap between these two types of social practices. To understand the potential for conflict such misunderstandings might cause, the social feedback factor is measured with reference to the individually formed cultural validation of particular norms. The empirical research seeks to reconstruct the varying links between formal validity, social recognition and cultural validation of a norm. This is important, since diverging interpretations of meaning may induce a clash of normative meanings and hence potentially present a source of conflict for politics beyond the state. The aspect which is particularly interesting to explore here is the question of whether globalisation and transnationalisation will contribute to 'solving' the problem or whether the reverse is the case and the level of contestation increases. While we can hypothesise that the more transnational a context of interaction, the less likely are clashes over norm interpretation, this hypothesis would work only if the process of transnationalisation turned out to be all-encompassing. Otherwise, transnational arenas might have to be added to the existing national arenas within the larger context of global politics, thus increasing the reference frames of social recognition and hence the potential for conflictive interpretation. Whether or not such an internationally caused conflict of meanings would necessarily lead to *political* conflict, or whether it could be considered as a way to enhance legitimacy remains to be addressed from a normative theoretical standpoint. I will engage with these options in some more detail when evaluating the findings of the case study and discussing them in chapters 8 and 9.

Types of norms

To enhance transdisciplinary accessibility of this research design, I propose distinguishing among three types of norms: fundamental norms, organising principles and standardised procedures (see Table 4.2).[7]

---

[7] Note a similar pattern of distinction by Dimitrova who distinguishes, however, between 'levels' not 'types' of norms with reference to one multilevel governance system (Dimitrova 2005).

Table 4.2 *Types of norms*

Type of norms	Substance[a]	Generalisation	Specification	Contestation
Fundamental norms	Sovereignty *Citizenship*[b] *Human rights* *Fundamental freedoms* *Democracy* *Rule of law* Non-intervention	More	Less	More
Organising principles	Proportionality *Accountability* *Responsibility* Transparency Flexibility Gender mainstreaming Mutual recognition International election Monitoring	Medium	Medium	Medium
Standardised procedures	Qualified majority voting Unanimous decisions Proportional representation	Less	More	Less

[a] The norms presented in the 'substance' column are listed as examples which are not all-inclusive.
[b] The norms printed in italics are addressed by the case study in chapters 5 to 7.

The types are distinguished according to their degree of generalisation and specification, as well as their moral and ethical scope, so that research conducted in different disciplines may refer to these generic types and engage in meaningful conversation with neighbouring disciplines.

The first generic norm type is called *fundamental norms*. They include core constitutional norms or metanorms – which are commonly applied with reference to modern constitutionalism – on the one hand, and basic procedural norms – which are commonly applied in International

Relations theory – on the other (Jackson 2005).[8] This type comprises citizenship, human rights, the rule of law, democracy, sovereignty, non-intervention, abstinence from torture and so forth. The second norm type is called *organising principles*. Organising principles are closely linked with policy or political processes. They inform political procedures and guide policy practices and include such principles as accountability, transparency or gender mainstreaming. The third norm type is called *standardised procedures*, which are identified as prescriptions, rules and regulations. This norm type entails, for example, electoral rules or assembly regulations which are clearly defined and expected to facilitate immediate and uncontested understanding.

It follows logically that the most contested norms are the least specific, i.e. the fundamental norms, while the least contested are the most specific, i.e. the standardised procedures. For example, fundamental norms are considered as the glue of a community. They express that what is agreed to. In domestic constitutional contexts these agreements typically reflect the organisational practices of modern nation-states. In turn, in the context of global politics, fundamental norms are agreed by the international interaction of 'civilised nations'[9] and are defined as 'basic procedural norms' including sovereign equality, respect for human rights and non-intervention in international affairs among others (Jackson 2005: 16–17). Organising principles evolve through the practices of politics and policy-making. They include, for example, accountability, transparency, gender mainstreaming, peacekeeping and peace-enforcement.[10] Standardised procedures are least likely to be contested on moral or ethical grounds. This norm type is not contingent and entails directions that are specified as clearly as possible, such as for example the instructions to assemble a flat-pack piece of furniture (Kratochwil 1989) or guidelines pertaining to electoral processes.

For all norms, the three conditions of contestation (Table 4.1) apply. That is, while they have been identified with reference to a specific context, in this case, modern constitutionalism as it evolved through the social practices of modern nation-state politics, they may well change in the light of on-going processes of contestation. In addition,

---

[8] I thank Martin Binder who raised the issue of this useful distinction during a discussion at the Science Centre for Social Research in Berlin, 8 June 2006.

[9] See Article 38(1)c of the Statute of the International Court of Justice at www.icj-cij.org/documents/index.php?p1=4&p2=2&p3=0 (accessed 24 July 2007).

[10] See, e.g., Locher 2002; Jackson 2005; Begg 2007; and Bovens 2007.

the way they work depends on how they are interpreted according to the three conditions of contingency, moving social practices and crisis. Since 'no rules in international law are absolute', indeed, 'nothing in this normative sphere is absolute' (Jackson 2005: 19), lawyers expect the interpretation of legal texts to depend on input through legal discourse, i.e. deliberation, jurisprudence, learned opinion and other discursive interventions. The contested issue regarding this input lies in different legal traditions. These can generally be distinguished according to a stronger disposition to interpret the letter of the law among continental lawyers, on the one hand, and a disposition towards a generally flexible quality of international law understood as evolving through the process of jurisprudence among Anglo-Saxon lawyers, on the other (Scott 2004). Nonetheless it can be argued that while considering the input of discourse at different stages, we can attribute a constitutive role to discursive interventions in the process of shaping and changing norms within international law.[11]

Variation in the interpretation of meaning

Considering that '*a constitution* can seek to impose one cultural practice, one way of rule following, or it can recognise a diversity of cultural ways of being a citizen, but *it cannot eliminate, overcome or transcend this cultural dimension of politics*' (Tully 1995: 6; my emphasis), the case study compares the input of cultural practices in an *emerging* transnational arena with those in *enduring* domestic arenas. While both types of arenas are part of the wider environment of the European Union, the second condition of enhanced norm contestation (see Table 4.1) suggests that contestation is a likely outcome of this comparison. Studying diverging, converging and diffused interpretations of

---

[11] As Finnemore and Toope summarise, 'Law is a broad social spectrum *deeply embedded in the practices, beliefs, and traditions of societies, and shaped by interaction* among societies' (2001: 743; my emphasis). Compare, however, the following observation: 'Customary international law displays this richer understanding of law's operation as does the increasingly large body of what has been termed "interstitial law", that is, *the implicit rules operating in and around explicit normative frameworks*' (*ibid.*). In this quotation the normative framework is explicit and the rules are implicit; however, this book considers the normative framework as fuzzy and composed of both organisational and cultural practices of constitutionalism. The rules are also considered as more clearly defined, reflecting the organisational practices of constitutionalism.

normative meanings may appear a rather elusive exercise. The challenge lies in locating the dimension of cultural validation analytically and in examining it empirically. It is crucial to identify indicators for diversity and commonality of meaning of fundamental norms at a level of deseg-regation that allows for the empirical assessment of meaning.[12] However, when considering that individuals are prone to carry norma-tive baggage wherever they go, normative interpretations achieve a considerable radius of input and therefore influence under conditions of transnationalisation. Most importantly, elites who have been socia-lised in domestic political contexts ('national' elites) will carry the respective domestically constituted normative baggage into interna-tional negotiation environments. In these environments conflict is there-fore more likely when decisions are taken by elites who have little experience in sustained and continuous transnational interaction and hence are unable to refer to a common reference framework. In the absence of a significant increase of transnationalised politics and policy processes, international politics remain just that, i.e. they are 'interna-tional' in the literal meaning of the word.[13]

While constitutive for political outcomes, interpretations of norms remain largely invisible. They are most likely to entail the hidden mean-ings which need to be made accountable to offer empirical reference points for a comparative assessment of divergence, convergence or diffusion of the meanings of fundamental norms. Following the distinc-tion between visible factors of a treaty or convention such as principles, articles and provisions, and invisible factors such as individual inter-pretations of fundamental norms, research on hidden meanings turns to the latter. Thinking about the constitution mobilises a variety of indi-vidual perceptions. It adds an intangible dimension to constitutional-ism. Searle points out that 'one reason we can bear the burden [of the day-to-day metaphysics which govern human activities, AW] is that the complex structure of social reality is, so to speak, weightless and

---

[12] For a project which brings together comparative research on the question of diversity and commonality of meaning of democratic principles and procedures in Europe, see, for example, Team A in Research Group 2 of the CONNEX Network of Excellence; see www.connex-network.org/ (accessed 25 July 2007). For published details, see Wiener 2007b and www.palgrave-journals.com/cep/journal/v5/n1/index.html (accessed 25 July 2007).

[13] See also chapter 1, footnote 1 for the specific focus on the literal meaning of the word.

invisible' (1995: 4; my emphasis). However, the point I wish to make here is rather the opposite. That is, the presence of the invisible constitution of politics, and the notable absence of learned knowledge about this feature, might be less blissful than the quotation suggests. While remaining hidden and unregulated, it can spark debate at best and major political conflict at worst. The better we get at identifying conflicting interpretations, the more likely we are to succeed in designing a pattern for conflict resolution. After all, the political role of fundamental norms and the interpretation of their respective meanings depend heavily on the social environment in which they are interpreted.[14]

The following develops a research design which will then be applied to make normative meaning accountable. The purpose of the case study is to unveil individually transported interpretations of normative meaning, following the argument that these are invisible, yet constitutive, for the constitution of politics. By making them visible, they become 'account-able' (Garfinkel 1967) for politics in their diverse, specific and contesting ways. To scrutinise assumptions about domestically established meanings that are often mistakenly labelled 'national' and their potential for being shared in other domestic or transnational contexts, the case study disaggregates the category of the 'national'. The difference in expectations towards meanings and the potential consequences for politics are well expressed by this German working in Brussels who said:

This is, by the way, a general experience which I have made again and again in Europe – with the Commission but also in Parliament or in the Committee of the Regions – that our considerably specific German thinking about norms – about norms not available in politics – is very difficult to relate to. That is, our German lawyers' orientation based on fundamental rights, subsidiarity and proportionality is almost incomprehensible.[15]

For the case study it is crucial to identify the normative baggage which individuals bring to international negotiations either by moving from domestic political arenas towards international negotiation contexts, or by moving from transnational political arenas to these

---

[14] For example, it has been demonstrated that while political ideas are spread across boundaries, they are interpreted anew and often quite differently depending on their new social environment of implementation (Hall 1989).

[15] Interviewee Brux/Ger H, 23 May 2001; this and all following interviews are on file with the author. Unless stated otherwise, all emphases are mine.

same contexts. By analysing social practices in context, it is possible to identify individual interpretations without falling into two caveats following from the conventional (or modern) constructivist approach. The first caveat is the bracketing of interaction and the assumption that stable norms structure behaviour. As a consequence, the very process of meaning construction is excluded from the analysis. The second caveat is the assumption of stable (or 'given') community identities. While as a precondition stable identities are important indicators for the analysis of national identity options, they prevent analytical appreciation of moving individuals and changing individually transported associative connotations as a result.[16]

Methodology and method

The focus on discourse analysis draws on insights from sociology, foreign policy analysis, anthropology and ethno-methodology.[17] The book works with a single case study to generate a working hypothesis for follow-up studies.[18] In distinction from long-term group constellations and individual input into transnational politics, the empirical focus is on interventions made by individuals who operate on a micro-level in 'settings of interaction' which are identified as 'locales' of day-to-day practice (Giddens 1984: xxv). In this case, such locales involve mainly the offices of the interviewed civil servants, advocacy group members, journalists, academics, politicians and consultants. Following the contingency condition of norms (see Table 4.1, *condition 1*), actors operate within a context that is constituted by the interplay between structures of meaning-in-use and individuals. The latter hold associative connotations[19] which become

[16] Note that the term 'associative connotation' is to be distinguished as defining an emotionally 'affective' notion rather than the legal notion of 'affectedness'. The latter defines the accessibility of the court to individual citizens. For details on the legal notion of 'affectedness', see, e.g., Beljin 2006: 19.

[17] See, e.g., Schutz 1932; Garfinkel 1967; Berger and Luckmann 1991; Doty 1993; Weldes and Saco 1996; and Milliken 1999.

[18] This type of case study focuses on exploration as opposed to description or the investigation of explanatory theories. For the distinction, see Titscher, Meyer, Wodak and Vetter 2005 [2000]: 44.

[19] Note that these associative factors differ from Max Weber's concept of 'affectional action' (Gerth and Mills 1946: 56), as they are not based purely on sentiment but characterise rule-following on the basis of perceived social norms (Finnemore and Sikkink 1998).

recognisable through interaction, that is, when identified as discursive interventions. The question is whether such discursive interventions are reduced to reveal diverging, converging or diffused patterns of meanings, or whether the frequency and place of interaction changes meanings. Following the rule-in-practice assumption the latter is expected; however, this assumption remains to be sustained by empirical research.

The purpose of the case study is to reveal 'the essential relevance ... of a concern for common sense activities as a topic of inquiry in its own right and, by reporting a series of studies, to urge its "rediscovery"' (Garfinkel 1967: 36). By bringing normative contingency to bear empirically, the case study seeks to investigate the 'constitutive phenomenology of the world of everyday' meanings in order to identify their impact on politics as 'background expectancies' which are individually transported. While Garfinkel's studies focused on enhancing '*sociological* inquiries' by making 'commonplace *scenes* visible' (1967: 37, cited in Schutz 1932; my emphases), I seek to fill a gap in the political science literature by making the impact of commonplace *meanings* visible for the study of politics. Following insights from discourse analyses especially in the field of foreign policy analysis, it is assumed that even if we know the words and speak the same language, a word in and by itself provides insufficient information about its meaning. To catch the meaning of a word or a phrase, we need to examine 'the cultural and social day-to-day context in which it has been used' and 'marked by indexicality' (Schutz 1932; Garfinkel 1967; Hauck 1984: 155). Associative connotations allow for an assessment of the degree to which the meanings of fundamental norms converge. This assessment provides information about individual dispositions towards these norms.[20] Understanding is never unmediated but subsequent to interpretation against the background of individual experience. Therefore,

[20] I distinguish between legal approaches to 'valuation' or the 'interpretation of values', on the one hand, and a sociological approach to demonstrate individually transported associative connotations which are of direct relevance for political strategising and decision-making in international contexts, on the other. The difference in approach follows the distinction between legal interpretation, on the one hand, and sociological interpretation, on the other. The former is conducted with reference to different types or traditions; in turn, the latter refers to the interpretation of meaning based on social practices. For the legal interpretation of values in the European constitutional literature, see, for example, Aziz and Millns 2007.

individually transported expectations hold the key for comparing normative interpretations in international settings (Shapiro and Bonham 1973: 165; Weldes and Saco 1996: 369).

While research on conflicting interpretations of norms is not specifically interested in 'positioning', Bourdieu's assumption about a meaningful system which evolves through permanent contradiction is a central element.[21] The emphasis on the dialectics of 'struggle' as a unifying element and an on-going process of contestation, on the one hand, and the notion of 'fields', on the other, is especially important for this research on the variation of normative meanings. Most significant is the incorporation of contestation and its role in the construction and use of meaning;[22] however, the process of creating the fields and the main norms that govern them, on the one hand, and the process of working with these norms and reacting to them, on the other, do not necessarily overlap. This is the condition for studying the way norms work in contexts which deviate from modern assumptions, i.e. by operating beyond the state rather than within nation-states. To access normative meaning and make it accountable, it needs to be revealed specifically based on discursive interventions. The following elaborates on the details of making meaning accountable by applying discourse analysis.

Discourse analysis

Discourse analysis offers a specific *perspective* on social phenomena that begins with the assumption of discourse as a social practice.[23] It does not offer an *approach* or a research *technique* for the analysis of

---

[21] As Bourdieu notes, 'When we speak of a *field* of position-takings, we are insisting that what can be constituted as a *system* for the sake of analysis is not the product of a coherence-seeking intention or an objective consensus (even if it presupposes unconscious agreement on common principles) but the product and prize of a permanent conflict; or, to put it another way, that the generative, unifying principle of this "system" is the struggle, with all the contradictions it engenders' (1993: 34; emphasis in original).

[22] That is, the emphasis on the formative process of these fields, and the speaker's evolving and changing power position, is left to one side for the purposes of this case study.

[23] It is 'a social practice through which thoughts and beliefs are themselves constituted' (Weldes and Saco 1996: 371).

texts such as qualitative content analysis or reconstructive analysis.[24] The choice of method for a specific text therefore remains to be made. For now, discourse is used as a cognitive map that will facilitate access to a more detailed understanding of fundamental norms than currently available.[25] These details are located in social practices that reflect experience within specific contexts. To grasp meanings that are attached to social practices, it is necessary to turn to reconstructive analysis rather than content analysis. While the latter will reveal constellations and frequency of code noted prior to the evaluation, the former offers interpretative tools with which meanings that are constituted prior to a discursive intervention can be uncovered. As a reflexive process, reconstructive analysis thus enables us to bring intangible aspects of discourse to the fore.[26] The process hence involves the steps of interview, transcription, excerpt compilation, evaluation and interpretation. Each step requires specific decisions with regard to technique and procedure. In any case, reconstructive analysis is always based on a basic text corpus (Huffschmid 2004). In this specific case, the text corpus is compiled based on micro-level interaction that generates discursive interventions. The evaluation of the text is conducted with a view to reconstructing the specific normative structure of meaning-in-use defined as 'intersubjective structures ... that provide the categories through which we represent and understand the world' (Weldes 1998: 218). The language used in discursive interventions is understood as constitutive in a Wittgensteinian sense, i.e. it not only functions to describe facts but also constitutes new meaning.[27] For example, at the meta-theoretical level, discourse analysis assumes that 'the meaning of a comment rests in its usage in a specific situation' (Titscher *et al.* 2005:

[24] See, for example, Bohnsack 2000 and Kruse 2007.

[25] See Weldes and Saco 1996: 373; Milliken 1999: 231; Schneider 2001; Hüllsse 2003: 39; and Titscher *et al.* 2005. Weldes and Saco define discourse as 'a *structure of meaning-in-use* that is both intersubjective and, in part, linguistic' (1996: 373; my emphasis).

[26] That is, '*meanings* produced through a discourse "pre-exist their use in any one discursive practice", or ... by any one individual. *Discursive practices*, in turn, *are social acts, enabled by a discourse*, through which some relevant aspect of the world is actively defined and constituted' (Weldes and Saco 1996: 343–4; c.f. Fiske 1987: 14; my emphasis).

[27] Compare, for example, Wittgenstein's demonstration of 'language as constitutive for the world' as opposed to the positivist 'set of labels which can be compared to the world' (Fierke 1998: 3).

146, cited in Wittgenstein 1984, para. 7). It follows that individually transported associative connotations about meaning are derived from and contribute to the structure of meaning-in-use.

To summarise, analysing discourse offers access to the space in which collective perceptions are present (Schneider 2001: 32). Access to and use of this space are therefore crucial for any work that seeks to assess the social recognition of norms. Since social practices, and more specifically cultural practices, have been identified as the key factor in this comparative study, the data are collected based on techniques generated by 'critical discourse analysis' (Wodak 1996). This type of analysis

sees discourse – language use in speech and writing – as a form of 'social practice'. ... [This] implies a dialectical relationship between a particular discursive event and the situation(s), institution(s) and social structure(s) which frame it: the discursive event is shaped by them, but also shapes them. That is, discourse is socially constituted, as well as socially conditioned. ... It is constitutive both in the sense that it helps sustain and reproduce the social status quo, and in the sense that it contributes to transforming it. (Titscher *et al.* 2005: 26; citing Wodak 1996: 15)

The following two subsections distinguish between the type of data that is to be collected and the approach to evaluating that data, respectively. This final subsection specifies the choice of indicators for the case study.

Data collection

To reconstruct hidden normative meanings I examine 'contemporarily produced texts' (Weldes and Saco 1996: 373; Bublitz 1999; Schneider 2001; Huffschmid 2004). In general, such texts may include a range of data sources, such as parliamentary debates, the media or interview transcriptions. The research at hand focuses on interview transcriptions as the primary data source. The intention is to obtain indirect references to fundamental norms that allow for an insight into the respective individual's – contextualised – cultural validation of a norm. The chosen interview technique therefore applies structured interviews that focus on generating the interviewees' 'gut' reactions to obtain 'expressive', that is, predominantly spontaneous and emotional, comments. The discursive interventions are set to take place in the interviewees' respective day-to-day context. They occur at the micro-level of this empirical investigation. The comments are detailed according to a selection of *keywords*. The keyword selection is inductive, that is, keywords are derived following the reading of the main text corpus. As heuristic constructs, keywords are thus considered as outcomes rather than coded input categories of qualitative text analysis.[28] The keyword selection is carried out on the basis of semantic references to specific fundamental norms. The cross-linkage between keywords and norms allows for a comparative distinction of individually transported associative connotations. With that in view, this case study's main data source consists of interview transcriptions in order to reconstruct the structure of meaning-in-use with regard to selected fundamental norms taken from the European Union's treaties. The compiled text includes fifty-three transcriptions of interviews that lasted about three-quarters of an hour each.[29] The analysis seeks to reveal the heretofore hidden meanings ascribed to these norms by individuals from three different contexts within the EU.

The interviews are conducted anonymously so as to create an environment that warrants spontaneous answers that reveal personal reactions or 'gut' feelings.[30] This emphasis follows the distinction between 'informative', 'expressive' and 'directive' uses of language where this case study sought to avoid informative or directive uses of language. Instead, it stressed the 'expressive' use of language to generate emotional responses.[31] That is, technical or other types of rationalised expert opinions that are likely to reproduce standardised rules and general guidelines rather than revealing 'emotive' personal views were not encouraged.[32] Such views would simply restate the formal validity of

[28] On this distinction see, e.g., Kruse 2007: 119 (original text in German).

[29] This text corpus encompasses about 1,000 pages and is on file with the author.

[30] All interviewees remain anonymous. The full references are on file with the author. Interviews were conducted by the author and two research assistants. Interview evaluation proceeds on a strict anonymity basis, i.e. providing letter-coded reference only.

[31] For this distinction of three different uses of language, see, e.g., Copi 1998 [1961], cited in Kalish 1964: 92. See also the distinction of different types of speech acts as 'directive', 'assertive', 'commissive', 'expressive' as well as a group of 'declaratives' in Nastri, Pena and Hancock 2006: 1029.

[32] See Holbrook, Krosnick, Carson and Mitchell 2000. Note that 'emotive meaning' indicates attitudes and feelings associated with the use of a word, phrase or sentence, in contrast to its literal significance. See, for example, Brandt's definition: 'To say a word has "blind emotive meaning" is to say it has a dispositional capacity to arouse emotive effects of substantial order, in certain

norms, and as such they would not be conducive towards the task of making the individually transported associative connotations accountable. 'Many of the most common words and phrases of any language have both a literal or descriptive meaning that refers to the way things are and an emotive meaning that expresses some (positive or negative) feeling about them. Thus, the choice of which word to use in making a statement can be used in hopes of evoking a particular *emotional* response.'[33] In addition, 'attitude questions' were raised in order to provide a cross-check for the interview database.[34] In sum, the empirical focus on discursive interventions is expected to reveal the intersubjective engagement *with* rather than the discourse *about* a particular issue. Once transcribed, the collection of spontaneous remarks constitutes the text corpus as the main database which also notes the interviewees' sociocultural context based on the question about their respective living and working circumstances during the decade prior to the interview.[35]

In sum, the case study allows for a shift in perspective from the discursive event at the *macro*-level as the level of high complexity (international politics) towards the discursive event at the *micro*-level (individually transported associative connotations) to reduce this complexity (Titscher *et al.* 2005: 27). The individual interview situation provides a setting in which interaction in context generates the text corpus as the empirical database. This database allows for identifying the structure of meaning-in-use. In this case, the discursive event at the macro-level that added complexity to International Relations studies was the transfer of policy sectors which were originally designed for modern nation-states into the supranational realm and hence beyond the boundaries of modern nations-states. The emerging 'finality' debate and the resulting constitutional push in European integration discourse are taken as the trigger of complexity in this situation. It is of general interest to reduce the complexity created by that situation, for example by reference to theoretical assumptions and by choice of empirical

---

circumstances, independently of any alteration the hearing of it introduces into the cognitive field (except for the sensory presence of the word itself)' (1950: 535).

[33] Kemmerling 2002 (my emphasis).

[34] For the evaluation of this cross-check, see chapter 8 in this book.

[35] For example, the questionnaire asked, 'How many times a month do you generally engage in international interaction i.e. in spoken language?' (on file with author).

Table 4.3 *Research assumptions about social practices*

No.	Assumption
1	Discourse is a social practice.[a]
2	Structures of meaning-in-use are constituted through social practices.[b]
3	Discursive practice represents the link between text and social practice.[c]

[a] See Wodak 1996; Titscher *et al.* 2005: 156; as well as Kruse 2007.
[b] See Weldes and Saco 1996; Milliken 1999.
[c] See Fairclough 1992; Titscher *et al.* 2005: 150.

design. The case study seeks to generate a working hypothesis for a follow-up project targeting, for example, a larger, more representative sample. During the individual interview situation, the discursive event takes place at the micro-level in the context of the interview situation. Following three basic assumptions about social practices raised by critical discourse analysis (see Table 4.3), qualitative expert interviews have been conducted on the basis of a guided questionnaire.[36]

Interview evaluation

The case study is conducted and evaluated by applying methodological 'triangulation' to the extent that qualitative and quantitative research methods are combined to analyse the invisible constitution of politics.[37] The evaluation period involves the following five empirical phases. In the first phase, interviews are conducted; during the second phase, interviews are transcribed and a general text corpus is compiled; the third phase involves text analysis using the techniques of excerption, keyword selection and deriving oppositions. In the fourth phase, the normative structure of meaning-in-use is reconstructed with reference to the relevant political

---

[36] The interviews took place in the time period that stretches from mid-2001 to mid-2003. Apart from a few exceptions, all interviews were conducted in the aftermath of the 9/11 atrocities in 2001.

[37] See, e.g., King, Keohane and Verba 1994; Tarrow 1995: 473; and Lustick 1996: 616. As Tarrow notes: 'Triangulation is particularly appropriate in cases in which quantitative data are partial and qualitative investigation is obstructed by political conditions' (1995: 473). My turn to triangulation reflects a lack of quantitative data and the additional problem of generating data based on the qualitative method.

arena, elite group and modern constitutional norm. Finally, in phase five, a quantitative evaluation of types of divergence, convergence or diffusion of meanings is carried out based on the set of associative connotations generated by the interviews to indicate a direction for larger quantitative studies.[38] This final step uses the method of 'structured, focused comparison' (King, Keohane and Verba 1994: 45) based on the systematic collection of information.[39]

Following the interview and the transcription phases, respectively, the text analysis engages in the *three evaluative steps*. Firstly, the text corpus is organised according to policy fields, each of which provides a framework with significant relevance for one of the three fundamental norms that lie at the centre of this case study. Secondly, the interview comments are sorted according to elite group and keyword families so as to garner patterns of associative connotations for comparison. All data are presented in one case excerpt document. As the script for the following evaluation, this document provides direct links between keywords and individual utterances.[40] The up to ten choices of associative connotations presented in keyword groups with reference to one of the three meta-constitutional norms are easily recognisable in the three major tables which are organised according to policy field, fundamental norm, associative connotations, political arena and elite groups. The table entries are identified by numbers (from 0 to 9) referring to the respective associative connotation uttered in the micro-context of the interview. While the numbers allow easy allocation with reference to the distinctive associative connotations, they also provide direct links to the specific discursive interventions uttered by each of the fifty-three interviewees. The text corpus is thus linked directly with the associative connotations and the norms presented in each table. Thirdly, these associative connotations are recalled and identified as

[38] This approach follows the research design and experience documented in Schneider 2001.

[39] It is important to note that in the present research design, the evaluation of divergence, convergence and/or diffusion of meanings involves comparing results which have been taken at one particular point in time (i.e. a snap-shot) rather than process-tracing. The factor of diffusion is defined as a range of choices regarding the meaning of a fundamental norm. It differs notably from the finding of converging associative connotations (i.e. within each domestic elite group sample) as well as from divergence (i.e. among various domestic elite group samples). Diffusion therefore differs from the finding of an either/or choice of meaning.

[40] The Case Excerpt is a 67,922-word (196 pp.) document, on file with the author.

sets of *oppositions* which derived from the text corpus of interview transcriptions.[41]

I distinguish between core oppositions and derived oppositions. Both are derived from the text corpus through induction; however, the core opposition also meaningfully relates to the academic literature that exists outside the text. The technique involves 'abstract[ing] from two particular oppositions to a *core opposition* underlying both' (Milliken 1999: 234; emphasis in original). Of interest here is whether core oppositions can be identified in each of the three policy fields and whether these core oppositions do prevail in the transnationalised context of the Brussels arena. The point of the research based on interviews is thus less one of demonstrating how one particular constitutional norm is interpreted; rather, it identifies the structure of meaning-in-use that will guide its interpretation and hence turn into the opportunity or constraint when interpreting supranational norms in a situation of crisis. I apply the method of deriving oppositions to the case excerpt as the reduced text corpus to which discursive interventions of a number of individuals, i.e. the interview situations which are identified as 'micro-events', have generated passages. It is divided into three parts so as to allow for a comparative reading according to the three distinctive sections of the questionnaire. Each section refers to a different policy issue: 'Schengen', 'Enlargement' or 'Constitutional Politics', respectively. Oppositions between domestic elites are derived first. These are then compared against the connotations displayed by the Brusselites.

The case study is designed to assess divergence, convergence or diffusion of meanings. An outcome that finds divergence of normative meanings rather than convergence to be the dominant pattern would indicate an absence of cultural harmonisation among elites. In turn, an outcome that found converging meanings to prevail would sustain the layer-cake assumption. Should the outcome entail both diverging and converging interpretations – and possibly a third pattern of diffusion as well – the variation will be according to type of divergence assessed. The question is whether the transnational elites' respective utterances

---

[41] The oppositions are rendered by single documents which are identified as 'the language practice of predication – the verbs, adverbs and adjectives that attach to nouns' (Milliken 1999: 232).

demonstrate a divergence from national domestic elites. Three types of variation are considered as indicators of divergence (see Table 4.4).

Table 4.4 *Types of divergence*

A: domestic vs transnational
B: domestic vs domestic
C: transnational vs transnational

Choice of indicators

The following turns to the selection of indicators upon which the empirical research is to focus as the final remaining detail of research operationalisation. The indicators include the following generic types: social groups, norms, political arenas and issue areas.

Elites

The decision to interview elites follows the bifocal approach of this case study. According to the empirical argument, the layer-cake assumption expects that of all social strata, elites are most likely to generate cultural harmonisation as a result of regional integration (Deutsch 1953). Research therefore focuses on interviews with elites to scrutinise this assumption of cultural harmonisation (Liebold and Trinczek 2003). According to the normative argument, elites are the social group most likely to achieve access to full participation in a political community, i.e. enjoying rights, access and belonging to political practices in the public sphere. It has been demonstrated, for example, that 'discourse elites' have 'influence for important decisions with regard to the entire society ... based on particular positions within public discourse' (Fairclough 1992: 212; Gerhards 1992: 307; Schneider 2001: 49 citing Hoffmann-Lange 1990: 11). Based on these two considerations, the selection of interviewees includes European Union citizens who enjoy full membership in the European political community and who operate either within the Brussels transnational arena or in domestic political arenas.

Crucial for the selection of interviewees was the consideration that each individual must enjoy active access to participation in the public sphere. For the purposes of the case study, elites are defined as citizens who enjoy access to contestation of the norms, rules and procedures which govern a community. This definition draws on the observation that, 'a free and democratic society will be legitimate even though its rules of recognition harbour elements of injustice and non-consensus if the citizens are always free to enter into processes of contestation and negotiation of the rules of recognition' (Tully 2000: 477). It implies a definition of citizenship that goes beyond the modern expectation of 'full membership in a community' (Marshall 1950: 8). While the former would follow the 'civil tradition' of citizenship, the 'civic tradition' considers active access to social practices that enable an individual's contestation of the rules that govern the governed as the key element of 'civicisation'. It stresses the egalitarian aspect of citizenship as a process of becoming citizens through practice. That is, an individual enjoys the power to engage with political discourse both as a recipient and as a setter of that discourse (Peters 2005; Tully 2007). Each interviewee must – in principle – be able to both make use of and shape the resources of the public sphere. Only thus is the individual's constitutive input on the interrelated dimensions of cultural validation, social recognition and formal validity, i.e. the dimensions which have been singled out as key to norm interpretation, warranted. This would involve, for example, the production of texts such as policy documents, draft legislation, newspaper articles, academic writing, official documents and so forth, in addition to access to information and use of resources. In sum, the interviewed elite samples involve a group of highly flexible, well-informed, and boundary-crossing citizens who are able to both influence and access public discourse. Like all individuals, these elites carry normative baggage which informs their respective expectations towards the meaning of norms. Unless contested by others, or within an otherwise non-agreeable context, the baggage will prevail, notwithstanding the crossing of societal or political boundaries. The baggage is conceptualised as associative connotations. The case study details its quality, quantity and durability.

Fundamental norms
To assess the range of interpretations attached to fundamental norms by elites from Germany and the UK both within and beyond the limits of modern constitutionalism, the case study examines the interpretation of the modern constitutional norms which have found their way into international treaties. They include citizenship, the rule of law and

democracy, and human rights and fundamental freedoms. This choice follows the liberal community hypothesis as all norms form part of the shared normative structure that binds civilised nations in world politics. For example, the Treaty on European Union (TEU) states in Article 6 that 'the Union is founded on the principles of liberty, democracy, respect for human rights and fundamental freedoms, and the rule of law, *principles which are common to the member states*' (my emphasis). Furthermore, the Treaty Establishing the European Community (TEC) stipulates Union citizenship in Articles 17–22. Both treaties have been signed by the EU member states' government representatives, among them the President of the Federal Republic of Germany and Her Majesty the Queen of the United Kingdom of Great Britain and Northern Ireland.

Issue areas

Three new policy fields have been selected as foci for discursive interventions during the interview process. The choice of policy field allows a focus for conversations that seek to reveal interpretations of the meaning of fundamental norms. Therefore, each selected field is considered as being of particular yet not exclusive relevance for a specific set of fundamental norms. For example, utterances regarding the Schengen policy field will be explored with a specific relevance for 'citizenship' indicators; the Enlargement field will be explored with particular relevance for 'democracy' and 'rule of law' indicators; and finally, the Constitutional Politics field will be scrutinised for 'human rights and fundamental freedoms' indicators. The selection of these particular pairings is based on the assessment of which keywords are most likely to be uttered in structured qualitative interviews that focus on these three respective fields. Note that this choice has been made primarily to provide a structure for the interview and keyword organisation. It does not assume to present an exclusive relationship between a particular policy area and a particular norm. The point is rather to demonstrate that, despite their all-pervasiveness, norms do retain different meanings to individuals. These come to the fore through the interaction of individuals in different contexts (Hall 1989; Jenson 2007). All new policy fields have been either sufficiently, and repeatedly, addressed by the media, or experienced by the elites themselves, for example through personal travel. The selection follows the *rule-in-practice* assumption which stresses the individual input in the formation of normative structures, i.e. elites will only refer to structures of meaning-in-use that are accessible to them. The three policy fields are considered as reference frames which allow for a structured approach to individual interviews. They all achieved a particular relevance in the post-Cold War era and, especially, the massive enlargement process of the EU which began with the Copenhagen Agreement in 1993 and ended with the accession of ten new member states from central and eastern Europe and Malta in 2004.

Political arenas

The case study examines elite interpretations of the meaning of norms in London, Berlin and Brussels as the political arenas in which elites operate. The choice to select long-standing EU member states which enjoy several memberships in supranationally formed communities follows the liberal community hypothesis which would assume that the more community memberships any two countries enjoy, the higher the shared recognition and appropriateness of fundamental norms is likely to be. Both Germany and the United Kingdom hold membership in various international organisations including NATO, the United Nations and, last not least the European Union, as well as the respective supranational communities which have been forged in their suite. This set of strong community memberships has been considered as generating a normative pull based on a shared identity as 'civilised' nations in the larger realm of world politics.[42] Of importance for the case study is furthermore that both the German and the British constitutions, respectively, are based on a power-limiting rather than a power-creating rationale. Despite their obvious difference in appearance as written or unwritten frameworks,[43] they were both intended to support the 'legalisation of politics' by securing the limitation of monarchic or feudal powers. Both countries thus shared a structural sense of appropriateness

---

[42] Note that there is a curious albeit still little discussed overlap between the role of identity in normative Kantian approaches and organisational sociology. What is of interest here is not the discrepancy between the original theories but the similarity assigned to the derivates of both theories which have found entry into International Relations scholarship on norms, i.e. this scholarship assigns a strong causal relation between community identity and norm-following behaviour.

[43] Note, however, that the 'unwritten' status of the British constitution is not uncontested. As Sartori holds, for example, 'it remains questionable whether it is really true that the British constitution is unwritten (I would be tempted to say that it is "written differently")' (1962: 862).

with regard to the constitutional rationale (Moellers 2003: 9). While the point that Germany and the United Kingdom follow similar, i.e. power-limiting, constitutional traditions, it could also be argued that if inter-action in context facilitates convergence and the lack of it divergent associative connotations with meanings, then the two different legal traditions in the United Kingdom and Germany would expect connota-tions to differ according to experience with common law and continen-tal law, respectively.[44]

Conclusion

The research project encompasses a comparative study of elite percep-tions of fundamental norms in three different political arenas (London, Berlin and Brussels) of two different types (domestic, transnational). The four interviewed elite groups include Londoners, Berliners and Brusselites with the last group being divided into German and British elites. The database is evaluated with a view to establishing diverging, converging or diffused interpretations of meanings of fundamental norms (citizenship, human and fundamental rights, democracy and the rule of law). Each norm is considered as being predominantly addressed with reference to one of three new policy fields. For example, the discursive interventions generated through conversations about 'Schengen' are linked with indicators on the meaning of 'citizenship'; 'Enlargement' is linked with 'democracy' and 'the rule of law'; and 'Constitutional Politics' is linked with 'fundamental and human rights'. Based on these data, the case study aims at identifying individually transported associative connotations. Once identified, these are coded according to keywords and families of meaning indicating their relation with fundamental norms.

It must be noted, however, that given the limited scale on which the empirical research is carried out, i.e. conducting fifty-three interviews only, the case study can be no more and no less than an indicator of variation. It is hypothesised that with increasing divergence, conflicting meanings in actual international negotiation settings become more likely. The scope of the case study is thus one of a pilot project. The intention is to generate a working hypothesis which will be applied as

---

[44] And this is, indeed, the underlying expectation for the case study which identifies derived oppositions.

the starting point for a larger and potentially more representative investigation. While social practices can be distinguished as organisational and cultural, this study focuses on the latter. Based on the choice of two rather more than less divergent legal traditions among EU member states, for this case study the following assumptions can be made. Firstly, if harmonisation between all four elite groups in the three arenas emerges, the layer-cake assumption and the liberal community hypothesis trump. Secondly, if divergence among two national sample groups in London and Berlin can be established, and in addition this divergence is maintained among the two national groups of German Brusselites and British Brusselites in the Brussels arena, then national identity options carry the day. Thirdly, if a new divergence between the London sample and the British Brusselites, on the one hand, and between the Berlin sample and the German Brusselites, on the other hand, is identified, then it is demonstrated that interaction in context has a decisive input on the interpretation of meanings of fundamental norms.

PART II

Case study: reconstructing the structure of meaning-in-use

5 | Citizenship

> The best approach is to view citizenship as a *dynamic institution that changed with respect to time and place* and with the developing sophistication of those who had to use and define it.
>
> (Riesenberg 1992: 141; my emphasis)

Introduction

Conflicting interpretations of the meaning of fundamental norms are perhaps most commonly and clearly stated by different conceptualisations of citizenship. Thus, modern approaches would define citizenship to mean a universal right, while other more contextual approaches would understand it as a particularistic practice.[1] Contextualised meanings of citizenship are made evident by comparing interpretations generated within different domestic political arenas horizontally. In addition, this book's case study focuses on a vertical comparison between transnational and domestic political arenas. To identify variation in the meaning of citizenship as a fundamental norm in international relations (compare Table 4.2, *norm-type* 1), this chapter begins to examine individually transported associative connotations in relation to a set of norms. As one of three chapters, it focuses on discursive interventions uttered by individual elites who work and live in political arenas which differ according to type and nationality. While some of the nationalities overlap (British and Germans) with the arena in which the individuals work and live (London and Berlin, respectively), others do not (British and Germans conducting their life in Brussels). The following proceeds in three further sections. The first introduces the stipulation of citizenship as a fundamental norm in European law in distinction from its definition as a modern constitutional norm, and then summarises the methodological guidelines of the

---

[1] For the former, see Brubaker 1989; for the latter, see especially Bös 2000.

case study evaluation. The second carries out the analysis of opposition-deriving. The final section provides a conclusive summary.

Citizenship: a new fundamental norm in European law

Despite the common language provided by the citizenship legislation of the TEU (Articles 17–22),[2] the expectation towards citizenship varies pending on where the interpreter stands. According to the rule-in-practice assumption, it is expected to find citizenship meanings to differ according to social practices in context. As has been demonstrated elsewhere, for example, 'citizenship practice' (Wiener 1998) as the process that contributed to the institutionalisation of the terms and substance of citizenship in 'Europe' differs from other 'national' experiences of citizenship practice (Wiener 2003b). The formal validity may be sustained by the social recognition developed through rights-based liberal organisational practices such as, for example, in the United Kingdom, or identity-based republican practices of citizenship such as, for example, in France and the United States. From a day-to-day perspective of cultural practices, it may involve standardised procedures which differ along the lines of either a duty to register the place of residence and to carry identity cards (Germany), or the right to not carry identity cards (UK) and so forth. In addition, different conceptual perspectives on citizenship prevail. While the concept of citizenship is generally understood to involve rights, belonging and access,[3] the understanding of how citizenship works as a fundamental norm differs significantly with respect to the emphasis attached to each of these three factors by the respective scholar's conceptual leaning. For example, liberal contract-based approaches emphasise the notion of citizens' rights,[4] communitarians emphasise the role of the community and republicans

---

[2] Throughout I refer to the Treaty on European Union (TEU) and the Treaty Establishing the European Community (TEC), respectively, when referring to the treaty which was in force at the time of the interview. See *Official Journal of the European Communities*, OJ325 Brussels, 24 December 2002.

[3] For work that builds on T.H. Marshall's notion of 'access' to citizenship rights (1950), see, among others, Jenson and Philips 1996; Wiener 1997, 1998; Lister 2003; Benhabib 2004; and Pfister 2007.

[4] As Kommers and Thompson summarise, for example, 'the essence of liberal constitutionalism is government grounded in, limited by, and devoted to the protection of *individual rights*' (1995: 24; my emphasis).

stress active citizenship as the on-going activity of defending rights.[5] Identity is granted qua status as bearer of rights and membership in a community. Belonging develops through citizenship practice (Kaplan 1993). Access to citizenship is distinguished by thin or thick conceptions of citizenship, with thin citizenship approaches assuming access to citizenship to be granted qua nationality, while thick citizenship approaches hold that access to citizenship requires a modicum of welfare rights (Marshall 1950).

Citizenship is in one way or another considered as a crucial foundation for political communities (Bendix 1964; Grawert 1973; Tilly 1975; Brubaker 1989). The way in which citizenship plays out as the glue of a community – or as the 'border of order' as Kratochwil has once called it (1994) – depends on the specific context. It depends on the substantive and structuring components of citizenship, which consist of historical and constitutive elements, respectively (Wiener 1998). The former have been identified as rights, belonging (or identity) and access, while the latter are the constitutive elements. They involve the polity, the individual citizen and citizenship practice as the relation between individual and polity. Citizenship has been called a 'developing concept'. That is, through practice and over time a specific 'citizenship ideal' is expected to develop in a given community (Marshall 1950: 28).

That citizenship ideal, entailing the historical elements of citizenship of rights, access and belonging, offers an empirical vantage point for research that seeks to establish the structure of meaning-in-use for citizenship in particular contexts. The historical elements are taken as the main analytical indicators for the reconstruction of the structure of meaning-in-use of citizenship. The goal is to establish converging, diverging or, in fact, diffused meanings in transnational and domestic political arenas in Europe. The indicators are taken from interview situations. These situations were conducted as interactive micro-events. That is, they were to take place in the distinct and specific contexts of the interviewee's day-to-day working environment.[6] The interview

---

[5] See an overview by Beiner (1995).

[6] Titscher, Meyer, Wodak and Vetter define such interview contexts for the type of case study which 'implies that the texts used for analysis do not "attach" to particular persons who represent something'; they hold that instead 'the transcribed communication serves as a depiction of some situation or topic area indicated by the research question as an object of study' (2005: 33).

evaluation focuses on responses to 'gut' questions regarding the new policy field of 'Schengen'. This policy field has been established with support from various portfolios in the member state governments. It developed around the 1985 Schengen Agreement among five European states.[7] It was first established to abolish internal boundaries among European Economic Community (EEC) member states. The Schengen Agreement (henceforth: 'Schengen') itself is not an object of this particular investigation. What matters, however, in relation with Schengen, is that as an *emerging policy field* beyond the state, it most closely addresses issues that fall into the portfolio of *justice and home affairs* in modern nation-states. As such, it was chosen as a policy field that offers links with issues of citizenship. That is, the substantive policy issues dealt with by Schengen are closely associated with keywords relating to inside/outside, migration, borders, security, civil rights and so forth. The associative connotations have therefore been coded according to the *keywords* set out in Table 5.1.

The discursive interventions on issues related to the Schengen policy field are used as the major text corpus, providing an empirical reference to reconstruct the structure of meaning-in-use on the basis of the critical discourse analysis that focuses on associative connotations in relation to the fundamental norm of citizenship. While not exclusive, the link is hardened by a significant range of utterances regarding rights, access and belonging as the historical elements of citizenship. The keyword selection listed in Table 5.1 allows for a sufficiently encompassing sample towards establishing the pattern of divergence, convergence or diffusion of meanings held in domestic and transnational political arenas, respectively. In addition, these indicators demonstrate the respective elite groups' understanding of citizenship as either internal and 'inclusive', or, as external and 'exclusive' (Shaw 2007). The respective input into the structure of meaning-in-use as the cultural reference frame for constitutional negotiations in the EU will critically depend on whether or not different European elites' associative connotations converge, diverge or diffuse on the issue of inclusion or exclusion. It thus provides

---

[7] For the text of the Schengen Agreement, see *EuroLex* at http://europa.eu.int/eur-lex/lex/LexUriServ/LexUriServ.do?uri=CELEX:42000A0922(01):EN:HTML (accessed 8 August 2007).

Table 5.1 *Citizenship: keywords – Schengen*

Keywords	Associative connotations
Security	Security matters, standardisation, control, police
Civil rights	Civil rights are to be guarded, importance of rule of law, fundamental rights, individual rights (to be protected against the state)
Travel	Pragmatism, approval based on personal experience, freedom of movement, opting-in advantage UK
Fortress Europe	Negative aspect, exclusive, unfair
Border control ineffective	Obsolete instrument (from world of nation-states), UK should become Schengen member
Community formation	Good for further integration, reference to larger project of integration
External border control	More control necessary to compensate loss of security
Asylum/migration	Visa policy, third country nationals
Cooperation	Political cooperation, market cooperation (positive aspect)

Source: Selection of utterances from the data set Case Excerpt (196 pp.) on file with author. This selection has been extracted from the data set 'Text Corpus' (*ca.* 1.000 pp.) which entails fifty-three transcribed interviews and is also on file with the author. They will be referred to as 'Case Excerpt' and 'Text Corpus', respectively.

a critical ideational input into the more general discussion of either 'maintaining' or 'overcoming' diversity.[8] The Schengen text corpus is analysed as one of three parts of the primary database examined in order to identify the structure of meaning-in-use with reference to the fundamental norm of citizenship. The information provided by this exercise will enable us to make individually transported normative baggage accountable for politics.

---

[8] See a summary assessment of various philosophical positions on the possibilities and conditions of a successful 'European' polity by Friese and Wagner (2002). For further discussion of the case study's implications on this debate, see chapter 9 of this book.

Deriving oppositions

The primary data allows for deriving two oppositions from the Schengen text corpus. As the interview excerpts and the following tables demonstrate in some detail, the empirical analysis suggests a clear pattern of strong divergence among the two domestic elite group samples, i.e. the Berliners and the Londoners. Each interviewee has been asked the same sequence of questions based on a guided questionnaire.[9] The evaluation technique of deriving oppositions by analysing the text corpus is applied as a tool to identify core associative connotations. Once these are singled out with reference to the keyword selection, they are quantitatively analysed as well. While the qualitative analysis allows for depicting the particular associative connotations in relation with context and specific group, the quantitative analysis generates insights into the specific pattern constituted by these connotations.

Opposition 1: free movement vs security

The evaluation of the text corpus takes up each of the questions raised by the guided questionnaire. The first set of replies was uttered in response to the question

What do you think of the Schengen Agreement?

The following section groups the discursive interventions uttered by the four elite groups during interview situations. The utterances have been evaluated according to the quantitative (tables) and qualitative (oppositions) indicators of divergence, convergence or diffusion. The indicators for the evaluation are identified with reference to the semantic context rather than frequency of appearance.

Londoners: 'free movement'
Overall, the elite group questioned in London – hereafter labelled '*the Londoners*' – were quite enthusiastic about the Schengen Agreement. Their spontaneous reactions reveal associative connotations that

---

[9] The one-paged guided questionnaire entails three central questions with regard to each policy field, and a number of additional questions which were raised as appropriate from the flow of the interview. It is on file with the author.

converge clearly on the practical advantages provided by Schengen, especially the *travel*-related issues. For example, this interviewee replied: 'Actually, I think it's been *really good* for the UK. Generally, I think it is a good thing, yes I do. The idea of duty-*free travel* for European citizens is one of the logical and clear and visible benefits of membership and the links with the European Union for all European citizens. It's one of those things you can *touch and feel and experience every day*.'[10] And another replied along a similar line, 'I think *Schengen is* a very *good thing* and it's of big *benefit to citizens*. It is *something that people can feel* ... it is something the EU has given them *in their daily life which is* more than their national government could have given them; it is a huge benefit.'[11]

While this is perhaps surprising, given that the United Kingdom's commitment to Schengen is based on an 'opting-in' arrangement[12] which maintains a strict regime of passport controls and identity checks at all British ports of entry, the personal experience of travel appears to have played a major role in the responses of many Londoners. The following replies reveal a considerable degree of convergence on this issue, usually referring to pragmatic and personal notions. Thus, there was an emphasis, for example, on '*the speedy movement of people* through ... well what we call ports of entry in Britain'[13] and '*free circulation of populations – that's the message*'.[14] The following remark summarises the general thrust of the Londoners' associative connotations in this way, 'In principle, yes I think *Schengen is a good thing*. I think ... if we are going to have a single market, we ought to have single borders and *free movement of people* within those borders.'[15] It is notable that only a very small number of Londoners stressed the benefits of 'police cooperation' in relation to the 'free movement' advantages when

[10] Interviewee UK C, 19 December 2002.
[11] Interviewee UK O, 26 November 2002.
[12] When the Schengen Agreement was transferred into the Treaty on European Union with the 1996 Amsterdam Treaty, the British government obtained the specific opportunity to opt in to various aspects of the Schengen Agreement rather than sign up to the entire agreement. For details, see Wiener 1999; for an update on the UK Participation in the Schengen *acquis*, see House of Lords 2000 Select Committee Fifth Report on European Union documents and matters related to the EU at www.publications.parliament.uk/pa/ld199900/ldselect/ldeucom/34/3402.htm (accessed 20 May 2006).
[13] Interviewee UK P, 18 December 2002.
[14] Interviewee UK D, 26 November 2002.   [15] Interviewee UK I, 10 May 2001.

travelling, like this interviewee, who said, 'Well, there is the cooperation among the police forces, there is the *principle of free movement* within the EU. A couple of years ago I was on holidays in France and when we crossed to Italy we realised we had no passports with us. ... Nobody was looking and that was *personally a positive aspect of EU membership*.'[16]

Berliners: 'security'

The responses of the elites interviewed in Berlin – hereafter called the '*Berliners*' – reveal an almost diametrically opposed connotation. Thus, the majority of Berliners raised issues of *security*. The emerging common view was that the Schengen Agreement involved considerable security threats. This interviewee's gut reaction is a good example for immediate reactions that point to the 'security' issue, stating, '*people have a need for security, to be sure*. That can be taken care of based on particular local policing activities. You need to see how this *need for security* can be faced. I always think it is a positive sign when the state keeps a certain restraint on itself in this regard.'[17] The following interviewee's discursive intervention sustains the strong concern for security in a similar way, 'securing external borders and a compensation based on an outstanding technical system with a view to the removal of personal controls at internal EU borders is the right way forward'.[18]

The following reaction summarises the Berliners' notable convergence on the security issue as the first gut reaction when asked about Schengen quite well: 'what it means? – Well, *removal of external borders further away* and unsolved migration and *border security problems*'.[19] It is interesting to observe that these comments were not necessarily raised as a consequence of personal experience with borders, as this interviewee does, in fact, point out on a more general level, 'As always, to begin with [an agreement like Schengen] comes with certain *worries*.' When asked what kind of worries these were, the reply was speculative rather than relying on a specific experience, 'Oh, well, the *concerns are*, as it were, *probably* that surrounding states, or at least some of them have more *relaxed standards* [*of security*] than we have, and this will imply that we will be drawn towards their level.'[20] Nor

---

[16] Interviewee UK K, 10 May 2001.
[17] NOTE: This and all following German interview excerpts have been translated by the author. Interviewee Ger J, 24 June 2002.
[18] Interviewee Ger P, 15 October 2001.
[19] Interviewee Ger R, 14 May 2002.   [20] Interviewee Ger U, 11 July 2001.

do these discursive interventions display any detailed views about the kind of threat that might be responsible for triggering this security risk other than the removal of internal border controls among the member states of *Schengenland*. 'One of the major tasks of the European Union and at the same time within this is as well – and that does not only refer to the Schengen agreements but also for all members of the European Union – *Security and Law*. Many tasks which come up, here, in the area of *Justice and Home Affairs*.'[21] And this interviewee points to two different security aspects of concern when saying, 'Schengen has two sides ..., *first, the security aspect*, which we have to treat with preference from the perspective of the police department, and then the other aspect of the achieved[22] freedom of movement for all citizens of the Schengen member states.'[23]

Among the Berliners, the worry about the loss of security does not really demonstrate a clear grasp of a specific threat, as this reply demonstrates: 'I believe that this is linked with, and you should not forget that – the formal end of border controls means at the same time a growing possibility for the policy within areas of close proximity to borders and considering the space, that is, the said *security deficit* which was to be expected with the abolition of border controls has been complemented by other *measures to increase security*.'[24] The majority of the Berliners raised the 'security' issue as a first spontaneous reply when questioned about Schengen. Security is the first associative connotation for these highly educated, moving and internationally well-connected elites.

Summary
So far, it can be concluded that the opposition between 'travel' and 'security', which was derived from the London and Berlin samples, respectively, substantiates the link with the concept of citizenship and its deeper meaning as a discourse about borders (Kratochwil 1994). Borders – whether providing the citizen with protective support or enabling the citizen to cross them – are central to the concept of citizenship that grants special rights exclusively to those who enjoy membership of a particular political community. Incidentally, it was precisely this conceptual underpinning which was picked up by the European

---

[21] Interviewee Ger A, 17 July 2001.
[22] German original text: 'gewonnenen', literally 'won'.
[23] Interviewee Ger F, 19 April 2001.   [24] Interviewee Ger E, 30 May 2001.

Union's (then EEC's) strategists in the first decade of citizenship practice in the 1970s. At the time, the decision to set up a European citizenship policy was motivated by the expectation that citizenship would give a long-needed boost to the construction of a European identity (Wiener 1998, ch. 3).

Further to the universally valid conceptual roots of citizenship, however, the historically generated and contingent interpretations of its meaning in daily life differ. The interesting finding from this first opposition-deriving exercise is that the core opposition entailed in citizenship (i. e. inside vs outside) appears as separated parts rather than in its entirety in the two questioned elite groups. The connotations uttered with reference to the introduction of the Schengen Agreement which abolished borders among a group of nation-states with either 'security' or 'travel' reveals such persisting contingencies based on individual experience.[25] While the Berliners express worry and concern and reiterate the importance of new external EU borders to replace those internal EU borders which had been abolished as well as coordinated policing, and a commitment to some measure of 'control' and standardised 'regulation', the Londoners express appreciation based on a pragmatic perception of personal experience often with reference to the principle of 'freedom of movement'.

To summarise the findings of the two elite groups situated in domestic political arenas, Berliners immediately point to the security issue as a notion of *threat*. In turn, the first issue that comes to the minds of the Londoners is generally associated with the issue of unlimited travel and the *freedom* of movement. The opposition derived from evaluating the utterances in reply to the first Schengen question is therefore defined by the derived opposition of 'security' vs 'travel'. It refers to a core opposition of 'inside' vs 'outside'. The finding hence suggests a core opposition based on associative connotations with external and internal citizenship rights, respectively, with a German preference for the external and a British preference for the internal foundation of citizenship. If that core opposition persists, the empirical research will need to establish firstly, whether the national identity-options assumption holds. If the results

---

[25] While it is important to note here that the United Kingdom has chosen to remain outside the Schengen Agreement, opting in only to a selected amount of measures, the interviewees nonetheless experienced 'travel' in the new borderless space of Schengenland when travelling outside the UK.

suggest it does, it follows that the opposition will also be identified when comparing Berliners and German elites in Brussels – hereafter the '*German Brusselites*' – on the one hand, and Londoners and British elites in Brussels – hereafter the '*British Brusselites*' – on the other.[26] Secondly, to scrutinise that assumption with reference to the primary database, the questions on other issues will need to confirm that core opposition. The following section examines the replies of the German and British elite samples questioned in Brussels to that end.

Brusselites: both/and

In distinction from the rather clearly opposed reactions to the general question about Schengen uttered by Londoners and Berliners, a quite different pattern emerges when comparing the British Brusselites on the one hand, and the German Brusselites on the other. Both groups have been living and interacting in the Brussels transnational arena usually for a period of at least five years. As the following will show, they do not display a pattern of divergence akin to the *type B* divergence (domestic–domestic; see Table 4.4). Instead, the Brusselites display a much more widespread or *diffused* range of associative connotations. The issues are often shared by both elite samples in this transnational arena. The elites operating in this transnational arena hence relate to a much more diversified structure of meaning-in-use than the ones available to the British and the Germans, respectively. The Brusselites' structure of meaning-in-use includes, for example, the issues of 'security', 'free travel', 'obsolete border control' and 'community formation' noted in utterances made by both German and British Brusselites. The following replies by British and German Brusselites are grouped according to these associative connotations.

While considering that 'Schengen is basically a good thing', the issue of 'security' has also been a concern for the following British Brusselite who points out, for example, that 'Schengen is *no real improvement on accountability*. And a lack of balance between the freedom and *security* of the external border is a side of Schengen.' Upon further questioning, this interviewee replies that the security side 'is dominating'.[27] The functionally important role of Schengen is acknowledged by this British Brusselite with a view towards establishing the international

---

[26] Note that the British Brusselites are indicated as 'Brux/UK' and the German Brusselites as 'Brux/Ger' in all following footnotes and tables.

[27] Interviewee Brux/UK A, 22 May 2001.

market. That is, 'It is certainly *essential for the internal market.* ... If you are creating an internal market, you have to deal with these issues, ... *also with the security side.*'[28] Others stress the importance of having border controls to a country which is geographically speaking an island.[29]

I think ... in British politics – that is a very difficult line to cross which is *giving up border controls*. In particular there is a clear difference here between a country like Belgium which is surrounded by other countries and the United Kingdom – Well Britain has a sea-border and the only *land border* is with the Republic of Ireland. ... I mean the difficulty is that it does not seem to work that *many immigrants, illegal immigration and asylum applications in Britain*, the whole problem with the so-called refugees, I mean, on the whole, the *policy does not seem to work*. But my personal assessment is that it might be more sensible for the UK to opt in fully into the Schengen system.[30]

Despite such 'security' concerns, most British Brusselites would favour full UK membership of the Schengen Agreement instead of the currently valid arrangement of opting in on selected issue areas.

The following British and German Brusselites display a spontaneous reference to the issue of 'travel'. The issue is usually not uttered as an isolated connotation but in relation with other issues. For example the promotion of European 'identity', 'community formation' or 'coopera-tion'. This interviewee stresses the link between movement and identity when replying: 'Oh absolutely yes, ... I think *it is an excellent initiative* and indeed the UK, although we opted out of Schengen, opted in to a number of measures, a lot of measures in fact. So, certainly I think it is one of the most visible manifestations of the EU in terms of *enabling a pro-movement*. And it is an extremely important one, and probably one, you know, the *people most closely identified* with. So I think it is extremely important, yeah.'[31] A similar link between associative con-notations is made by this British Brusselite here: 'I think it is *an excellent idea*, the Schengen dismantling of what had caused bureaucratic delays in *travelling*; scandalous previously, up to Schengen was implemented

---

[28] Interviewee Brux/UK C, 26 February 2003.
[29] While this is a popular perception, it has been argued at the 1997 Select Committee Hearing on Schengen in the House of Lords that the geographical situation of the UK is not entirely dissimilar compared with other EU member states who did sign the Schengen Agreement (Wiener 1999).
[30] Interviewee Brux/UK H, 26 February 2003.
[31] Interviewee Brux/UK B, 27 February 2003.

having to queue to show your passport, to go from one member state to another. You always had to show your identity card, you know. ... It is just the speed of *travelling and also the police cooperation*, you know and it should be, but there is not on asylum cooperation.'[32]

Similar to the Londoners, both British and German Brusselites are enthusiastic about the travel opportunities, stating, for example, as this British Brusselite does, 'I am definitely in favour ... certainly in the democratic setting of the European Union *it is a wonderful thing*. And it is unfortunate, in my opinion, that the UK is not a full member of the Schengen Agreement. ... I am all *in favour of abolishing border controls*. In fact, I am all in favour of abolishing nationalism and *working for what I consider a supranational ideal*.'[33] And, the following German Brusselites echo such spontaneous praise of free travel, when saying that 'personally you become actually aware of this when *crossing borders*, that is, when you travel by plane or car and may join a choice of queues, or, when you not even notice that you cross the border when actually driving across it. *I perceive that as an advantage*.'[34] And this German interviewee in Brussels echoes that personal experience when replying, 'I would agree for sure that Schengen is a success story ... that has, of course a *private background which is very positive – the possibilities of travel, everybody moving by car and hence has to cross borders, can do this these days*.'

This German Brusselite highlights the ambiguity of expectations related to the Schengen Agreement when stating

in such a particular problem area that deals with the internal security of member states, the decision has quite simply been ... in favour of a construction outside of the EC. ... I can obviously see that, for example in the area of external borders, if you want to conduct something akin to migration, that might be contradictory ... and, well, as a normal citizen I assume I am also *afraid of organised crime*. And that has not become particularly easier with eastern enlargement, to be sure, and ... yes, there is also some loss of internal security ... based on the opened borders.[35]

Asked what the negative sides of Schengen were, if there were any, this interviewee replies: 'Negative? Yes, because there are, in a way, no more

---

[32] Interviewee Brux/UK J, 6 September 2001.
[33] Interviewee Brux/UK E, 28 August 2001.
[34] Interviewee Brux/Ger D, 28 August 2001.
[35] Interviewee Brux/Ger D, 28 August 2001.

border controls. I am not sure whether there are statistics on that, that specific areas of criminal activity benefit, or drugs, whether this has increased after Schengen. But I could imagine that this is a negative aspect. But otherwise, I assume, the positive aspect clearly trumps with Schengen.'[36] Some interviewees raise the more general issue of 'obsolete border controls', for example as this interviewee points out, 'I think *there are more sophisticated ways of securing and ensuring security other than having a pretty artificial border control.*'[37] And another British Brusselite replies, 'I think the British *should be in Schengen*, because ... *border controls* is *not a dramatic issue.*' However, referring to the situation in other European countries as well, the same interviewee then states 'I think border controls still – in people's minds – it still has an important psychological importance.'[38] These observations are made, once again, by both groups though a stronger tendency is found among the British sample.

And finally, associative connotations with the keyword 'community formation' are uttered by both groups, yet they are more popular among the German Brusselites than with the British Brusselites. Nonetheless, this British Brusselite makes a strong point for British full Schengen membership with a view to establishing a European 'identity' based on the enjoyment of 'free movement' when saying that: *'It is a pity that the UK is not a full member of Schengen.* It is *both a psychological and a political thing.* I am not a security expert but I think people do not learn to appreciate what it means to travel without being checked all the time. If you fly from Paris to Berlin you can feel it, but the people in Britain are simply not used to learn how to find about the good sides Europe can have for them.'[39] And this British Brusselite links the two core issues of the European citizenship package, i.e. the issue of 'free movement' and the right to vote in European elections, when pointing out that: 'The abolition of *personal checks, the systematic personal checks at the internal borders of the European Union* had been one of the demands of the European Parliament since its first direct election – and also to my own. I consider this as *great progress within the European Union.*'[40]

---

[36] Interviewee Brux/Ger F, 21 May 2001.
[37] Interviewee Brux/UK E, 28 August 2001.
[38] Interviewee Brux/UK A, 22 May 2001.
[39] Interviewee Brux/UK G, 27 February 2003.
[40] Interviewee Brux/UK G, 29 August 2001.

Findings

Instead of indicating a foundation of cultural convergence as the basis of an emerging supranational political community, these discursive interventions indicate diffusion. That is, rather than convergence, which would reflect a shared recognition of constitutional discourse in the early 2000s, we find a new pattern of diversity based on the comparison of the four elite samples in London, Berlin and Brussels. It is important to note that this pattern is not manifested along the lines of nationality, which would have produced two derived oppositions rather than three. According to the associative connotations noted in this case, two types of divergence and one pattern of diffusion which had not been anticipated were found. The first two include divergence between the two distinct domestic groups (compare Table 4.4, *type B*), and divergence between the domestic and the transnational groups (*type A*). The third pattern shows diffusion between the transnational groups (*type C*). In other words, the evaluation of this case finds an 'either/or' pattern for the two domestic groups (*type B*), on the one hand, and a 'both/and' pattern for the transnational groups, on the other.

The distinguishing factor is – according to this sample – the context of day-to-day interaction. While this finding requires further empirical proof before any general insight might be stated, it is important to note that a new pattern is emerging in the transnational arena. In this arena, while not converging on one associative connotation, two different national groups diverge from the clear patterns derived from the two national groups in the domestic arenas. For example, both the British and German Brusselites' respective responses display a strong leaning towards the connotation of 'travel' with the British elites including the reference to 'community formation' and some German elites' insistence on 'border control' in addition to a generally shared, often personal, appreciation of the realisation of freedom of movement. Most Brusselites' utterances display little concern for border controls in order to achieve or maintain 'security' in the light of the abolition of internal border controls. Table 5.2 shows the quantitative evaluation of associative connotations by grouping the individually uttered connotations according to particular keywords and relating them to actor (type of elite group) and context (type of political arena). The percentages for this and all following tables are considered as follows: 50 percent or larger demonstrates a 'significant majority' of the sample; 30 to 40 percent demonstrates a 'significant group' out of one sample; more

Table 5.2 *Citizenship opposition 1: free movement vs security*

Arena	Domestic		Transnational	
Keywords / Elite groups	Londoners	Berliners	Brux/UK	Brux/Ger
Security		35	20	20
Civil rights				
Travel	69.2		40	30
Fortress Europe				
Borders obsolete			10	
Community formation			30	20
External border control				
Asylum/migration/visa				
Cooperation				

Source: 'Text Corpus'. The percentages indicate the frequency with which associative connotations to one keyword were uttered in response to particular policy field questions; author's calculations in this and all following tables displaying the results of the opposition-deriving exercise.

than 10 and less than 30 percent demonstrates 'a small group' out of one sample; and finally 10 percent or less indicates 'a few'.[41]

The evaluation demonstrates that the respective associative connotations uttered by the four different interviewed elite groups are unlikely to generate a single shared framework of reference. They thus question the expectation of a substantively socialised elite group pattern suggested by the liberal community hypothesis or the cultural harmonisation expected by the layer-cake assumption. Note in this regard, the opposition between the Londoners and the Berliners oscillating between the two rather opposite interpretations of Schengen as a 'security' risk or as a 'travel' opportunity provider on the one hand, and the diffused pattern of diversity emerging in Brussels, on the other. The data presented in Table 5.2 stands to be scrutinised by the opposition-deriving exercises which follow in this and chapters 6 and 7. For now, Table 5.3 summarises the emerging pattern of *types of divergence*

---

[41] In real numbers, this and all following case study tables are based on interviews with thirteen Londoners, twenty Berliners, ten German Brusselites and ten British Brusselites. The percentages are calculated accordingly and are on file with the author. Please note that the percentages reflect utterances with reference to the keyword list only. For guidance with regard to preparing the quantitative evaluation, I am thankful too Dorothee Wiegand.

Table 5.3 *Citizenship: core and derived oppositions (1)*

Core opposition		Derived opposition	Core opposition	
Divergence (either/or)				
Domestic arena 1			*Domestic arena 2*	
London			**Berlin**	
Inside			Outside	
		Security	[shaded]	
[shaded]		Travel		
Diffusion (both/and)				
Transnational arena			*Transnational arena*	
UK/Brux			**Ger/Brux**	
Inside	Outside		Inside	Outside
	[shaded]	Security		[shaded]
[shaded]		Travel	[shaded]	
	[shaded]	Border control obsolete		
[shaded]		Community formation	[shaded]	

Source: Table 5.2 and Case Excerpt.

according to Table 4.4. It also stands to be substantiated further in the following opposition-deriving samples. These will ultimately provide the basis for the reconstruction of the normative structure of meaning-in-use with regard to the three sets of fundamental norms (see chapter 8).

To summarise the findings of this first of seven opposition-deriving exercises, the Berliners focus on a perspective of concern about how to protect the borderless interior space from threats that are looming on the outside. In turn, the Londoners focus firmly on the inside of the European Union. Perhaps not surprisingly, the British elites' spontaneous reactions bear a reflection of internal sovereignty casting light on the sentiments of individuals and how their movements might be enhanced or hindered by a liberal state, while the German elites' reactions demonstrate a strong concern for upholding the markers of external sovereignty thereby displaying a thorough trust in their own state. Importantly, the Londoners' associative connotations suggest a view of 'the state' as 'other' while the Berliners construct a picture of 'the state' as 'self'.

Opposition 2: civil rights vs external borders

The next field of indicators derived from the Schengen text corpus is established with reference to compensatory security measures following the abolishment of internal border controls by the Schengen member states. The question targets associative connotations with the three core flanking measures, such as, for example, the Schengen Information System (SIS), the practice of police spot checks on individuals and the measure of upgrading external EU borders and ports of entry from non-Schengen countries to Schengen member states.[42] The core innovation of the SIS consists of linking police computers among Schengen member states so as to provide improved data access through exchange.[43] The spot-check instrument enables police to conduct passport controls in border areas, on trains and at train stations without any specific reason. A second question follows up by addressing more specific details about policing practices, success and political outcome associated with the abolishment of internal border control among the Schengen countries. The following set of questions was raised.

What do you think about the complementary measures of the Schengen Agreement such as, e.g., the 'spot-check' mechanism?

The replies were, where appropriate, encouraged to be more specific based on a reply to this additional question:

[42] For details, see Den Boer 1997; Petite 1998; Geddes 2000.

[43] On a summary of the history and current contents of the SIS as well as its legal integration into the EU's treaty framework, see *Development of the Schengen Information System II, Communication from the Commission to the Council and the European Parliament*, COM(2001) 720 final, Brussels, 18 December 2001. For the Schengen *acquis*, see 'The Schengen *Acquis*: Agreement between the Governments of the States of the Benelux Economic Union, the Federal Republic of Germany and the French Republic on the Gradual Abolition of Checks at their Common Borders', *Official Journal L 239, 22/09/2000 P. 0013–0018* http://europa.eu.int/eur-lex/lex/LexUriServ/LexUriServ.do?uri=CELEX:42000A0922 (01):EN:HTML (accessed 15 February 2006).

What is your view on the Schengen Information System?

The individually transported associative connotations are displayed in some detail by the replies to these questions, which are grouped according to political arena and elite group.

Londoners: 'civil rights'

The Londoners' replies on the compensatory measures following the removal of internal border controls with the implementation of the Schengen Agreement converge on a predominant concern about *data protection*. The view is that the protection of individual British citizens from insufficiently transparent mechanisms of state interference must be based on a protected respect of civil liberties. For example, as this Londoner stresses, 'there are *worries about rights and about data protection* ... I often feel bad when I see somebody being stopped basically because of what they look like – *because of the colour of their skin* or the way they are dressed.'[44] Another interviewee's associative connotation with the 'important protection of *privacy*, etc., perspectives; and *that obviously has not been dealt with in a very good way in the Schengen context*[45] reveals a similar concern. It is even more detailed by this interviewee's reactions: 'There is *considerable concern about privacy and civil liberty issues*. Schengen involved much more sharing of data about individuals between immigration and law enforcement agencies in all the member states which operate on the Schengen Agreement. ... The UK historically has quite a *strong civil liberties tradition and awareness among the civil liberties* NGOs, I mean, not least organisations like Liberty and Justice and others.'[46]

As would be expected in the context of a liberal political culture, these concerns display strong reservations against the interference of 'the state' in the individual affairs of individual citizens. The sceptical distance assumed with regard to state interference in private affairs, which establishes the state as 'the other', is particularly well described by the following reaction: 'I am always *very sceptical generally when governments use the term "freedom"* because what they mean is the right to police freedoms more generally, and this is why I'm deeply sceptical

---

[44] Interviewee UK O, 26 November 2002.   [45] Interviewee UK N, 8 May 2001.
[46] Interviewee UK H, 9 May 2001.

about it because it is a *huge extension of a state's policing powers.*[47]
The concern is reflected in expectations about the potential impact of
the Schengen flanking measures, as the same interviewee continues to
point out civil rights issues, now with a view to these measures:

And that's what worries me more I think, the Schengen Information System, the
increase in requirements of identity cards, ... some people would use it [the
Schengen system, AW] in terms of it might allow police to stop and search and
all those things ... My concern is how it is used for the transmission of information from police forces, from one to another; how it's being used, if you like, for
the accumulation of *data about individuals* – which is not a traditional civil
liberties concern but *strikes me as deeply worrying,* that *this huge concentration
of police knowledge about me or anyone else* which represents me in a particular
way and I'm not quite sure where that information ends up. (*ibid.*)

   In addition, the convergence regarding the associative connotations
with 'civil rights' and 'data protection' issues reveals a strong concern
about 'fairness' regarding the implementation of complementary security measures. This interviewee's reaction with a view to future European
Union practice is based, for example, on experience in the British
domestic context:

I am in particular thinking obviously here with regard to the potential of *having
racially motivated priorities in this stop and search tactic.* There have been long-
standing complaints not just in Britain but in other member states as well, that,
for example, police appeared to be targeting specifically *black citizens or black
persons* in the streets. And obviously when we are talking about *spot checks* at
the European level as a response to a borderless Europe, there would be similar
concerns and problems that the EU would be faced with.[48]

Asked about the flanking measure of the SIS and, especially, its central
role in providing cross-national access to a single electronic police
database, this interviewee replied,

I have *strong reservations* about it. This kind of information gathering – *I don't
really know where the information goes or where it ends up.* ... I'm pretty
comfortable with cameras – I know this is full of contradictions here, but on
the other hand I do feel slightly safer in the streets. Certainly I feel cameras are
useful in places like 'the tube' ... in the British tube nasty things do happen quite
frequently. So in that sense there is a direct tangible benefit you feel.[49]

---

[47] Interviewee UK M, 9 May 2001.
[48] Interviewee UK B, 8 May 2001.   [49] Interviewee UK D, 26 November 2002.

The next interviewee's reaction stresses a feeling of loss of control to state interference in personal matters when pointing out that,

basically everywhere when you really needed cooperation or where, you know, *from a civil liberties view there will be a sinister aspect of it.* That cooperation will take place anyway. ... Well, that you could basically follow people with the cooperation of police forces in other countries, for instance, you politically didn't like. ... I think it is pretty obvious that the police collaboration in itself is good, the question is just then, what limitations are there on sharing information and of course that has an *important protection of privacy* etcetera?[50]

Berliners: 'external borders'

In turn, the Berliners, when asked specifically about data protection, display a considerably higher degree of tolerance towards the flanking measures such as the spot-check policy and the SIS. Their first reactions converge on the association with security problems and the increasing importance of *external borders*. For example, they consider a particular level of standardisation regarding data transfer and control which could be brought about by the transnational SIS as necessary, when pointing out, 'I believe there was no alternative to Germany joining the Schengen Agreement which is now being included and integrated into the Treaties. After all, *the Schengen Agreement's aim of securing the external borders as well as providing compensation based on an outstanding technical system with a view to the abolition of personal controls at the internal European Union borders is the right way forward.*'[51]

This interviewee speaks for many when stressing the issue of standardised cooperation between national police organisations: 'if we are to secure an area of law where those who are criminals move abroad within Europe, we need to make sure that he will be taken into custody and extradited under the same conditions as in this country. Well, we can't possibly let it happen that Europe allows you to be criminal in one country of the Union and then ask for asylum in the neighbouring country, so to speak, and that extradition does not work.'[52] And this interviewee stresses the point of view of a new need for stronger internal security control based on police cooperation when saying that, 'Once you open borders *you naturally have to create compensation,* and that's

[50] Interviewee UK N, 8 May 2001. [51] Interviewee Ger P, 15 October 2001.
[52] Interviewee Ger S, 10 July 2001.

what this Schengen Information System is. It provides for a corrective measure in case of crimes, so that criminals who obviously can cross borders as well can be caught.'[53] In addition, the Berlin elites' connotations converge on the importance of cooperation and external border control. This interviewee's reply expresses very well the view of the overwhelming majority of Berliners:

Well, the possibilities, err, regulations of data protection are regulated in utterly different ways in each nation-state. I could imagine there to be a certain standard on the European level which could be agreed upon. Obviously, this standard has to comply with particular aspects of security and data protection, not that suddenly there is an absolute control on the European level which is in breach with the traditions of data protection established in the nation-states. However, there is no alternative to harmonisation, to be sure. ... According to me *only a European approach* to such regulation is sensible.[54]

Other Berliners' utterances reveal an equally sound confidence in cooperation in the area of border control. This trust in the flanking measures is paralleled with the associative connotation of a feeling of threat towards input from 'outside' the European Union's external borders, and a particular wariness about the level of trust to be invested in some EU member states' attitude and ability to comply with these measures. A reaction reflecting this line of thought is, for example, displayed by this interviewee: 'it is *an advantage*, if, for example, *German security interest* is realised not only at a German external border, but at a French Schengen border. And this has become possible with the creation of the *Schengen Agreement*.'[55] The combination of a concern about security with mistrust of some European member states paired with a generally sound confidence in the EU system is also displayed by this reply which stresses the control at external borders as the main issue: 'the main criteria of compensatory measures are, in my view, the Schengen Information System and external border controls. ... Regarding the Schengen Information System the additional keyword is the question of input. Search data need to be established and collected. That means work. ... However, the overwhelming part of

---

[53] Interviewee Ger C, 29 May 2001.   [54] Interviewee Ger J, 24 June 2002.
[55] Interviewee Ger H, 19 April 2001.

these data is provided by Germany and a few other member states, and many others don't comply.'[56]

While generally optimistic about the possibilities of integration, the connotations display a prevailing reservation about the compliance potential of some member states and the security potential of external borders in general. This interviewee, for example, does not express a general feeling of threat, yet at the same time displays a considerable lack of trust towards some member states in particular.

I don't believe that security is really threatened by the opening of the borders. Yet, when imagining how borders might be secured at the Romanian eastern border or ... wherever else, and comparing this to what is usually done by our border police is currently doing at the Polish border – that can create a difference by all means. And when you hear about these Romanian gangs who appear suddenly here in Berlin or elsewhere and crack shop windows and within three minutes empty the office or the shop, and with machine guns, and then disappear, then, I believe you cannot apply too low an estimate to the *security aspect. It definitely matters.*[57]

Most interviewees echo this concern about a lack of security and the importance of external borders.[58]

When asked about a potential critique of the Schengen Agreement, this interviewee points to the problem of the new external EU borders as cutting down the formely established ways of access and communication, stressing that this matters in particular for those citizens who belong to different countries (by passport) while belonging to the same nationality. Hungary and Romania are examples where such a situation occurs.

I see problems at the future external borders of the EU, because the forth-coming enlargement of the EU and the Schengen regime will cut through some very vital developments which have been established in some areas. Such problems exist for example between Hungary and Romania ... *the problem is that the rather rigid external border regulations might create something akin to a new Iron Curtain* at the eastern and south-eastern borders of the Schengen area.[59]

Among the positive associative connotations uttered by Berliners with reference to the Schengen Agreement is the appreciative reference

---

[56] Interviewee Ger F, 19 April 2001.   [57] Interviewee Ger L, 1 June 2001.
[58] Interviewee Ger M, 15 October 2001.   [59] Interviewee Ger B, 31 August 2001.

to Europeanisation and the creation of a common European identity. Both are considered as a good thing as this reply demonstrates:

That these controls are not carried out at borders but within a larger space, ... is an expression of *Europeanisation* which, I believe, is sensible ... since Europe is increasingly understood as relating to a single identity, it is good for controls to adopt the same character across Europe as at internal German borders between different stations in the German *Länder*. These are practically invisible and, of course, this touches the quality of external border controls, for sure, at the borders of the Schengen zone. Both *contribute to identity formation, that is, to the process of Europeanisation, which I welcome.*[60]

It is notable that only a minority of Berliners would spontaneously make reference to the lack of control, for example, based on the rule of law and, like this interviewee, consider that situation as problematic: 'I do see a problem of lacking control based on the rule of law.'[61]

Findings

While commonly referring to the problems perceived as a consequence of the abolition of internal borders within the Schengen territory, a marked opposition has emerged between the connotations displayed by the Londoners, on the one hand, and the Berliners, on the other. The majority of the Londoners included references to the issue best summarised by the keyword of *'civil rights'*, i.e. by suggesting that data protection and individual liberties protection required further consideration. Their main concern was one of preventing the violation of individual civil rights against interference through, for example, common police regulation. Subsequently, the associative connotations displayed a general mistrust of the new EU government as the 'other'. In turn, most Berliners' connotations included issues that are best summarised under the keyword of *'external border control'* and *'cooperative policing'*. Here the concern was whether or not border control could or, indeed, should be upgraded in order to provide a firm and safe substitute for the abolished internal borders (compare with Table 4.4, *type B*).

---

[60] Interviewee Ger E, 30 May 2001.   [61] Interviewee Ger G, 15 October 2001.

While these connotations share a general element of mistrust with the Londoners, it is important to note that the Berliners' mistrust is directed towards other member states or candidate countries rather than towards the EU as 'other'. Indeed, the Berliners' associative connotations regarding the EU differ quite substantially from that of the Londoners in expressing *trust* rather than mistrust in the capability and scope of EU governance, for example, demanding better and/or more standardisation as well as regulation of compensatory measures. The opposition derived with respect to measures of border control involve the Londoners' sceptical assessment of the SIS and increasing data collection as interfering with civil rights, on the one hand, and the Berliners' concern with pressure on unsafe external borders combined with lacking police collaboration and sustaining the loss of security following the removal of internal border controls, on the other.

Brusselites: both/and

Unlike the rather clear-cut opposition between the Londoners' and Berliners' respective associative connotations with the Schengen compensatory measures, such a notable distinction cannot be observed with the Brussels samples. In the transnational arena, the associative connotations are much more *diffuse* than those uttered by elites interviewed in the two domestic arenas. Yet, there is more diffusion of issues among the German Brusselites than the British. While the German Brusselites' connotations involve the issues of 'civil rights', 'obsolete border controls', 'security', 'cooperation' and 'external borders', the British Brusselites diffuse on the issues of 'civil rights protection' and 'obsolete border controls', only. The German and British Brusselites particularly share the view that border controls have become 'obsolete' in an age of globalisation. They are not the most efficient measures to catch criminals in the twenty-first century and therefore not preferable.

As this British Brusselite notes, 'well I think that [you can] possibly [count] on one finger the number of terrorists that have been caught as a result of border control. The number of drug traffickers who had been caught on border control methods. ... I think there are more sophisticated ways of securing and ensuring security other than *having a pretty artificial border control*.'[62] And, this German Brusselite confirms this view stating, when asked about spot checks, that as

---

[62] Interviewee Brux/UK E, 28 August 2001.

a *mechanism*, this is rather annoying, yet on the other hand, it is a necessary measure and the burden should not be too much for the citizen ... and there is the additional question of whether this is efficient, isn't it? ... Well, I think – as one does notice – that such border checks, for example, on trains crossing the border, and the kind of *habitus* with which people act there, well I could personally live without that. And I assume that this does relatively little to prevent illegal border crossings or what have you, or catch somebody. I don't think so.[63]

This German Brusselite also stresses the importance of spot checks in comparison with the outdated measure of catching criminals at borders: '*Spot checks* ... are not only helpful at external or internal borders, ... *systematic border controls* – we have seen that in England contribute comparatively little in the fight against crime. ... why borders are supposed to be a particular space where crime can be detected particularly easily and criminals can simply be caught and controlled is beyond reason.'[64]

The Brusselites also demonstrate a shared reference to concerns about 'civil rights', as this British interviewee replies: 'but even then, what *right of the state to ask a citizen anything?* Unless they are suspect they have a reasonable ground to suspect something is wrong. And there is [Napoleonic vs Rome], you know the UK common law position. ... for example, Ireland and the UK and the classic answer of the Napoleonic system, should they account to the state for their action if requested? Or is that the other way round, the state should account to the citizens?'[65] And this British Brusselite's reply adds that the Schengen Agreement 'also means ... other potential *infringements of human rights* in terms of ... *fingerprinting*, much more kind of *control, surveillance*. It reinforces, if you like, the channels of a police nature of keeping people within the EU and outside the EU ... and the *spot checks* ... we are not happy with that.'[66] A German Brusselite echoes that concern with civil rights protection when stating,

that is an area where we need to pay attention, as it were. That is what in our jargon we call the rule of law *acquis*, should not get lost through the transfer of competences onto the European level, for example, in case they are not

---

[63] Interviewee Brux/Ger D, 28 August 2001.
[64] Interviewee Brux/Ger H, 23 May 2001.
[65] Interviewee Brux/UK J, 6 September 2001.
[66] Interviewee Brux/UK D, 22 May 2001.

accompanied by *instruments which we know with reference to civil protection at the national level*, shouldn't it? That is unacceptable and we need to be very careful there. According to my knowledge it is still the case that everything that happens on the European level does *not represent a direct interference with the individual rights of citizens.*[67]

And this German Brusselite confirms the problematic view on rights protection saying: 'Yes, that is a bit of *a problem for me*, indeed. I mean, you read in the papers that *spot checks* involve individuals who do not look particularly super Germanic.'[68] Similarly, this British Brusselite emphasises a civil rights concern: 'I think each citizen should have *access to the data which concern her.*' However, this interviewee feels that data collection is quite common in both the public and private sectors: 'So, one shouldn't be shocked by that. But obviously *one doesn't want the use of personal data to be abused.*'[69]

Another British Brusselite points out, 'what we probably need is some kind of regulation which would apply the *principles of anti-discrimination clauses* in the Treaty ... if you carry out *spot checks* you can't just concentrate on people who have a *different colour.*'[70] And yet another British Brusselite adds that '*free movement*' while '*a big plus on the citizen side of the EU*' was 'good in a context where everything was focused so much on goods and services – although it has some *problematic aspects on the civil liberties side*', adding that it was 'not balanced; pretty much intergovernmental' and '*not democratically controlled*'.[71] This German Brusselite concurs when pointing out that judicial control in Schengen matters is adamant. That is, '*yardsticks at the European level are therefore rather vague and unspecific*; because different from the German context, they are not subject to the strict *obligation to respect fundamental rights.*[72] ... The problem of control and competence of the ECJ [European Court of Justice] ... still exists, to be sure. ... I think it is important to secure the juridical control of what Europol does, and, what the migration authorities[73] do on the basis of European law.'[74]

---

[67] Interviewee Brux/Ger J, 21 May 2001.
[68] Interviewee Brux/Ger J, 21 May 2001.
[69] Interviewee Brux/UK E, 28 August 2001.
[70] Interviewee Brux/UK A, 22 May 2001.
[71] Interviewee Brux/UK G, 27 February 2003.
[72] German original text: 'Grundrechtsbindung'.
[73] German original text: 'Migrationsbehörden'.
[74] Interviewee Brux/Ger H, 23 May 2001.

This interviewee weighs the idea of free movement against the practice of setting up a 'fortress Europe' by enforcing external borders. 'I think our *concern about Schengen* is that [with] free movement within the EU the price we pay is ... having much [higher control, AW] of borders around the EU and to that extent we are quite concerned about it; we are not in favour of it, really, because it just makes *much stronger borders around the EU* and we enforce this idea of *fortress Europe. ...* So, to that extent, *we don't think that Schengen is a good idea.*'[75] The strong diffusion among the German Brusselites' replies involves the emphasis on more cooperation and parliamentary control.

[I] think that *Europol is still far too embryonic.* Surely, the executive needs to obtain authority, yet other aspects need to be taken away. That is, the immunity clause must go, and parliamentary control must come. ... I rather wonder somewhat whether the ... right measures have been created or are used towards working with truly European controls. That is not to imply that a European super policy mingles with domestic police affairs. That would be ill advised. Instead, there should be cooperation.[76]

Similarly, this German interviewee in Brussels answers when asked about the SIS, 'well, to me that keyword means difficult technical compatibility, according to my knowledge this always fails because of standards that remain unclear'.[77] These German Brusselites display a relatively strong overlap with Berlin German officials' associative connotations when stressing '*security*' as the recurring connotation to Schengen all the way through the interview. 'Of course citizens rightfully expect to live safely in a Europe without borders. And it cannot be that the freedom of movement for capital, goods and services is bought on the basis of less security. Nobody would understand that, I think, and that depends in the end and in no small part on the people's acceptance of European politics.'[78] Questioned about the SIS, this interviewee points out that it is 'indispensable for providing the security of the member states'.[79]

[75] Interviewee Brux/UK D, 22 May 2001.
[76] Interviewee Brux/Ger B, 12 June 2002.
[77] Interviewee Brux/Ger D, 28 August 2001.
[78] Interviewee Brux/Ger C, 30 July 2002.
[79] Interviewee Brux/Ger G, 29 August 2001.

Table 5.4 *Citizenship opposition 2: civil rights vs external borders*

Arenas	Domestic		Transnational	
Keywords / Elite groups	Londoners	Berliners	Brux/UK	Brux/Ger
Security				
Civil rights	84.6	5	60	40
Travel				
Fortress Europe		5	10	
Border control obsolete			10	10
Community formation		5		
External border control		65		50
Asylum/migration/visa				
Cooperation		5	10	30

Source: 'Text Corpus'. The percentages indicate the frequency with which one keyword was uttered in response to particular policy field questions; author's calculations.

Findings

The second exercise of deriving oppositions generated an equally clear and sound opposition between the Londoners and the Berliners, with the Londoners stressing the role of 'individual rights' and their concern for the respect for them by the European Union as the 'other' (see Table 5.4 and compare Table 4.4, *type B*). In turn, the Berliners' main concern lies with 'external borders' and the related assumption that these borders are not safe and that 'others' may enter the European Union in a presumably unlawful and/or threatening way.

This finding resonates well with the conventional (or modern) constructivist work which found distinct national identity options indicating a British view of the EU as the 'other' and a German view of the EU as 'more of the same' (Marcussen, Risse, Engelmann-Martin, Knopf and Roscher 1999). With regard to the layer-cake assumption about more or less cultural harmonisation among European elites, however, it is interesting to compare the second result of the opposition-deriving technique, i.e. the Brusselites' cross-check sample. Here the British and German elite groups' utterances no longer focus on a clear opposition based on two keywords of oppositional meaning. Instead, and similar to the previous opposition-deriving exercise on the Schengen policy

Table 5.5 *Citizenship: core and derived oppositions (2)*

Core opposition		Derived opposition	Core opposition	
Core opposition		Derived opposition	Core opposition	
Divergence (either/or)				
Domestic arena 1			*Domestic arena 2*	
London			**Berlin**	
Inside			Outside	
		External borders		
		Civil rights		
Diffusion (both/and)				
Transnational arena			*Transnational arena*	
UK/Brux			**Ger/Brux**	
Inside	Outside		Inside	Outside
		External borders		
		Civil rights		
		Border control obsolete		
		Community formation		
		Fortress Europe		
		Cooperation		

Source: Table 5.2 and Case Excerpt.

area, the references are much more diverse. That is their meaning is diffused, if not in a homogenous way that is often attached to the process of norm diffusion. For example, both British and German Brusselites mention a concern with 'civil rights', with the British still quantitatively leading over the Germans (see Table 5.4).

In addition, the concern lies with 'fortress Europe' among the British and 'border control ineffective' as an obsolete measure with both the British and the Germans, and a stress on 'community formation' and 'external border control' as well as 'cooperation' with the German Brusselites (see Table 5.5).

Conclusion

The Brusselites both of British and German national origin display little evidence of stable or 'sticky' national identity positions. In addition, the results caution against the expectations of harmonisation among elites following regional interaction raised by the layer-cake assumption. While harmonisation does remain as a potential outcome, it is, however, more likely to occur in transnational arenas than in an all-encompassing way which would extend into and across domestic political arenas. We can conclude, for now, that based on the first data set garnered from the Schengen policy field, the degree of harmonisation appears more likely to develop in correlation with the frequency and place of interaction than national identity. The elite groups acting predominantly in domestic political arenas, i.e. Londoners and Berliners, appear to sustain the impression suggested by popular clichés suggested in numerous contributions to the literature. They confirm the national identity-options assumption which has been established by political science research that found three different types of national identity options for France (upgrade to Europe), Germany (more of Germany) and Britain (Europe as the other) (Marcussen *et al.* 1999). In addition, the work of lawyers who proposed distinguishing between different legal cultures in, for example, Germany and France based on the different understanding of the rule of law (Preuss 1994) or different constitutional practices.[80] The more interesting aspect is the diverging interpretations of meaning when comparing the elite groups of the same national origin and which are demonstrated by the Brusselites' utterances.

In sum, this chapter has confirmed the national identity-options assumption which found a convergence among the national samples interviewed in London and Berlin, respectively. For example, the British saw the European Union as the 'other' and for the Germans it represents 'more of the same' (Marcussen *et al.* 1999); that is, the Germans tend to understand the EU as 'us' rather than 'them'. However, confirmation of the national identity-options assumption is limited to the Berliners and Londoners who operate mainly within a single domestic political arena. Notably, therefore, the influence of nationally derived primordial identity options does not allow for making predictions about

---

[80] See, e.g., Moellers 2003, who acknowledges the same 'power-limiting' constitutional tradition yet points to different constitutional systems today.

associative connotations held by elite groups operating in the transnational political arena in Brussels. Here, the findings suggest a number of variations with regard to a particular national pattern. While no one single pattern that is shared by both transnational groups is identifiable (yet?), this diffused pattern is indicative of the deconstruction of national identity options based on interactions within a transnational context.

Given the limited data set of fifty-three interviewees questioned with reference to one policy field (Schengen) and one fundamental constitutional norm (citizenship) only, no conclusive remarks can be offered at this point. Suffice it to say that the 'outside' vs 'inside' interpretation of citizenship derived from the core opposition among Londoners and Berliners does not hold in Brussels. The Brusselites' interviews suggest that in this transnational arena, a 'both/and' interpretation is emerging (Beck 1993). Of key importance for International Relations students is, thus, whether an on-going tendency towards a transnational interface of associative connotations can be observed while domestic associative connotations remain stable, i.e. maintaining the pattern of divergence. If this tendency can be sustained by further empirical research, it can be concluded that the transnationalisation of politics establishes an additional layer of diversity. Instead, it supports the new observation that 'pockets of Europeanisation' emerge thereby challenging the layer-cake assumption and the liberal community hypothesis, respectively. The following two chapters seek to scrutinise these findings with reference to the same group of interviewees, yet focusing on two further policy fields, i.e. 'Enlargement' and 'Constitutional Politics', which are associated with two further sets of fundamental norms including 'democracy and the rule of law' and 'human rights and fundamental freedoms', respectively.

6 | Democracy and the rule of law

The rule of law thus stands in the peculiar state of being *the* pre-eminent legitimating ideal in the world today without agreement on what precisely it means.

(Tamanaha 2004: 4; emphasis in original)

Introduction

Two changes in world politics have contributed to the enhanced contestation of normative meanings. Firstly, increasing interaction between communities which are considered – and consider themselves – as belonging to the group of civilised nations in world politics has raised the level of contestedness of norms (compare Table 4.1, *condition 3*). Secondly, the increasingly routine application of fundamental norms as conditionalities that stand between candidacy and membership of international communities has turned fundamental norms into organising principles. It has also undermined the role of these norms, as substantive meaning has given way to function as a hurdle of sophistication with regard to 'universal' standards of democratic governance.[1] In the light of the on-going enlargement negotiations at the time of the interviews (2001–3), which referred to the fundamental norms of democracy and the rule of law, among others, as a condition for membership, this chapter examines the substantive meanings of these norms from the perspective of selected elites from EU member states. The following comparative evaluation indicates an emerging pattern of diversity with regard to these meanings. Thus, it will be demonstrated that fundamental norms (whether they are 'core constitutional norms' derived from domestic constitutional frameworks or 'basic procedural norms' in world politics, compare Table 4.2,

---

[1] Note that universalist approaches would often confound mastering this hurdle with 'civilisation'.

norm-type 1) have sometimes taken on a more shallow meaning.[2] It will further be shown that the substantial normative interpretation of their meaning differs as well. If the latter can be sustained, this would suggest that the assumption of stable norms and related expectations of behaviour in world politics require substantial revision.

This chapter continues to examine individual interpretations of normative meaning with a view to understanding the impact of cultural validation in addition to the formal validity and social recognition of norms. This second step towards reconstructing the structure of meaning-in-use with regard to fundamental norms sets the focus on *democracy* and *the rule of law*. The four elite groups in London, Berlin and Brussels have been questioned with regard to enlargement policy. In the last decade this new policy field has been managed by the Commissioner for Enlargement.[3] More generally, the policy is part of the larger umbrella of external or foreign policy (Smith 2003). Substantially, enlargement policy would be most closely linked with the responsibilities and policies dealt with by the Foreign Office in modern nation-states. In the past decade the most influential decision with regard to enlargement policy was the decision to conduct a massive enlargement process involving ten new member states, most of them former command economies.[4] As before, the field has thus caused suffi-cient public debate to be of interest to the sample groups interviewed here. The questions were intended to generate expressive, discursive interven-tions so as to indicate the specific individually enacted associative connota-tions and conduct a comparative evaluation of each elite group sample. The next section turns to the fundamental norms of democracy and the rule of law. Subsequently, a section identifies group-related associative connota-tions based on the method of deriving oppositions from the interview

---

[2] See also Rosert and Schirmbeck's (2006) work on the 'erosion of international norms' with reference to the nuclear taboo and the UN convention against torture.

[3] See the current Commissioner for Enlargement, Olli Rehn's website: http://ec. europa.eu/commission_barroso/rehn/press_corner/speeches/index_en.htm (accessed 12 August 2007); the previous holder of this Commission portfolio was Günther Verheugen.

[4] On 1 May 2004, ten new members joined the EU after a decade of accession negotiations and enlargement politics. They include Estonia, Latvia, Lithuania, Poland, the Czech Republic, Hungary, Slovakia, Slovenia, Cyprus and Malta. For details of the process, see http://europa.eu/scadplus/leg/en/lvb/e50017.htm (accessed 10 August 2007). Among numerous academic discussions of the process, see especially Schimmelfennig and Sedelmeier 2002 and 2005.

transcripts. The final section assesses the findings that ensue from three such opposition-deriving exercises.

Democracy and the rule of law: fundamental norms in European law

The rule of law and democracy are modern constitutional norms which have achieved a considerable degree of acceptance and legitimacy beyond modern boundaries, to the extent that they are both stipulated in legal contexts outside the constitutional limits of modern states. As fundamental norms, they are not only central to national constitutions but also accepted as peremptory norms of international law. That is, each of these norms is 'accepted and recognized by the international community of states as a whole as a norm from which no derogation is permitted and which can be modified only by a subsequent norm of general international law having the same character'.[5] In addition, both are also included in Article 6 (TEU) and therefore carry formal validity qua treaty law for all European Union member states – regardless of whether the document is called a 'treaty' or a 'constitution'. Norm contestation, however, is enhanced under three conditions: contingency, moving social practices and crisis.[6] As Philip Green has emphasised, we therefore require empirical data to shed light on the tension between the 'normative although impossible ideal', on the one hand, and the 'concrete, yet quite different, contemporary reality', on the other (1993: 30). This tension between ideal and perceived social fact contributes to the notion of 'essentially contested' concepts.[7] Thus, even though considered as shared values of (modern) political communities and stipulated by the TEU, the understanding of democracy and the rule of law are

---

[5] The Vienna Convention on the Law of Treaties, 1969, Article 53 states, 'A treaty is void if, at the time of its conclusion, it conflicts with a *peremptory norm of general international law*. For the purposes of the present Convention, a peremptory norm of general international law is a norm accepted and recognized by the international community of states as a whole as a norm from which no derogation is permitted and which can be modified only by a subsequent norm of general international law having the same character.' See www.un.org/law/ilc/texts/treaties.htm (accessed 6 January 2006); my emphasis.

[6] For the three conditions that enhance the contestation of norms, see Table 4.1.

[7] See Gallie 1956 for the term 'essentially contested concept'; for a discussion of citizenship as an essentially contested concept in the EU, see Shaw 2007; for the rule of law as a contested concept, see Tamanaha 2004: 3.

expected to be contested. After all, assumptions about the universality of norms must always be understood as just that, normative theoretical assumptions which remain an 'impossible ideal', unless and until conditions and possibilities of approaching this ideal are specified by empirical research. Only then can the actual meanings of norms be accounted for and compared, so as to examine if and when their respective meaning is shared and, in fact, understood. The moment of shared acceptance of a norm following the solemn signing of a treaty, therefore, reveals little about the actual degree of shared social recognition or, for that matter, cultural validation. Both require empirical demonstration based on specific and detailed research.

As in the previous chapter, the following applies the technique of deriving oppositions from the text corpus with reference to the spontaneous utterances of fifty-three individuals belonging to four different elite groups. This time, the questions addressed enlargement policy to reveal associative connotations with the norms of democracy and the rule of law.[8] The resulting associative connotations of the four elite groups of Londoners, Berliners and British and German Brusselites, respectively, are compared with reference to the list of keywords displayed in Table 6.1 by deriving oppositions. Continuing with the qualitative and quantitative evaluation of the text corpus, the interviews focus on the issue of 'Enlargement' as the reference frame for assessing the degree of divergence, convergence or diffusion of interpretations of democracy and the rule of law. Pending on the keyword link that is generated by specific utterances, both derived and core oppositions are identified. The *core opposition* in the enlargement policy field is defined by the distinction between *society* and *community*. This distinction follows comparative research on 'polity ideas' which suggests working with two basic views on statehood. It distinguishes, for example, between situations of 'national statehood' and 'beyond statehood', respectively (Jachtenfuchs, Diez and Jung 1998: 419). The point is that, following the preferred option used in a specific text, further choices regarding models of governance ensue. Considering that this chapter's leading questions relate exclusively to the European Union's enlargement process, the 'beyond statehood' option applies throughout.

---

[8] For three different norm types including fundamental norms, organising principles and standardised procedures, recall Table 4.2.

Table 6.1 *Democracy and rule of law: keywords – Enlargement*

Keywords	Associative connotations
Compliance	Obey treaty, comply with conditionality, interest in political stability justifies means, interest in membership justifies conditionality
Fairness	Differentiate in fairness
Value-export	Peace, order and good government, multi-party democracy, historical trajectory, values and identity
Inclusion	Access to participation, debate, public information, transparency, equality
Integration (political stability)	EU action potential matters to the interviewee, cooperation
Wealth export (economic stability)	Stabilise market, promote economic prosperity
Finality	Further deepening, enhanced integration

Source: 'Text Corpus'.

In keeping with the model, two legitimacy options apply to the specific setting of this case study. Both involve either output-oriented or input-oriented legitimacy, where output-oriented legitimacy is related to efficient performance and input-oriented legitimacy is linked with the electoral process.[9] According to the polity-ideas research frame, two types of polity ideas are relevant. The first type focuses on 'legitimation by output' following the concept of an 'economic community', the second type refers to 'legitimation by participation and identity' following the concept of a 'network community' (Jachtenfuchs, Diez and Jung 1998: 419). The case study applies this distinction. However, it works with the slight alteration of defining 'output' as facilitated by both economic and political performance. The indicators are accordingly based on a selection of keywords that suggest, for example, the production of 'wealth', 'security', 'stability' and so forth (see Table 6.1). These keywords connote functional definitions of a political organisation based on the concept of *society*. In turn, the input-oriented legitimacy option which is linked with the connotations of 'community of values', 'identity'

[9] See, e.g., Scharpf 1995 as well as Leibfried and Zürn 2005.

and 'inclusion' indicate a preference for the more emotionally rooted and identity-oriented concept of *community*.[10] The complete selection of keywords and associated connotations applied to the interview evalua-tion with regard to discursive interventions on enlargement policy is listed in Table 6.1.

The distinction between the concept of society as functional and the concept of community as emotional reflects a rather general distinction between republican and communitarian approaches to political order in world politics. For this specific research context, it is less important what the specific and complex substantial aspects of both entail, than finding an opposition that allows for situating the respective interview-ees' utterances within the structure of meaning-in-use relating to the fundamental norms of democracy and the rule of law. Accordingly, the evaluation looks for an expression of different views on and expecta-tions of the state within the context of a particular polity. The following turns to the case study which conducts and compares three opposition-deriving exercises based on the interview transcriptions.

Deriving oppositions

Opposition 1: fairness vs compliance

As an organising principle on a procedural level i.e. a *norm-type 2* 'fairness' indicates a condition of 'generally accepted principles of right process' (Franck 1990: 24). As a fundamental norm in democratic polities, i.e. a *norm-type 1*, it raises the expectation of equal access to participation for all.[11] With regard to the European Union's eastern enlargement process, the principle of 'fairness' on the one hand and the expectation of 'compli-ant' behaviour, i.e. candidate countries' respect for the conditions of membership set by the 1993 Copenhagen Agreement, on the other revealed a derived opposition.[12] The following interview evaluation demonstrates

---

[10] See, e.g., Barry Buzan who proposes to distinguish between a purposeful organisation of *society* and a more emotionally based glue of a *community* in international relations (1993; see also Toennies 1988). And Deutsch defines '*society* ... as a group of persons who have learned to work together, and a *community* ... as a group of persons who are able to communicate information to each other effectively and over a wide range of topics' (1953: 169; emphasis in original)

[11] Compare Table 4.2 for both norm types.

[12] On critical assessments of these criteria, see e.g. Witte 2000 and Schwellnus 2007.

that both meanings are present in the interviewees' discursive interventions. The starting questions were as follows:

> What do you think of the current enlargement process?
> Should it, for example, proceed at a different speed?

The additional question with reference to this policy field was:

> Should the full *acquis communautaire* – including the Schengen
> *acquis*[13] – be applied by candidate countries?

Londoners: 'fairness'

Many of the Londoners raised a spontaneous concern with a lack of *'fairness'* in the enlargement process. Yet, at the same time, these interviewees also tended to prefer to maintain the 'rules of the club'. As this interviewee states, for example: 'Well personally I do not consider it fair, and I think that this different treatment of existing member states and future member states, I am sure that will at least potentially create problems with regard to the acceptance by the general public in the new republican state with regard to the European project.'[14] The issue of fairness is put down to the fact of lacking standards and a feeling that the added conditions of entry may result in double standards. As this interviewee points out,

I am not so worried about adding conditions because so long as it's all the member states agree then it's not one member state picking on a candidate country; for example, it is not that Austria was not able for the Czechs to

---

[13] The House of Lords Select Committee's Fifth Report defines the 'Schengen *acquis*' as 'the collective term for an intricate body of rules establishing an area free of internal frontier controls. The UK and Ireland are the only two EU Member States to have remained outside the Schengen free movement area. Although the Amsterdam Treaty 1997 brought the Schengen *acquis* within the framework of the European Union, the UK (and Ireland) secured an opt-out while retaining the possibility, subject to the agreement of the other Member States, of opting in to some or all of the provisions comprising the *acquis*.' House of Lords, 15 February 2000, at www.publications.parliament.uk/pa/ld199900/ldselect/ ldeucom/34/3402.htm (accessed 20 May 2006).

[14] Interviewee UK B, 8 May 2001.

close down the Treblinka power plant. What I am worried about is the fact that the EU does not have very clear standards in most of these areas; it does not have an *acquis*. And so that's where it becomes a *double standard*. ... So, for example, we can all agree to the Rule of Law, Democracy, Human Rights, Respect and Protection of the Rights of Minorities, but that is 'motherhood and apple pie' – we've never defined what that means, even rule of law. And that gives the EU much more policy entrepreneurship in defining the conditions. It allows for *discriminatory behaviour towards certain countries*.[15]

Asked whether the candidate countries ought to accept the existing *acquis*, this interviewee replied, 'The existing *acquis*, yes, and they have to accept flexibility to future developments but not to the existing one.'[16] This is confirmed by the next interviewee who also thinks that it is important to 'take over the whole *acquis*, certainly'.[17] Much of these utterances refer to the perception of the EU as a club – rather than a community. As this interviewee explains, 'I mean basically if you want to join a club you have to accept its rules, but you try and reform from within – it is that basic.'[18] Asked about the inclusion of minority rights in the accession *acquis*, this interviewee replies,

I think it was the right thing to do although, of course, the accusation will come through of *double standards* and that we demand more of candidate countries than we demand from ourselves. But here are particular problems left over from history in the candidate countries like the Russian minority left in the Baltic states particularly in Latvia, or the Roma across much of Central Europe, other little minority groups around the place and we have extended, far extend the process to Turkey by giving them a date, a conditional date to start negotiations, and there in Turkey, these problems are very real. They are very important. So what we have done for the Central Europeans is a signal to the Turks. It is also a signal to the Balkan states. ... Their treatment of the Serb and Bosnian minorities in Croatia, it's something ... we've made a lot of progress on and we've got to continue putting the pressure on, and these political criteria of minority rights will be important with them too. So, it has been essential to create this extra bit of the *acquis*.[19]

Asked about transition rules which do, for example, include an albeit limited period during which time the accession countries' citizens will

---

[15] Interviewee UK O, 26 November 2002.   [16] Interviewee UK K, 10 May 2001.
[17] Interviewee UK L, 10 May 2001.   [18] Interviewee UK E, 26 November 2002.
[19] Interviewee UK C, 19 December 2002.

not enjoy the full range of citizenship rights[20] and, instead, will earn the right to free movement of persons based on a step-by-step approach, this interviewee replies:

I think actually, that is a very attractive idea and it would make me feel more confident to get the police mechanism working, and you could see the flaws and defects in them, and if they would not be working, you would have the chance to remedy them. Against that is that *you are creating two classes*, aren't you? You are creating a second class of European citizens. ... It will be acceptable if that is for a short period only, two or three years. You couldn't do it for ten years.[21]

Berliners: 'compliance'

With reference to the enlargement field, the associative connotations displayed by Londoners and Berliners are not as diametrically opposed as in the Schengen policy field. This is likely to be a reflection of the personal distance experienced by individual elites from foreign policy issues. Those interviewees whose work is unrelated to Foreign Office issues are especially less likely to be able to draw on practical experiences with implications for the enlargement process than on, for example, 'travel' experience with regard to the Schengen policy field; however, despite a relative overlap regarding the quantity of the *acquis*, i.e. the spontaneous approval of incorporating the full *acquis* in the enlargement conditions, the Berliners' respective associative connotations with enlargement diverge regarding the quality of the process. That is, they demonstrate a far less prominent concern with 'fairness' and express a concern with '*compliance*' instead. This interviewee stresses that reaction briefly and clearly when stating 'I am decidedly in favour of the candidate countries' *duty to comply* with the Schengen *acquis*.'[22]

This interviewee's reaction points in more detail to a substantive link between integration and compliance with the existing *acquis* when saying, for example, 'the EU has a particular *acquis*, not just the legal

---

[20] For example, decisions about the free movement of workers have been delegated to the EU member states. Subsequently only a few member states have opened their labour markets either under specific conditions such as Denmark, the UK and Ireland, or fully such as Sweden, whereas most of the other member states have chosen to apply 'transition periods' which restrict labour market access for citizens of new member states; see, e.g., Brücker 2005.

[21] Interviewee UK A, 8 May 2001.   [22] Interviewee Ger P, 15 October 2001.

acquis ... and, as part of the historical development, now a number of states join later in the process, if you wish. To question this – except for transition periods which are there, to be sure, and which do create a Europe of different speeds no doubt about that – would mean negotiating backwards. ... To detangle the *acquis* ... is not useful for the adaptation period.'[23] Referring to other exceptions in the full compliance practice, for example regarding the UK's decision to opt out of Schengen, all Berliners' react with a no-nonsense reaction, favouring a clear all-or-nothing approach. Asked whether the new member states will have to accept the Schengen *acquis* in full, this interviewee replies, 'Yes, ... that is out of the question: *all of Schengen or nothing*. In other words, no cherry-picking as I said. And with Britain the situation is different. Britain belongs to the founding fathers of the EU, well not really, but in any case it belongs to central Europe [*sic*] shall we say, and the intention was to entice Britain with the further development of Schengen, and therefore this special regulation was set up.'[24]

In addition, the discursive interventions display an associative connotation with political power and strategic input, for example when stating, 'when they come to the EU we have the right to say *you must comply* with the *acquis communautaire*, including the social *acquis*, the umbrella mantle *acquis*, well, all these *acquis* that we have. This also implies that whatever we accuse them of now, for example, price dumping, environmental dumping and so forth. All that we cannot accuse them of in the future because *they have to comply* with the *acquis*.'[25] The substantive input of compliance is sustained by a spontaneous link with further integration. As this interviewee points out, 'the Copenhagen criteria are part of the European Union's self-perception ... as the practice shows. The old member states are also scrutinised according to these conditions which are called Copenhagen criteria [*sic*].'[26]

Unlike the Londoners' perception of the European Union as a club, the Berliners' discursive interventions indicate the contrary. As this interviewee says, for example, 'I cannot say, I want to join the EU but I do not want Schengen. I compare that a bit with a sports club. If I wish to join a sports club, then I cannot say, I join, but I do not wish to

[23] Interviewee Ger R, 14 May 2002.   [24] Interviewee Ger F, 19 April 2001.
[25] Interviewee Ger S, 10 July 2001.
[26] Interviewee Ger J, 24 June 2002. Note that this interviewee is mistaken to the extent that scrutinisation does not actually take place in the old member states. For details, e.g. on the case of minority rights, see Wiener and Schwellnus 2004.

accept its statutes. Either I accept them or I do not. However, if I was a founding member of the club, then I might have achieved an exceptional status – otherwise the club might not have been put together in the first place.'[27] And this intervention displays an associative connotation with 'community' building rather than 'club' membership when stating, 'our proposal was an expression based on the background of experiences with our [German, AW] process of unification, that is, that the entire accession process is not just understood as a, well, "joining the club", but as an interactive process. As far as this is concerned, I believe we would have imagined some more openness. After all, these countries also have quite a bit to offer.'[28] In addition, this interviewee's discursive intervention reveals a connotation with 'fairness' which is exceptional compared with the Berliners' overall compliance expectations.

> I think, it is a fundamental problem of the enlargement process that all those freedoms of opting-in and out, differentiated regulations which old member states have allowed themselves over the past years, now are not supposed to apply to the new member states as a matter of principle, and instead they are confronted with the alternative of 'take it or leave it'. And that's what I see as a big problem, especially the application of the Schengen Agreement in some new member states.[29]

Summary

Evaluated in quantitative terms, the opposition-deriving exercise reveals an opposition between reference to fairness 'fairness' expressed by the Londoners, and 'compliance' based on substantive views on enlargement as a part of the larger process of integration on the part of the Berliners (compare Table 4.4, *type B*). The Londoners are quite happy with the reference to the European Union as a club that works based on the principle of fairness. That is, formulated in more general terms, they follow the 'society' approach to the EU. In turn, the Berliners generally prefer to think about the EU as a 'community'. The interviewees refer, for example, either to the candidates' 'duty to comply' with the rules of the 'club', or they take a more inclusive view and stress the importance

---

[27] Interviewee Ger K, 26 April 2001.   [28] Interviewee Ger G, 15 October 2001.
[29] Interviewee Ger G, 15 October 2001.

for new members' 'inclusion' in the process of constructing the EU further as a community.

Brusselites: both/and

While the associations uttered by the two respective domestic elite groups in London and Berlin display domestic convergence and international divergence (compare Table 4.4, *type B*), the British and German Brusselites' connotations are not in tune with either of the two domestic groups, nor are they converging on one keyword amongst themselves, however (*type A*). Instead, they are constitutive for a more diffused pattern. Thus, in comparison with the domestic elite groups, the range of associative connotations has doubled in the transnational arena. Now the relevant list of keywords includes 'fairness', 'integration', 'compliance' and 'finality'. The following substantiates this finding in some more detail with reference to the individual discursive interventions.

The German Brusselites' reactions to the question regarding compliance with the full *acquis* and exceptions from it point out that 'this would be a system of second-class citizens, and while you can work with transition periods, to be sure, you must not question the principle'.[30] And another interviewee's reactions sustain this point by stating, 'I think that we must be clear about that, that if the entire meaning of the EU's *acquis communautaire* is asked for, then I must not choose *second-class members*. And there I cannot help but get the impression that particular areas move in that direction. ... Especially structural policy, freedom of movement and, I mean, freedom of movement is one of the basic foundations of the European Union.'[31] In addition, some British Brusselites' associative connotations display a rigorous opposition to the idea of the European Union as a 'club', when saying, 'This sort of idea of a club – I have always been opposed to the Europe club mentality as a young Labour militant who was pro-European; I always objected to a capitalist club tag that was put on the European idea. To my mind the *European Union idea is not clubbish, but the reverse*. ... I certainly know my field of social policy: the *acquis communautaire* is going to be extremely difficult for candidate countries to match.'[32] The

---

[30] Interviewee Brux/Ger H, 23 May 2001.
[31] Interviewee Brux/Ger F, 21 May 2001.
[32] Interviewee Brux/UK E, 28 August 2001.

connotation of 'justice' and 'fairness' is pronounced even more strongly by this British Brusselite's utterances which link the enlargement procedures with the constitutional process: 'And you certainly get this in the candidate countries, I mean, people have a right to know what they are joining.'[33] This German Brusselite equally raises the issue of 'fairness' when pointing out that 'many of the new members will have enormous difficulties with adapting to the *European standards*'.[34] German Brusselites notably tend to refer to the experience of their own country's process of unification. As this statement demonstrates, that process raises questions about the degree of 'fairness' applied to the procedure. 'It is an enormous task for these countries to prepare according to the conditions of the European Union and to adopt the rules of the club and then actually implement them at home. And we can see how difficult this has already been for us, as the wealthy Federal Republic of Germany in relation to the then GDR. That is not an easy process, but it is a process without any political alternative.'[35] In addition, the possibility and quality of independent action is raised by this German Brusselite: 'The bulk simply must be swallowed by the candidate. Well, he [*sic*] knows that. That is, of course, I won't say a struggle, but it is a situation of enormous dependence that is presented to and asked of someone.'[36]

In turn, other German and British Brusselites' respective connotations display no problem with the 'club' association. For example, when asked whether more possibilities of interaction among member states and candidate states should be created in the enlargement process, this German Brusselite responds:

No, I don't think so, no, when you consider this on a quasi game-theoretical level, it follows that these are rules that have been identified by some. And when they [others, AW] want to join the club, if you wish, then these rules must be complied with for starters. Everything else can be negotiated once they are members of the club, I think. ... The set of rules has always been developing and changing, and that will continue. Yet, for accession, I think, *you should set a hurdle* so that they are confronted with the rules and understand and accept

---

[33] Interviewee Brux/UK A, 22 May 2001.
[34] Interviewee Brux/Ger A, 26 February 2003.
[35] Interviewee Brux/Ger C, 30 July 2002.
[36] Interviewee Brux/Ger B, 12 June 2002.

them, as it were. That means, overall, even with the consequence that under certain circumstances they may not join.[37]

And this British Brusselite fully matches that view when stating, '*It is a club*; you should accept the rules, the constitutional background. It is not pick and choose, pick and mix, which some of the Conservative Party would like in the UK. *It is either all or nothing*.'

Asked whether the practice of enlargement that has been used before, i.e. the 'all or nothing *acquis*' should be kept, this interviewee replies: 'Yes, it has to be.'[38] This is echoed by a German Brusselite who also supports the approach to the EU as a 'club' (rather than a 'community') when stating:

> The European Union does not have to enlarge. The central and eastern European countries plus Cyprus and Malta want to join. We have not asked them to. They have applied for accession, and if they are ready and obviously prepared, and if the timing and transition periods and *all our conditions are met*, then there can't be any political reason to deny them their wish to join. They themselves must decide whether they want to or not. The decision is not ours; we can only open the door. It's up to them to walk through it.[39]

Findings

In a similar fashion, yet not as significantly as with the Schengen policy field, the associative connotations uttered by the Brusselites in response to the questions about enlargement demonstrate diffusion rather than divergence according to nationality. While the Londoners stressed the issue of 'fairness', and the Berliners' connotations converge on 'compliance', the Brusselites refer to both. The Brusselites' individually transported connotations do not, however, clearly confirm the pattern of diversity which had been established with regard to the Schengen policy field. Nonetheless, it is important to note the consistent divergence (*type A*) demonstrated by the British Brusselites' reference to 'finality' as opposed to the Londoners' references to 'fairness', as well as 50 percent of the German Brusselites' connotations stressing 'fairness' as opposed to 5 percent of the Berliners' connotations (see Table 6.2 for the display of results).

---

[37] Interviewee Brux/Ger D, 28 August 2001.
[38] Interviewee Brux/UK J, 6 September 2001.
[39] Interviewee Brux/Ger G, 29 August 2001.

Table 6.2 *Rule of law opposition 1: fairness vs compliance*

Arena	Domestic		Transnational	
Keywords / Elite groups	Londoners	Berliners	Brux/UK	Brux/Ger
Compliance	38.5	40	10	60
Fairness	23.1	5	20	50
Value-export				
Inclusion				
Integration				
Wealth export				
Finality			10	

Source: 'Text Corpus'. The percentages indicate the frequency with which utterances related to one keyword in response to particular policy field questions; author's calculations.

Table 6.3 offers an overview over the qualitative results of the first opposition-deriving exercise. It demonstrates the consistency of the *core opposition* of 'society' (Londoners) vs 'community' (Berliners) based on *derived opposition 1* ('fairness' vs 'compliance') in the domestic political arenas. In turn, the transnational political arena sustains a pattern of diversity. It does not display any distinction according to nationality between the two interviewed elite groups.

In sum, it is noted that with reference to the rule of law, the associative connotations of 'compliance' with a view to community formation as opposed to 'fairness' in the process of carrying out the enlargement procedure reveal no indicators of a major opposition that would confirm the *core opposition* of society vs community types of governance. The next section focuses on the *derived opposition 2* of 'value-export' vs 'inclusion' to scrutinise this finding with regard to the fundamental norm of democracy.

Opposition 2: value-export vs inclusion

In addition to the first opposition of 'compliance' vs 'fairness' which was derived in the previous section, the following conducts another opposition-deriving task to add to interpretations of the fundamental norm of democracy. This time the evaluation focuses on the opposition between democracy as an *export* item and democracy understood as a principle

Table 6.3 *Rule of law: core and derived oppositions (1)*

Core opposition		Derived opposition	Core opposition	
Divergence (either/or)				
Domestic arena 1			*Domestic arena 2*	
London			**Berlin**	
Society			Community	
		Compliance		
		Fairness		
Diffusion (both/and)				
Transnational arena			*Transnational arena*	
UK/Brux			**Ger/Brux**	
Society	Community		Society	Community
		Compliance		
		Fairness		
		Finality		

Source: Table 6.2 and Case Excerpt.

which enables equal access to participation in constructing democratic *values*. Again, as in the previous chapter on citizenship, the discursive interventions display a significant difference in adopting positions which can be distinguished with reference to 'us' versus 'them' as the respective central factor underlying the derived oppositions. The following question was raised with reference to the enlargement policy field:

> What do you think about the transition rules?

And an additional question was:

> Has democracy been a key element in the process?

Londoners: 'value-export'

With regard to the transition rules which had been set up to facilitate gradual adaptation to the innovations brought about by the enlargement process, on the one hand, and the role of democracy, on the other, most Londoners stressed the importance of exporting democratic values to the candidate countries. The concern was one of stability and security. Historical responsibility was often raised as an associative connotation among the domestic elite sample of the Londoners. As this interviewee stresses, for example: 'And also the implicit sort of security guarantee it gives as well. ... Just because of the history of the European countries and ... you know, the fact that they have been under Communist regimes for so many years, I think it is fairly important to be within a group of countries which is perceived as being founded on civil liberties, fundamental rights. That sort of thing is very important.'[40] The following connotations with 'moral obligation' sustain the attitude of reaching out with a helping hand while keeping an interest in enhanced stability which enlargement would bring to mind in the West: 'Because in some ways we have a *moral obligation* to other countries, in some ways I think it is beneficial for our own stability and security.'[41]

This interviewee's connotations echo the mix of a perception of 'responsibility' towards the East and the advantage of enhanced 'stability' for the West that is linked with that same process.

I am instinctively in favour of enlargement because I don't want Europe simply to be a club of the wealthier countries of western Europe. I mean, I think that is both selfish and in the long run risks creating an unstable Europe, because the newly emerged democracies in central and eastern Europe are still relatively fragile and could revert to communism or, worse, fascism. So I think *western Europe has a duty* towards the countries of eastern and central Europe to research and seek to integrate them within the European Union.[42]

The following utterance offers another good example of the Londoners' converging connotations of duty and responsibility. 'I am optimistic that although we have clearly taken them in before they are properly ready, that political gesture is the right one I think to make and to submit democracy and stability in these countries – and they will catch up quite fast. I think they will catch up much faster, most of them, than Greece has.'[43]

---

[40] Interviewee UK E, 26 November 2002.　　[41] Interviewee UK I, 10 May 2001.
[42] Interviewee UK H, 9 May 2001.　　[43] Interviewee UK C, 19 December 2002.

Berliners: 'inclusion'

In comparison with the Londoners, the Berliners' associative connotations are more focused on the input-factor of 'community formation' and 'inclusion' than on the output-factor of creating 'stability'. This interviewee addresses the critical issue of equality during the accession period, for example: 'Well, *de facto* the candidate countries collaborate everywhere on an equal basis, *de facto*.'[44] And this interviewee raises the issue of lost and regained sovereignty with a view to accepting the *acquis*. The associative connotations with the problematic perception of 'pooled sovereignty'[45] and issues of participation in a process demonstrate a concern for input-oriented issues of community formation rather than a more functionally based perspective on the expected outcomes of enlargement for the West when stating: 'The Poles have acquired sovereignty ten years ago. For them it is therefore much more difficult than for us or others to turn parts of their sovereignty in which they had just gained. Of course, it is difficult given that this *acquis* is increasingly non-negotiable. The real message to the accession countries should be "you join a European, a political federation and may participate in changing it".'[46]

Again, as with the previous enlargement question, these connotations reflect individual experiences gained from either the German unification process as the previous utterance demonstrates, or from the expectation of actively participating in the European Union's enlargement process, as the following statement demonstrates.

I have been a number of times in Poland now and have the impression that the declining preparedness to welcome accession, the declining support for accession depends largely on the fact that the *acquis* is felt to be an affront rather than something socially constructed, or where one might be included in the process of construction. Instead, it is increasingly perceived as a pattern of rights and norms which considers the individual citizen more as an object than

---

[44] Interviewee Ger J, 24 June 2002.
[45] The term 'pooled sovereignty' indicates the transfer of sovereign decision-making rights to the EU, e.g. in matters in the area of the market, the environment and other policies that fall within the so-called first pillar of the EC Treaty.
[46] Interviewee Ger O, 13 July 2001; note that this interviewee makes an additional reference to negative experience for East Germans with German unification; German original word for 'federation': 'Bund'.

as a *citoyen*, that is, as an active citizen, who is able to contribute to and influence social relations.[47]

And this interviewee echoes the emphasis on 'inclusion' in the enlargement process when saying, 'There are numerous [forums which offer opportunities for participation, AW], and, I think they are generally adequate. Yet, on the other hand there is the candidate countries' wish to be involved in other issues such as, for example, the preparation of the 2004 intergovernmental conference. We consider that as appropriate. *They should participate.* ... They should be able to have a say about the future of the European Union.'[48]

Brusselites: both/and

The Brusselites do not display as significant a diffused pattern with reference to the second derived opposition of 'value-export' vs 'inclusion' which regards the position of the candidate countries in the enlargement process. A notable change was displayed by the British Brusselites whose associative connotations demonstrate a decline in the issue of 'value-export' in favour of a preference for 'inclusion'. As this British Brusselite states, for example, 'I think that large parts of EU decision-making are still far too un-transparent and incomprehensible.'[49] And this interviewee stresses the development of democratic participation within the candidate countries: 'The development of civil society, the organising of civil society in the candidate countries was and is progressing certainly in some countries – like Hungary. There is still a vacuum that has been left after the fall of dictatorship; it hasn't been fully filled by new social movements which are totally functioning.'[50]

Another interviewee echoes the Londoners' stress on exporting democracy to the candidate countries; however, stressing the participatory effect enlargement has as a whole for the citizens in the European Union, rather than the utilitarian interest in stabilising a previously unstable region.

I think that enlargement is one of the most tangible projects that the EU has undertaken in the past few years, and it is probably the one that in a way has

---

[47] Interviewee Ger O, 13 July 2001.   [48] Interviewee Ger A, 17 July 2001.
[49] Interviewee Brux/UK F, 28 August 2001.
[50] Interviewee Brux/UK E, 28 August 2001.

brought it close to its citizens. ... Actually our labour and economists have access to a bigger market, you know, you are promoting democracy and stability in these countries, peace and security at the same time of economic benefits all around. I think that in a sense does bring the Union closer to its people to show that it is a living dynamic entity, and it is not just a lot of bureaucrats in Brussels imposing rules. ... It is one of the things the EU has been historically extremely good at. ... It has been sort of entrenching democracy in countries there [in candidate countries during accession processes, AW].[51]

Like the Berliners and the British Brusselites, the German Brusselites stress the importance, and criticise the often still looming absence, of transparency and inclusion. 'With secrecy and secretive diplomacy on a political level I mean that it is basically, well that basically *there is no transparency* in politics.'[52] This German Brusselite raises critical questions about democratic procedures in the enlargement process, specifically with a view to the practices of Brussels institutions, noting that 'what is related directly with this is the question of *transparency* or *bureaucratic legitimation*, as I see it. To put it rather simply, the more mingling in the Council, the less transparency in the decision-making process.'[53]

Findings

This second comparison of discursive interventions that address the enlargement policy field confirms the pattern of divergence generated by the previous two opposition-deriving exercises (compare Table 4.4 types *A* and *B*). To probe the consistency of this finding, the *derived opposition* of 'value-export' vs 'inclusion' now stands to be compared with the *core opposition* of output-oriented perception of 'society' vs input-oriented perception of 'community'. While the emerging pattern is not as distinct as those emerging in connection with the Schengen policy field, a difference in associative connotations is still observable. That is, the individually transported meanings of the fundamental norms of 'the rule of law' and 'democracy' suggest variety rather than harmonisation, As Table 6.4 demonstrates in quantitative detail,

[51] Interviewee Brux/UK B, 27 February 2003.
[52] Interviewee Brux/Ger I, 23 May 2001.
[53] Interviewee Brux/Ger J, 21 May 2001; German original text: '*je mehr im Rat ausgeklüngelt wird*'.

Table 6.4 *Democracy opposition 2: value export vs inclusion*

Arenas	Domestic		Transnational	
Keywords / Elite groups	Londoners	Berliners	Brux/UK	Brux/Ger
Compliance				
Fairness				
Value-export	53.8		10	
Inclusion	7.7	20	20	30
Integration				
Wealth export				
Finality				

Source: 'Text Corpus', author's calculations.

associative connotations held by individual domestic elites in London and Berlin diverge. In addition, and notably, this pattern of divergence according to domestically converging connotations – as the national identity-options assumption would expect[54] – is not maintained when comparing domestic and transnational political arenas.

For example, the Londoners' spontaneous replies to the question of whether or not the transition rules were acceptable and whether or not the interviewee might expect more democracy in the enlargement process display a link with the core opposition (society vs community). While they value 'society', the Berliners' utterances indicate associative connotations with the EU as a 'community'; however, and this is slightly different from previous findings, both the German and British Brusselites' connotations display less diffusion. In this case, the domestic and transnational samples show continuity among the two German groups. Nonetheless, there is a shift from the Londoners' connotations with 'stability' and 'value-export' towards a more diffused and hence balanced focus on 'inclusion' as the outcome of the British Brusselites. The qualitative evaluation displayed by Table 6.5 links the patterns of associative connotations according to both the *derived opposition 2* (inclusion vs value-export) and the *core opposition* (society vs community).

---

[54] Note that the national identity-options assumption would expect connotations to converge with reference to national 'identity' as opposed to this study's finding of convergence according to 'interaction in context' – notwithstanding nationality (for details of this finding, see chapter 9).

Table 6.5 *Democracy: core and derived oppositions (2)*

Core opposition		Derived opposition	Core opposition	
Divergence (either/or)				
Domestic arena 1			*Domestic arena 2*	
London			**Berlin**	
Society			Community	
		Inclusion		
		Value-export		
Diffusion (both/and)				
Transnational arena			*Transnational arena*	
UK/Brux			**Ger/Brux**	
Society	Community		Society	Community
		Inclusion		
		Value-export		

Source: Table 6.4 and Case Excerpt.

The following demonstrates the findings of a third set of questions and the related opposition-deriving exercise. The important question with regard to the emerging pattern of types of divergence is whether the lack of diffusion with the German Brusselites indicates a stable pattern, or whether it can be regarded as an exception with reference to the keyword of 'democracy' in the enlargement field only. The following questions centre on the derived opposition of 'stability' vs 'political finality'.

Opposition 3: stability vs finality

This final set of questions on enlargement policy focuses on the meaning of the rule of law. Here, the emphasis is put on the difference between enlargement towards more integration based on connotations with either 'stability' defined in terms of strengthening the European Union's action potential, its so-called actorness as a political and economic actor in world politics,[55] or in terms of enhanced constitutional integration towards a political 'finality'. This is the question which was raised:

> Would you propose more or less enlargement (why)?

Londoners: 'stability'

This Londoner's associative connotations with the issue of more or less enlargement are in their overwhelming majority focused on the issue of *stability*. The connotation is distinctive and repeatedly and clearly expressed. As the following quotations demonstrate, enlargement is perceived as a 'good thing' because it is functional. In addition, there appears to be a sense of momentum that would suggest that stepping back to pause and reconsider was less of an option than going on. Enlargement, it seems, could apparently not be avoided. Thus, this reply states, for example, that enlargement 'is a very good thing, certainly for political reasons, and it is absolutely necessary to unite Europe. I mean one of the foundations of European integration certainly is to unite the continent *for peace and stability reasons*, so I think for that reason it is very important, you cannot draw a line somewhere.'[56] Enlargement is understood as a duty or a consequence which is to be taken on board, whether enthusiastically welcomed or not, so that stability can thrive. As this interviewee says, for example: 'The prize is to unite Europe and to achieve in Europe what has been done in the United States, which is to *produce a stable and prosperous bloc*. And without obvious rifts inside it, if that can be achieved it is terrific.'[57]

The following interviewee elaborates on the functionality of enlargement in more detail. By pointing to its relation to political deepening as well, the following connotation sustains a utilitarian connotation.

There is a potential conflict between enlargement and deepening. And yet, deepening in the sense of *more efficient, stronger* institutional decision-making procedures is essential to make an enlarged EU work. ... We need a more integrated community if it is going to remain a coherent entity able to operate effectively and take positions. On the other hand, the wider you diversify it by the membership in terms of numbers and levels of development, the more

---

[55] See, e.g., the work of Whitman and Manners 2000; Manners 2002, 2006; Smith 2003; and Sjursen 2006.
[56] Interviewee UK L, 10 May 2001.   [57] Interviewee UK A, 8 May 2001.

difficult it is to see how they can operate effectively if it is some sort of a deeply integrated community. This is a contradiction which I have not quite resolved in my mind as to what the outcome should be.[58]

Further to the distinctive approaches regarding fast enlargement versus slower enlargement, this interviewee points out that, 'we can also see the big historical gain here which is to end forever the post-war divisions of Europe and to ensure they never recur – and that is quite a prize'.[59]

Berliners: 'finality'

In contrast to the Londoners' quite detailed elaborations on why and how enlargement matters to both political and economic stability in the West and in the entire European region, the Berliners' connotations are less pointed either way. Instead, they display a generally positive perception of enlargement as being part of the political *finality* of the European Union. In this utterance, even a concern with deepening before enlargement comes to the fore. 'Under general political considerations I welcome the enlargement process, the accession in particular of central and eastern European states. The question is, however, whether the European Union won't be paralysed in the light of the large number of member states, twenty-five or twenty-six. Well, the task is difficult to achieve a deepening of the Union at the same time. And that is something akin to squaring the circle.'[60] Another Berliner stresses the lack of adequate procedures available to conduct the process of enlargement in a democratic way when explaining, 'I think that Nice has brought a number of technical improvements for the enlargement and deepening. Yet Nice is also something of a symbol for a club attitude of the governments in Europe and this club has relatively little interest in supporting democratic and public debates.'[61] And finally, this Berliner offers a generally deviating view that the most important issue of enlargement is 'naturally and classically stability with regard to politics and the economy, that's the banal reason'.[62]

Brusselites: both/and

The Brusselites' associative connotations do not display much evidence of strong convictions in one way or another. The most notable result emerges from the quantitative as opposed to the qualitative evaluation.

---

[58] Interviewee UK K, 10 May 2001.   [59] Interviewee UK C, 19 December 2002.
[60] Interviewee Ger N, 26 April 2001.   [61] Interviewee Ger O, 13 July 2001.
[62] Interviewee Ger S, 10 July 2001.

Here, a significant divergence emerges not only between the two domestic groups but also between the two British elite groups operating in the political arenas of London and Brussels, respectively. While the Londoners' utterances reveal a preference for 'stability', the British Brusselites' utterances display little concern for the question of 'more/ or less' enlargement. As with the German Brusselites, in the transnational context, enlargement appears to be a given rather than something considered as subject to debate. As this German Brusselite states, for example,

I think that we need to be quick now. ... That is quite tangible for the internal progress of the Union, for progress with integration, if the enlargement process now also grinds to a visible halt, then we have a major crisis, haven't we? ... Here, cultural integration and political integration are also involved. And I consider that as very, very important with regard to integration, this balancing of the community, since Poland and Hungary will support the continental position somewhat, I assume, which has been somewhat weakened after the northern enlargement. I harbour certain hopes in this regard.[63]

While these connotations sustain the Londoners' stress on political stability, this British Brusselite does specifically emphasise the importance of 'inclusion': 'It was political union and the need to give some participant identity [and] political security to a country that has been living just a few years ago under dictatorship [that] was an imperative.'[64] And this German Brusselite's connotation with timing echoes concerns with momentum based on the promises which had been made, and the prospect of further political integration which may suffer from a loss of credibility if enlargement does not proceed.

I also think that the argument of being late matters. The Poles have a point in reminding us that both Chirac and Kohl spoke of time horizons which now are far behind when the Iron Curtain fell. Well, I think that enlargement should have been completed already. ... If you look at the historical time span and state that at the best of times we are now in year twelve, well and nobody of them is in at all, then the Sunday speech[65] of the unification of Europe and the reunification of Europe will be detected as a lie.[66]

---

[63] Interviewee Brux/Ger H, 23 May 2001.
[64] Interviewee Brux/UK E, 28 August 2001.
[65] German original text: 'Sonntagsrede'. This term indicates something akin to painting a rosy picture which is quite removed from the real facts.
[66] Interviewee Brux/Ger B, 12 June 2002.

Table 6.6 *Rule of law opposition 3: stability vs finality*

Arenas	Domestic		Transnational	
Keywords / Elite groups	Londoners	Berliners	Brux/UK	Brux/Ger
Compliance				
Fairness				
Value-export	7.7			
Inclusion				
Stability (Wealth export, Integration)	53.9	5		10
Finality	7.7	10	10	20

Source: 'Text Corpus', author's calculations.

Findings

The divergence between the associative connotations of the Londoners and the Berliners is notable if not as strong as in the Schengen case. It concurs with the previous opposition-deriving analysis on *opposition 2* in the enlargement field (value-export vs inclusion). For now, it is interesting to note that both opposition-deriving exercises refer to the same *core opposition* of 'society' (London) vs 'community' (Berlin). In turn, the Brusselites' connotations remain somewhat inconclusive. Thus, the replies display a German preference for 'community'. And, while the British sample displays a reference to 'community' as well, this reference is based on the utterance of only 10 percent of the interviewees.

More specifically, and comparing domestic and transnational cultural validation, the third opposition-deriving exercise reveals a notable swap between the associative connotations displayed by the Londoners, on the one hand, and those uttered by the British Brusselites, on the other. Whereas the Londoners have a clearly expressed high expectation of the enlargement process as providing political (and economic) stability and security to both the European Union and the candidate countries (note the distinction and the link between *derived oppositions 2* and *3* where the Londoners clearly opt for an export of democratic values), the British Brusselites do not consider the topic of sufficient interest to raise it in the first place (see Table 6.7).

Table 6.7 *Rule of law: core and derived oppositions (3)*

Core opposition		Derived opposition	Core opposition	
Divergence (either/or)				
Domestic arena 1			*Domestic arena 2*	
London			**Berlin**	
Society	Community		Society	Community
		Finality		(shaded)
(shaded)		Stability		
Diffusion (both/and)				
Transnational arena			*Transnational arena*	
UK/Brux			**Ger/Brux**	
Society	Community		Society	Community
		Finality		(shaded)
		Stability		

Source: Table 6.6 and Case Excerpt.

Conclusion

The evaluation of the discursive interventions on enlargement policy supports the findings of *type A* and *type B* divergence, yet not *type C*, that were noted in the previous chapter where questions on the Schengen policy were evaluated in relation to the fundamental norm of citizenship. This chapter's findings reinforce the notion of divergence both among domestic elites, and among domestic and transnational elites. Yet, there is no clear divergence between the two national elite group samples operating in the transnational arena. Here, the evaluation points to an emerging pattern of diffusion of associative connotations which is shared by both transnational samples (keywords vary, indicating various possibilities of interpretation of meaning), rather than convergence on one specific keyword (indicating one specific preference for the interpretation of meaning) among each respective elite group. As Tables 6.8 and 6.9

Table 6.8 *Domestic arena: core and derived oppositions (1–3)*

Fundamental norm: democracy and the rule of law		Domestic arena	
		London	Berlin
		Society	Community
Core opposition *Divergence (either/or)*			
Derived opposition			
	Derived opposition 1		
	Compliance		▓
	Fairness	▓	
	Derived opposition 2		
	Value-export	▓	
	Inclusion		▓
	Derived opposition 3		
	Stability	▓	
	Finality		▓

Source: Tables 6.3, 6.5, 6.7 and Case Excerpt.

demonstrate, the expectation of a general pattern of increasing *diversity* rather than harmonisation akin to the expectations raised by the layer-cake assumption is sustained.[67] Accordingly, the core opposition of 'society vs community' demonstrates the findings with regard to the interpretation of meanings to the fundamental norms of democracy and the rule of law most clearly. The three derived oppositions based on the evaluation of associative connotation with regard to the enlargement policy field (Table 6.8, *derived oppositions 1–3*) therefore include firstly, 'compliance' vs 'fairness', secondly, 'value-export' vs

[67] With regard to the EU, more recent work would theorise 'harmonisation' as 'Europeanisation'. For details and distinctions, see the discussion of the layer-cake assumption, the liberal community hypothesis and the identity-options assumption in chapter 3.

Table 6.9 *Transnational arena: core and derived oppositions (1–3)*

Diffusion (both/and)				
Transnational arena		*Derived opposition*	*Transnational arena*	
UK/Brux			**Ger/Brux**	
Society	Community		Society	Community
Opposition 1				
▨	▨	Compliance	▨	▨
▨	▨	Fairness	▨	▨
Opposition 2				
▨	▨	Value-export	▨	
	▨	Inclusion		
Opposition 3				
		Stability		
	a	Finality		▨
		Constitution		▨

a Note: There was one deviating utterance.
Source: Tables 6.3, 6.5, 6.7 and Case Excerpt.

'inclusion' and, thirdly, 'stability' vs 'finality'. All relate to the core opposition of 'society' versus 'community' as an either output-oriented or input-oriented definition of legitimate governance. Tables 6.8 and 6.9 summarise the findings.

In sum, the predominant pattern of diverging associative connotations that were established with regard to the fundamental norms of democracy and the rule of law is one of divergence between the two domestic elite groups. By and large, this finding would have been expected by the national identity-options assumption which would have predicted persisting national identities. These would also have been expected in light of the two constitutional traditions, i.e. the British tradition of common law and parliamentary sovereignty, and the German dogmatic continental law tradition and the constitution (i.e. the Basic Law) as the *locus* of sovereignty. The pattern of divergence between the domestic and the transnational groups that share the same national identity, however, does make the finding of diffusion among the Brusselites all the more interesting because it suggests that national identity options do not prevail when individuals move on from one context to another, for instance as in this case from the domestic to the transnational arena.

In turn, the liberal community hypothesis and the layer-cake assumption would have expected a stronger pattern of Europeanisation, i.e. divergence *types A* and *B* would contravene the expectation of this hypothesis. That is, the rather clearly established pattern of divergence among the two domestic groups also cautions against the expectation of Europeanisation on a short-term basis. This finding stands to be further scrutinised by the next chapter's opposition-deriving exercise. It is expected to shed light on the question of whether divergence rather than convergence among national groups can be expected as a general pattern. Such an outcome would be indicative for diversity patterns that evolve through social practice in context rather than according to national origin as the rule-in-practice assumption would expect. If this can be demonstrated, the implications for the theoretical discussion about fundamental norms such as equal access to participation and non-discrimination stand to be reviewed with a view to social practice rather than group-differentiated patterns based on skin colour or choice of religion, for example.[68]

---

[68] On this pattern of diversity based on interaction in context, see also Ireland's (2004) discussion of the social integration of migrant groups in different European countries.

7 | *Human rights and fundamental freedoms*

> Covenants and contracts are not identical synonyms for the constitution. The former term carries more communitarian, the latter more functional connotations, but both imply that a constitution is an enactive document consummating the creation of a polity.
>
> (Hart 2001: 154)

Introduction

In the best-case scenario, a constitution is not only signed by a constitutional convention. It is also the outcome of an on-going process of deliberation among those affected by the rules within it. Following from the ideal of that best-case scenario of a constitution, embedded in and targeted by on-going dialogue, two functions of a constitution stand out. They oscillate between the assumption of a constitution's role as part of the political organisation of a community, on the one hand, and constitutional rules as the focal point of political deliberation within a community, on the other. In contrast to this theoretical ideal, questions of whether constitutions trigger the creation of a community based on a constitutional moment,[1] and whether they enhance the perception of legitimacy in a polity are debated issues. The creation of a community and a perception of legitimacy remain to be established empirically on a case-by-case basis that takes the different time and shape of a polity into account.

While constitutions have both an organisational and a cultural dimension and hence involve two sets of practices,[2] their organisational role can be identified according to expectations towards that role at different times. Three positions can be meaningfully distinguished.

---

[1] On the constitutional moment, see Ackerman 1991; with regard to world politics, see Slaughter and Burke-White 2002.

[2] For details, see chapter 2.

Firstly, in the early stages, a constitution may be a 'documentary record of a settlement of conflict' (Hart 2001: 153). Secondly, over time, constitutions are expected to 'organize the political' within a community (Preuss 1994). And thirdly, constitutional documents might be considered as 'living constitutions', a position which had been supported by former Canadian Prime Minister, Pierre Trudeau, and which proposed a continuous engagement of Canadian citizens in discussions about the Charter of Rights.[3] As it was argued at the time, such engagement could be 'a meeting ground, a site for civil dialogues among citizens' (Hart 2001: 61; citing Vipond 1996: 181; Cairns 1989). Ultimately, the most visible aspect of a democratically legitimated constitution will be the quality of the citizens' access to rights. The next section summarises the place of fundamental norms in constitutional texts as well as the role of these texts themselves. A further section then carries out the third opposition-deriving exercise with a view to analysing divergence, convergence and diffusion of meanings of fundamental norms. The final section offers a summary of the findings.

Placing human rights and fundamental freedoms in constitutional texts

Several policy documents in the run-up to solemnly passing the European Union's Charter of Fundamental Rights at the Nice Summit in 2000 offer insight into the intentions behind constitutional policy-making by the political organs in Brussels including the European Council and the European Commission. For example, the European Council stated that with regard to the EU Charter of Fundamental Rights:

The European Council takes the view that, at the present stage of development of the European Union, the *fundamental rights* applicable at Union level should be consolidated in a Charter and *thereby made more evident*.[4]

---

[3] The model of a 'living constitution' has been playing a crucial role in the development and analysis of the Canadian constitutional discourse; see, e.g., McKenna 1993 and Cairns 1989: 38.

[4] See Presidency Conclusions, Cologne European Council 3–4 June 1999; http://europa.eu.int/comm/justice_home/unit/charte/en/mandates.html (accessed 29 June 2006); my emphasis.

And, at its meeting in Cologne, the Council agreed on the following decision towards drafting a Charter of Fundamental Rights:

Protection of *fundamental rights* is a founding principle of the Union and an indispensable prerequisite for her legitimacy. The obligation of the Union to respect fundamental rights has been confirmed and defined by the jurisprudence of the European Court of Justice. *There appears to be a need, at the present stage of the Union's development, to establish a Charter of fundamental rights in order to make their overriding importance and relevance more visible to the Union's citizens.*[5]

Accordingly, the Charter is expected to fulfil a particular function in the process of European integration. This function lies in bringing aspects of already existing rules and regulations to the fore by enhancing their visibility vis-à-vis the citizens and based on the Charter as an added public relations tool. As the preamble of the Charter states,

This Charter reaffirms, with due regard for the powers and tasks of the Community and the Union and the principle of subsidiarity, *the rights as they result*, in particular, *from the constitutional traditions and international obligations common to the Member States*, the Treaty on European Union, the Community Treaties, the European Convention of the Protection of Human Rights and Fundamental Freedoms, the Social Charters adopted by the Community and by the Council of Europe and the case law of the Court of Justice of the European Communities and of the European Court of Human Rights.[6]

---

[5] Annex 4 'European Council Decision on the Drawing Up of a Charter of Fundamental Rights of the European Union', Annexes to Presidency Conclusions 26/28, *Bulletin EU* 6, 1999; my emphasis; http://europa.eu/bulletin/en/9906/ i1064.htm (accessed 29 June 2006).

[6] See *Official Journal of the European Communities*, C 364, 18 December 2000, Charter of Fundamental Rights of the European Union, Preamble, p. 8; my emphasis. The reassessment of the Treaty under the German Presidency involves the decision to move towards Treaty reform taken at the Brussels European Summit on 21–22 June 2007. According to the Council Decisions, 'the Charter of fundamental rights will *not* be included in the Treaty'. See Council of the European Union, CONCL 2, Brussels European Council 21/22 June 2007, Presidency Conclusions, 111777/1/01, REV1, CONCL2, ANNEX I, p. 17; my emphasis. Note, however, that according to the Council Decisions – which remain to be debated in the forthcoming Intergovernmental Conference meetings – it is noted that the Charter 'shall have the same legal value as the Treaty' (*ibid.*: 25). The latter has been opposed by the UK and hence been added to the UK's opt-out list from the *acquis communitaire*.

The debate over the Fundamental Rights Charter includes the contest among the leading organs in the Europolity (i.e. the Court, the Commission, the Parliament and the Council) for mastery of the increasingly densely organised and powerful space in the European Union.[7] The most important questions with regard to the largest group of addressees of the constitutional document(s) is not only whether these respective processes are constitutive towards establishing the same rights for all member states, but also whether the meanings held by different groups of citizens create sufficient overlap to facilitate democratic legitimacy and political efficiency. There is an increasing worry among both political scientists and lawyers that the case law of the European Court of Justice is not evolving as a 'true dialogue' with 'other political actors' in Europe which is considered necessary for the European constitutional project (Witte 2002: 42).

Since putting the European Union's own constitutional moment on the political agenda with the post-Nice process, these questions have acquired some political urgency in Europe.[8] Especially after the Brussels Intergovernmental Conference (IGC) in June 2004, public reactions in the EU member states have varied considerably in their perception of what a European constitutional treaty might imply. As the electoral campaigns in the run-up to the 2004 European Parliament elections have demonstrated (e.g. in the UK), the discussion also focused on whether to support membership in the EU. At the time, Patricia Hewitt, the Trade and Industry Secretary, noted that a 'no' vote in a referendum 'would have the effect, and would be intended to have the effect, of putting Britain on the margins, and probably on the road to withdrawal' from the EU.[9] In turn, German public discourse focused on the question of whether to hold a referendum on the constitution in the

---

[7] See, e.g., Weiler's observation that 'While the "surface language" of the Court's human rights jurisprudence, as it first emerged in *Stauder*, is about human rights, its "deep structure" is *not* about protecting individual rights but rather about supremacy' (Weiler 1986: 1119; emphasis in original).

[8] This process was initiated after the European Council meeting in Nice, 7–9 December 2000. The Council welcomed the proclamation of the Charter of Fundamental Rights, and at the same meeting the Intergovernmental Conference agreed on the draft text of the Treaty of Nice on the basis of the texts in SN 533/1/00 REV 1. It was agreed that the final legal editing and harmonisation of the texts was to be carried out with a view to the signing of the Treaty in Nice early in 2001; see http://ue.eu.int/ueDocs/cms_Data/docs/pressData/en/ec/00400-r1.%20ann.en0.htm (accessed 19 April 2006).

[9] See *euobserver.com*, 24 June 2004.

first place.[10] The reactions in both member states as well as the debates accompanying the Dutch and French referenda on the constitution demonstrate a notable lack of public understanding, insight and knowledge about the constitutional text itself. For politicians the issue of dealing with the negative outcome of the referenda was particularly pressing since misunderstanding was likely to trigger conflict, potentially resulting in the rejection of further integration.

It can be assumed that, had the Intergovernmental Conference discussed *treaty* revisions rather than a document that was explicitly presented as of *constitutional* quality – as in previous decades – no particularly controversial public debate would have occurred on either side of the Channel. The involvement of voters and the resulting – albeit critical – debate amongst the public are new phenomena. And, as the negative vote in the referendum on the constitutional treaty suggested, the omission of public debate over matters in Brussels was detrimental to the appreciation of any document from Brussels. One insight gained from the Dutch and French 'no' votes was the confirmation of citizens' access to public debate as the cornerstone of democratic politics. The input of public debate matters both prior to and following the production of a constitutional document.[11] Strategically, the timing and conditions of such debate are critical. Substantively, the discourse about 'constitutional politics' as an emerging policy field in a beyond-the-state context offers important pointers to the meaning of fundamental norms under conditions of transnationalisation.[12] This chapter therefore picks up on the Aristotelian view of the constitution as an immanent organising principle of communities, on the one hand, and an understanding of the constitution as entailing both organisational *and* cultural social practices, on the other. The constitutional meaning as 'a way of life' is brought back by the following evaluation. As in the previous two chapters, this third

---

[10] See, e.g., 'Verwirrende Vorführung: Wie Müntefering die Union mit dem Thema EU-Verfassungsreferendum stellen wollte und nun Ärger in der eigenen Fraktion hat', in *Süddeutsche Zeitung*, 17 December 2004, 5; and 'Referendum per Gesetz', in *Süddeutsche Zeitung*, 14 December 2004, 5.

[11] For a discussion of participatory democracy, see Pateman 1970: 110; for the argument about participatory constitutionalism, see Tully 1995; Wiener and Della Sala 1997; and Hart 2001; see also Cairns 1989: 38.

[12] Compare the three conditions that enhance the default contestedness of norms as displayed in Table 4.1.

step towards reconstructing the structure of meaning-in-use involves a systematic reconstructive text analysis. This time the questions address the field of Constitutional Politics.

The choice of this particular policy field follows from the observation that, despite being a desirable policy for bringing the European Union closer to its citizens – like citizenship – constitutional politics is prone to create unintended consequences. That is, based on past *experience* in modern constitutional settings in each EU member state, *expectations* towards a constitution vary. While it can be argued that unless major changes considering the legal stipulations within the document are carried out, the branding of the document as either a 'treaty' or a 'constitution' will play a minor role, experiences with constitutional documents in different contexts have created divergent expectations towards the same set of fundamental norms. It is these expectations which need to be considered when assessing the likelihood of a political backlash being triggered by bringing such expectations to the fore during the current constitutional process itself. In addition, contextually forged diverging expectations may also reappear at international negotiations at a later stage, when the normative baggage held by individual – elite – negotiators comes to bear. It is this latter potential of diverging interpretations of normative meaning which the case study addresses. The key question is whether expectations will diverge or converge according to nationality or whether transnational contexts of interaction will make a specific difference. Such a difference could lie, for example, in more convergent or more diffused interpretations of meanings. The former would enhance homogeneity, the latter flexibility in assumptions about norms. To answer this question, conversations about the field of constitutional politics seek to allocate a systematic assessment of variations in interpreting the meaning of fundamental norms – not least, the term 'constitution' itself in EU member states.

The core opposition for the following opposition-deriving exercise lies between constitutions perceived as 'covenants' or 'contracts'. This distinction is based on the literature on constitutionalism which alerts us to the fact that 'the contract is signed, the covenant made' (Hart 2001: 155). With a view to reconstructing the variation in structures of meaning-in-use, it can be noted that a covenant entails *more of a promise* with reference to a subjective or emotional dimension, while a contract represents *more of an agreement*. While the former sets the

Table 7.1 *Fundamental and human rights: keywords – Constitutional Politics*

Keywords	Associative connotations
Symbolic function	Deepening, community building, finality, emotions, identity
Single framework	Repackaging, simplifying what's already there, functionality of constitutional arrangement as framework rather than substance
Identity	Human Rights declaration creates identity, constitution as emotional symbol, community of values
Participation	Individual participation, democracy, legitimacy, transparency, constitutional convention, understanding matters, public debate
Fundamental rights	Charter into treaty
Responsibility	More important than accountability
Accountability	More important than responsibility

Source: 'Text Corpus'.

basis for dialogue, the latter entails a documented agreement between two parties. For example, Jackson holds that the concept of 'global covenant' in global politics 'emphasize[s] that contemporary international relations is far more than a narrowly defined Machiavellian world of "power politics" but is also far from an expansively defined Kantian "community of mankind"'. Importantly, the 'global covenant' represents 'a world of dialogue' (Jackson 2005: 16). Table 7.1 shows the keywords which were identified as indicators for the interpretation of meaning of the fundamental norms of human rights and fundamental freedoms.

Deriving oppositions

Opposition 1: single framework vs finality

The first and most general question with a view to generating associative connotations in relation to *human rights* and *fundamental freedoms* during conversations about the field of constitutional politics was the following:

> What is your impression of the European Union's constitutional process?

In addition, and where appropriate, interviewees were asked whether they thought that the constitutional debate reflected their personal expectations of a constitution.

> Does it meet your expectations of a constitution?

The questions were put to the elite groups in London, Berlin and Brussels. The replies are grouped according to type of political arena i.e. transnational or domestic. The combined qualitative and quantitative evaluation based on the method of deriving oppositions demonstrates that the majority of the German and British Brusselites consider the Constitutional Treaty to be an opportunity to *simplify* the currently existing treaties rather than as a vehicle of *symbolism* and *community building*. In other words, the majority of this group did not dwell on the issue of creating a communitarian identity. Instead, their associative connotations indicated a concern about aspects of 'repackaging', 'simplicity' and 'public understanding'. In turn, the domestic elite groups in London and Berlin, respectively, reveal considerably stable positions which converge among the elites interviewed within one domestic arena, and diverge between the two different domestic arenas. As the following demonstrates in more detail, the Londoners regard constitutional politics as a contribution to simplify the treaties towards creating a 'single framework', whereas the Berliners see it as potentially activating a deeper 'symbolic function' of the constitution with a view to fostering a 'community of values'.

Londoners: 'single framework'
The expectation of a constitution's functional role combined with an underlying scepticism towards its flexible potential is depicted by the following intervention of a Londoner: '*Constitutions are ... very inflexible things* – so that would be part of our reservation; I'm sure that we think constitutions are more permanent.'[13] The following

---

[13] Interviewee UK D, 26 November 2002.

interviewee sustains this view on the constitutional process as making the treaties more accessible and the framework 'clearer' when saying, 'the idea of a constitution is, I think, a good one because I think it is important for people to be able to see in a way that *is a lot clearer than the existing Treaties*, you know, *where some of the boundaries are* and broadly *what the European Union stands for and what it stands on.* ... And *you really do need something like a Constitution to do that* I think.'[14]

This interviewee reveals a generally sceptical view vis-à-vis most written documents that are produced in Brussels yet stresses once again the pragmatic hope of clarification as the outcome of the constitutional process when saying, 'I don't think the British would be up there shouting, saying "we need a constitution". But we do think there are *advantages* to it and they are *to do with accessibility and clarity; and simplicity; and efficiency*.'[15] And, this Londoner echoes that view by stating: 'The other reason for having a constitution is simply to ensure people understand, including me; I'd like to understand exactly what the EU is trying to do, and I think this *functional document rather than an existential* document would be better.'[16]

Berliners: 'finality'

In turn, the Berliners' associative connotations generally carry an expectation of emotional and symbolic values attached to the constitutional process, a perspective which is well expressed by this interviewee's comment. 'What I would wish and what should be the plan is the consolidation of the treaties into one and not two instruments, *a text that would resemble a little more what is considered as a constitution*.'[17] This reply sustains the expectation of something monumental and moving.

An *impressive deal must be put on its way* – since previous constitution-making based on intergovernmental conferences has failed, and so far, agreement has always been based on the smallest common denominator. ... if we recall particular declarations such as the human rights declaration and so forth, then these are *identity-creating signifiers* and, I think, one should consider these, so that Europe is not exclusively based on the understanding

---

[14] Interviewee UK E, 26 November 2002.
[15] Interviewee UK C, 19 December 2002.
[16] Interviewee UK O, 26 November 2002.   [17] Interviewee Ger L, 1 June 2001.

of being an economic community but first and foremost, we are of course in every way a *community of values. And that must be demonstrated more strongly to the outside.*[18]

This Berliner also stresses the importance of enhanced community values when stating, 'what I would wish for this finality, is something rather *community-focused* which maintains, however, a lot of plurality and public debate. That would be crucial for me.'[19]

The following displays a deviating view from a Berliner with a long-time Brussels experience who replies that '*the simplification of the treaties as well as the limitation of competences,* both must be included, and that indicates a kind of constitutional process after all. Basic rights, the simplification of the treaties, the inclusion of the Charter of Rights and the role of national parliaments, these are the four Nice points, all with a view to creating more democracy and transparency. That is, in the end, what you could call a constitution. ... These elements do exist there.'[20] While revealing a preference for more simplified procedures, this interviewee's connotations do stress the key role of 'responsibilities' and the expectation that the ways of tracing responsibility will improve: 'Well I do see the possibility of trying to simplify the institutional setting so that the delimitation of *responsibilities* is clearer and the complexity of the decision-making processes will be reduced.'[21]

Brusselites: both/and

While they do not display as wide a range of diffusion of meanings as in the previous two chapters, both German and British Brusselites generally refer to both 'simplicity' *and* 'symbolism' in their expectations and impressions of the constitutional text. As this British Brusselite states for example:

I know this talk of having a referendum and all the rest of it, to endorse this new document – Constitutional Treaty, whatever you want to call it – ... for me, it has *more* an impact as *label* than an actual *substance*, because I don't believe [that] in substance we are going to be doing really radical things with the European Union. ... The one advantage of the *Constitution* of course is to suggest something *permanent*. A *treaty* is something *temporary*, which

---

[18] Interviewee Ger J, 24 June 2002.   [19] Interviewee Ger O, 13 July 2001.
[20] Interviewee Ger A, 17 July 2001.   [21] Interviewee Ger Q, 26 April 2001.

may be subject to change. ... On the other hand, *'constitutional' is a holy word.* I know, it has got an *emotional context.*[22]

And this German Brusselite's connotation is rather similar in its spontaneous reference to both symbolism and simplicity: 'Yes, *I deem a constitution important.* It has, of course, *an enormous symbolic meaning*, but I consider that as *positive, by all means.* ... I prefer to call what we now have *framework treaties. That is not a constitution yet.* For that you would need something like the convention. That *symbolic meaning is crucially important* indeed. I myself have written an article in which I call it *our new basic law for Europe.*'[23]

The following statement by a British Brusselite reflects more closely the Londoners' connotations with 'simplicity' than the Berliners' reference to 'symbolism'. 'Having a very *simple basic text* and then more powers delegated to the institutions, ... I think that is a strong idea behind the push in Germany for the constitution. ... *you ought to see what this is.* And you certainly get this in the *candidate countries*, I mean; *people have a right to know what they are joining.*'[24] The following German Brusselite's utterance echoes this view however.

How you call it afterwards – *constitutional treaty, or treaty constitution, or somehow structure and constitution*, right, that does not matter to me at all. *What matters in the end, is how the power questions are addressed.* And the power question, that is a bit more complicated than commonly viewed, since this relates very very centrally to the question of which goal we have as Europeans. And that is, which goals do we leave within national frameworks. ... *who does what,* .... that is part of the power question, *and who is entitled to do what,* that is the second part of the power question, *and how both questions then, are going to be answered, that is, according to all the political texts one has come across during the past 2,000 years, a factual constitution.* How you label that thing afterwards does not matter at all.[25]

Other Brusselites, like this German interviewee, display a more pragmatic view when stating that constitutional politics are not really new. 'Well, I mean, we do not need to reinvent the wheel. That must be said. *We do*

22 Interviewee Brux/UK C, 26 February 2002.
23 Interviewee Brux/Ger A, 26 February 2003.
24 Interviewee Brux/UK A, 22 May 2001.
25 Interviewee Brux/Ger B, 12 June 2002.

have, if you wish, a constitution with the treaties.'[26] This observation is supported by another German Brusselite:

[B]*y now we do have something akin to a constitution*, surely, even if it has the form of an international treaty. Of course, *whether you need a constitution in Europe is an open question*, in the light of the fact that there is one member state and not even a small one, that has been coping pretty well without a written constitution of this type; and it is even considered as a prime example for democracy, still ... Well, *the treaty does, of course, have the character of a basic law*. And therefore we do have a written ... stipulation of basic principles and goals of the community which has been ratified by all. ... Things are in flux, whether you want to stretch the term "constitution" or not, *de facto, there is something like it, isn't there? That is a stipulation of basic rules.*[27]

Finally, the following interviewees stress the necessity for simplicity by bringing in the notion of rigorous constitutional spring-cleaning rather than a less spectacular tidying-up exercise. As this British Brusselite's expressive response brings to the fore rather vividly: 'My constituents will probably not ask very much about the constitution, yet *it is very important to have a constitution, but a trimmed down one* which focuses on the major issues of the European Union specifying on a few areas of the *acquis communautaire*. ... *I would love to use a hatchet to change the acquis communautaire, to cut it down,* to revise it towards its necessity today.'[28] And, as this German Brusselite says, the

EC Treaty is the single most important treaty in this context. While its preamble states something about an ever closer Union ... among its members, this is the result of a pragmatic approach. It includes the most astounding details. And changing these details is as difficult as changing fundamental issues. In so far as the proposal of the European University Institute entails particular wisdom, namely to agree on basic principles which are to be laid down in a first constitution or in the first constitution-like part of the treaty. And ... to keep the threshold for change rather very high and to *clear out* – excuse my language – *the junk of all technically detailed regulations.*[29]

[26] Interviewee Brux/Ger C, 30 July 2002.
[27] Interviewee Brux/Ger D, 29 August 2001.
[28] Interviewee Brux/UK D, 28 August 2001.
[29] Interviewee Brux/Ger D, 29 August 2001.

Table 7.2 *Human rights and fundamental freedoms opposition 1: single framework vs finality*

Arena	Domestic		Transnational	
Keywords / Elite groups	Londoners	Berliners	Brux/UK	Brux/Ger
Finality		25	20	30
Single constitutional framework	46.1	15	50	40
Identity				
Participation				
Fundamental rights				
Responsibility				
Accountability				

Source: 'Text Corpus'. The percentages indicate the frequency with which one keyword was uttered in response to particular policy field questions; author's calculations.

Findings

As with reference to the previous conversations about the new policy fields of Schengen and enlargement policy, respectively, the Brusselites' associative connotations with constitutional politics turn out to be much more diverse than the two domestic groups' respective views (see Table 7.2).

The Londoners' associative connotations with constitutional politics reveal an understanding of the constitution as a text with a mission to provide simplicity and clarity, or as a policy tool which can be strategically applied to put an end to the process of further deepening. That is, their connotations do not centre on the keyword of 'finality'. The associative connotations of 'repackaging', 'simplifying', 'clarifying', 'accessibility' and so forth indicate a preference for a power-limiting interpretation of constitutional politics (see Table 7.1). In turn, the Berliners see the constitutional text as bringing together an identifiable 'community of values' which is to be achieved by 'further deepening' and the 'symbolism' attached to constitutional politics. To the Londoners a constitution represents a barrier against 'creeping political power'. A constitution is seen as marking the end rather than the beginning of a process. It is, then, first and foremost a power-limiting document to the Londoners. In turn, many of the Berliners see constitutional politics as marking the beginning of a process of further deepening

Table 7.3 *Human rights and fundamental freedoms: core and derived oppositions (1)*

Core opposition		Derived opposition	Core opposition	
Divergence (either/or)				
Domestic arena 1			*Domestic arena 2*	
London			**Berlin**	
Contract			Covenant	
		Finality		
		Single framework		
Diffusion (both/and)				
Transnational arena			*Transnational arena*	
UK/Brux			**Ger/Brux**	
Contract	Covenant		Contract	Covenant
		Finality		
		Single framework		

Source: Table 7.2 and Case Excerpt.

and, possibly, the creation of a community. Accordingly, the majority of the Berliners' connotations converge on the expectation of the constitution as 'enabling' and/or as carrying 'symbolic meaning'. A constitution, these connotations reveal, is more than a framework or a simple text. It entails the power if not the single purpose of creating identity.

Table 7.3 summarises the findings based on the first opposition-deriving exercise which identified the opposition of a 'single framework' expectation in London and a focus on 'finality' in Berlin. Thus, *derived opposition 1* reflects the deeper distinction of the *core opposition* of 'contract' vs 'covenant'. The Londoners' associative connotations express a contract-based, more functional meaning of the constitutional text whilst the Berliners' associative connotations reveal a covenant-based meaning indicating communitarian roots. The domestic groups thus sustain the finding of a *type B* divergence. In turn, both the British and German Brusselites who have been operating within the context of the transnational political arena in

Brussels for an extended period of time demonstrate associative connotations that depict constitutional politics as entailing a mission to provide a simple framework, however, one that is not entirely lacking symbolic meaning. The Brusselites' discursive interventions therefore do not reveal a *type C* divergence. That is, significant differences in correlation with national origin in the transnational arena are not observed. At the same time, *type A* divergence among two groups of the same nationality such as, e.g., the Londoners and the British Brusselites on the one hand, and the Berliners and the German Brusselites on the other, have been confirmed (compare Table 4.4).

Opposition 2: participation vs identity

To probe whether the divergence between the Londoners' connotations with contract-based keywords, on the one hand, and the Berliners' case of covenant-based keywords, on the other, holds, this sub section carries out one further exercise of deriving oppositions from the main text corpus.[30] The second set of questions has been raised as a follow-up to the first question where appropriate.

Why do you consider the constitutional process as positive (negative)?

And the additional question was:

Is this assessment based on specific institutional conditions, for example, or concern about the lack of democracy?

Londoners: 'citizen participation'
Overall, the Londoners' utterances display associative connotations which are predominantly linked with the keyword of 'citizen participation'. This trend is demonstrated by this interviewee who reveals, '*I think we should have a written constitution.* I think there should be more attempts to make the whole thing *open up and make it more democratic.* But I don't think it is easy.'[31] And this interviewee summarises that there is a need for '*more participation and citizens need to*

---

[30] See 'Text Corpus' on file with author.   [31] Interviewee UK A, 8 May 2001.

be more involved and understand what it is all about'.[32] This stress on access to participation is echoed in the following interviewee's associative connotations of the constitutional convention as 'an opportunity to look at the way the European Union has developed, which is organically over various IGCs, and see if we can find the structure and explain it to citizens in a way that makes sense ... set out a way that people can understand and something you can teach in schools'.[33]

This Londoner's discursive intervention demonstrates a lack of appreciation for symbolism and a strong preference for a pragmatic approach to constitutional politics:

We need radical, far-reaching reform in Brussels. ... It has failed miserably over the years in explaining itself. Being a sort of club, an exclusive club, institutionally aloof from the electorate, it has never felt this need to explain itself because ... *it's Byzantine, a monolith and incomprehensible to most people*. ... *Who needs a faraway place? It's bureaucratic*, it's sort of international or supranational ... it's an alien institution that is not identified as British or national.[34]

This interviewee again stresses the importance of an accessible constitutional text: 'The constitutional lawyer in me, or the constitutional designer, favours a governance model which would be *much simpler for the European citizens to understand*, which has *stronger checks and balances* incorporated within it.'[35]

Berliners: 'identity' and 'participation'

While often agreeing, in fact, with the utterances of the Londoners, for example in considering the Charter of Fundamental Rights as a key text, the Berliners' discursive interventions display a different connotation with the meaning of such a charter. This Berliner's reference to constitutional symbolism and values demonstrates such a connotation. 'I think the Charter of Fundamental Rights *is fundamental*. It is first and foremost *a moment of identity* for the European citizens, ... *a system of values for the EU*, which has now been agreed upon as binding and what differs clearly from US models of values and which therefore *creates a factor of recognition* is surely equipped to be the first part of what we will *hopefully be able to call the European constitution*.'[36] The next

---

[32] Interviewee UK L, 10 May 2001.   [33] Interviewee UK C, 19 December 2002.
[34] Interviewee UK D, 26 November 2002.   [35] Interviewee UK H, 9 May 2001.
[36] Interviewee Ger S, 10 July 2001.

Berliner echoes this associative connotation of rights with the creation of identities, when stating, 'definitely, it should be integrated in the treaties as legally binding because, like Union citizenship and similar to the free movement of persons or the internal market in general, this is what it takes to make Europe real for its citizens as well. This will create another *push for identity* if individuals ... are entitled to sue for their rights on the basis of a European charter of fundamental rights.'[37] Finally, this utterance reveals a link with values. Such a link would have been expected in relation to the inclusion of the Charter, once again stating that it is an important *'foundation of values'* and therefore 'should definitely be included in the treaties'.[38]

Compare this Londoner's connotation which stresses 'equal access to participation' as a condition for the new member states with regard to the Charter of Fundamental Rights. 'I think it's important for the acceding countries because *fundamental rights are very, very important to them given their history*. But I think if you have to have a basis for an *identity, for a European identity*, that should be it. ... Well I mean, this is a very personal view, but I do think that's kind of quite a defining thing of a *European identity*. Not necessarily the Charter of Fundamental Rights but the whole idea of Fundamental Rights.' Asked whether the Charter should be included in the Constitutional Treaty, the same interviewee replies, 'Yeah, I certainly would.' And asked for reasons, this same interviewee replies, 'Because I just think, if we are moving towards a constitutional settlement the *treaty just needs an expression of fundamental rights, and of the values the EU* is based on and what it was intended for to show to the citizens and clarify what the EU is all about but also to make it binding for them to know they can challenge it, if their rights are violated. ... I think, ... at this stage, the EU ... *definitely needs an explicit statement of the rights it is based on and which rights it protects.*'[39]

Finally, this Berliner stresses the 'effect' of the constitutional process when stating, 'this constitutional process also has the purpose of making something transparent to the citizen, and to reassure and to demonstrate the obligation of member states as well, to recall what they want with this, doesn't it? And in this context I would suggest, the *Charter is a factor that matters in its external impact – on the outside.*'[40] And another Berliner's utterances reveal the connotation of particular

---

[37] Interviewee Ger M, 15 October 2001.   [38] Interviewee Ger O, 13 July 2001.
[39] Interviewee UK L, 10 May 2001.   [40] Interviewee Ger K, 26 April 2001.

importance with regard to the issue of leading a debate about the Constitutional Treaty in the '*European* public sphere' when stressing that it 'is currently led in the public sphere and that is the right way to do it. There is no other way. And *within a European public sphere at that*.'[41] This associative connotation with a particularly 'European' public sphere once again stresses the Berliners' connotative link between constitutional politics and the creation of a community notwithstanding the beyond-the-state context.

Brusselites: both/and

The Brusselites' associative connotations in reply to the question about constitutional politics reveal a shared reference to 'participation'. Compared to the framework of the core opposition, this indicates that both Brusselite groups' utterances indicate a preference for a contract-based rather than a covenant-based constitutional document. To the majority, this document's comprehensibility ought ideally to be enhanced by the 'Convention process' as opening up a site where teaching and learning in the form of public debate about the constitutional details takes place.[42] In the words of one German Brusselite, 'we also have to try and enhance understanding [of the constitutional or treaty text] and make it simpler and more comprehensible for the citizen. *That's what the Convention is all about*.'[43] And, as this British Brusselite says,

the outcome of the *Convention will be a fairly nice and neat repackaging* of what we already have, with some adjustments around the edges, but not changing the fundamental jelly, ... a *simplification exercise* which also repackages all treaties and presents them in a ... more approachable way. But ... how many people sit down and read the German constitution, ... or the French constitution? Most people are happy because they know they *feel* comfortable with the constitutional arrangement that applies to them. They are happy with the system because they *understand* the basic principles underpinning the system.[44]

---

[41] Interviewee Ger B, 31 August 2001.
[42] See Walker's summary of both the Laeken Declaration and the following Convention on the Future of Europe as 'the first explicit attempt by the European institutions to discuss the future of the European Union in constitutional terms' (Walker 2003: 374). For a critical assessment of the convention process, see De Burca and Walker 2003: 296; Breda 2006: 341–2.
[43] Interviewee Brux/Ger C, 30 July 2002.
[44] Interviewee Brux/UK C, 26 February 2002.

The focus on a wish for clearly expressed and simple statements offered by the constitutional document is notable. The following utterance sustains that feeling. 'I think you should *make things clear*, because you know ... one of the problems that people have – not just in Britain – is that nobody quite knows, who chairs, where the competence is. And that is the practical [aspect].'[45] And as this interviewee points out, the constitution 'needs to be something which young adults – *sixteen-year-old people – can read and understand.* ... The best chance is to try to *explain [to] people* [in Britain] what it is and *what their democratic rights are* – to make it more democratic and to make it more open.'[46]

The German Brusselites' associative connotations echo this concern with easy access to participation and simplicity. As this interviewee points out, for example, 'politics about Europe leaves quite a bit of margin for improvement [in Germany]. However, that is what the Lower House should be doing, e.g. hold discussion groups parallel to the debates of the working groups in the [Brussels convention].'[47] And another interviewee's point is similar to the British concern with the constitutional process as a process that involves teaching and learning: 'It should be *clearer to the public and in the public sphere* who is responsible for what in the European Union, and who does not have any responsibilities.'[48] This German Brusselite stresses that the process of constitutional change 'can only be discussed in public, otherwise you experience once again in the light of the ratification of a new treaty that the population in a country where a referendum must be carried out, people will say, "that is incomprehensible. I don't follow you any-more." And hence, the "No" in Ireland was probably quite healthy. ... Because it made clear that a specific distance from the citizen is obviously part of Europe, and that cannot be.'[49]

Findings

A clear distinction regarding the associative connotations uttered by the elites in London and Berlin, respectively, is notable in these discursive interventions. While the Londoners make exclusive

[45] Interviewee Brux/UK H, 26 February 2003.
[46] Interviewee Brux/UK G, 27 February 2003.
[47] Interviewee Brux/Ger A, 26 February 2003.
[48] Interviewee Brux/Ger G, 29 August 2001.
[49] Interviewee Brux/Ger D, 29 August 2001.

Table 7.4 *Human rights and fundamental freedoms opposition 2:*
participation vs identity

Arenas	Domestic		Transnational	
Keywords / Elite groups	Londoners	Berliners	Brux/UK	Brux/Ger
Finality				
Single constitutional framework				10
Identity		35	10	
Participation	38.5	33	40	40
Fundamental rights				
Responsibility				
Accountability				

Source: 'Text Corpus'; author's calculations.

reference to an expectation of a 'clearer' and 'more transparent' and generally more 'democratic' and 'accessible' document – whether it is called a constitution or not – the Berliners display a strong leaning towards a more 'value-oriented' and 'identity-based' expectation of the text and generally expect it to be called 'a constitution'. In turn, both British and German elites in the Brussels transnational arena stress the importance of 'participation,' 'public debate' and 'accessibility' (see Table 7.4).

Interestingly, and different from the interviews with the two domestic groups, it is the British elite group in Brussels that generates more 'identity-based' and/or 'value-oriented' associative connotations (which the Londoners do not display) than the German Brusselites who do not mention such issues (while the Berliners do). As Table 7.4 demonstrates, in this particular case both Berliners and Londoners diverge in particular on the keyword of 'identity' (London: 0 percent, Berlin 35 percent). The Brussels groups converge on the issue of 'participation' which is associated by 40 percent of each group. And unlike the Londoners, the British Brusselites' connotations also include reference to the issue of 'identity'.

In sum, the figures obtained in this chapter (see Table 7.5) demonstrate a more significant result of convergence following (elite) interaction in transnational arenas. This finding differs from the previous

Table 7.5 *Human rights and fundamental freedoms: core and derived oppositions (2)*

Core opposition		Associative connotations	Core opposition	
Divergence (either/or)				
Domestic arena 1			*Domestic arena 2*	
London			**Berlin**	
Contract			Covenant	
		Identity		
		Participation		
		Single constitutional framework		
Diffusion (both/and)				
Transnational arena			*Transnational arena*	
UK/Brux			**Ger/Brux**	
Contract	Covenant		Contract	Covenant
		Identity		
		Participation		
		Single constitutional framework		

Source: Table 7.4 and Case Excerpt.

policy fields, in so far as the first five opposition-deriving exercises found that the Brusselites' associative connotations pointed to a range of different keywords, therefore suggesting *diffusion* rather than *convergence* in the transnational arena. If the finding of convergence in the transnational arena can be confirmed by follow-up research that is based on a larger sample, or that extends the range of comparison, it could be concluded that in the absence of regular interaction in transnational contexts even elite groups are likely to diverge in their interpretative patterns. Non-interacting elite groups are therefore likely to sustain diverging associative connotations based on the specific distinctions derived from national identity options. The following turns to the final comparative aspect of this case study. This final step has been conducted as a cross-check exercise. At this time, attitude questions rather than explorative interviews provide the material for evaluation.

Attitude questions: accountability vs responsibility

The final set of questions regarding the constitutional politics field addresses the norms of 'accountability' and 'responsibility'. Unlike fundamental norms that provided the focus in the earlier interviews based on guided questionnaires, these norms are defined as organisational principles. They are less general and more specific and entail a closer link with day-to-day procedures in politics and policy-making.[50] Following the distinction provided in Table 4.2, organising principles are a more specific than fundamental norms, yet less clearly defined than standardised procedures. This type of norm predominantly evolves through interaction in policy fields. Its purpose lies in regulating processes and procedures, for example by warranting the system of checks and balances based on the principles of efficiency, transparency, accountability or responsibility.[51]

At this point, the interviewees are not expected to generate associative connotations through discursive interventions at a micro-event (the interview situation). Instead, the following questions are 'attitude questions ... with simple dichotomous affirmative and negative response options' (Holbrook, Krosnick, Carson and Mitchell 2000: 465). They are carried out to cross-check the positioning of the four elite groups achieved on the basis of qualitative text analysis. They allow for an assessment of the interviewees' normative baggage with reference to a choice of organising principles rather than targeting the interpretation of meaning of fundamental norms. So far, the selection of keywords has allowed for the allocation of reference to associative connotations and, based on the opposition-deriving exercise, derived oppositions were linked to predefined core oppositions so as to qualify the structure of meaning-in-use, for example 'inside–outside' with reference to citizenship (chapter 5); 'society–community' with reference to the rule of law and democracy (chapter 6); and 'contract–covenant' with reference to human rights and fundamental freedoms (chapter 7).

---

[50] Compare Table 4.2 on the distinction of three types of norms, including fundamental norms, organising principles and standardised procedures.
[51] See, e.g., Bovens 2007; Puntscher-Riekmann 2007; and Begg 2007.

The concept of accountability has gained particular salience in processes of governance beyond the state. It is considered a prime organising principle to maintain a system of checks and balances. As Mark Bovens (2007) writes, for example, 'accountability comes from accounting'. He defines it 'as a relationship between an actor and a forum, in which the actor has an obligation to explain and to justify his or her conduct, the forum can pose questions and pass judgment, and the actor may face consequences' (*ibid.*: 107). While the principle of accountability is more strictly linked with types of action within a particular position in politics or policy-making, the principle of responsibility has a stronger moral underpinning.[52] Responsibility suggests a Kantian moral obligation. With regard to the European Union's constitutional process, it has been defined as 'a global and social environmental demand' (Shaw 2001: 8). The principle of responsibility thus evokes a link between rights and obligations that classically arise for citizens from their status as rights holders, or, indeed, for sovereign states vis-à-vis their citizens (Chyrssouchoou 2002: 8). Taking these details into consideration, the final part of the empirical case study keeps with the 'gut' question approach of encouraging expressive or emotional rather than explanatory replies from the interviewees; however, in distinction from the previous evaluation and interview technique, the following examination does not prompt interviewees to elaborate on their respective preference. The choice is simply noted and listed.[53] In this case, the interviewees have been presented with the choice between 'accountability' and 'responsibility'. The following question was asked:

> Which concept matters more to you (your own work), 'accountability' or 'responsibility'?[54]

---

[52] For a definition which distinguishes between political accountability and legal responsibility, see Bogdandy 1999: 905–7. In turn, Della Sala observes that enhanced cooperation and flexible governance 'cloud the lines of responsibility and accountability for the citizen' in the EU (2001: 15).

[53] However, many found the question required some explanation and offered either that, or elaborated on their respective preference. In those cases, that explanation is brought to bear in the evaluation as appropriate.

[54] While the German translations of 'responsibility' (*Verantwortung*) and 'accountability (*Rechenschaftspflicht*) were used for the German interviewees, interviewees often spontaneously preferred using the English term of 'accountability' whilst otherwise speaking German.

Table 7.6 *Attitude questions: preference for accountability vs preference for responsibility*

Arenas	Domestic		Transnational	
Keywords / Elite groups	Londoners	Berliners	Brux/UK	Brux/Ger
Responsibility (more important than accountability)	46.15	70	0	30
Accountability (more important than responsibility)	61.54	25	70	60

Source: 'Text Corpus'. Note that 'both/and' replies have been counted towards both values.

As Table 7.6 demonstrates, the Berliners' replies reveal a preference for responsibility (70 percent while the Londoners are at 46.15 percent), whereas the majority of the Londoners stress the significance of accountability in their day-to-day environment (61.54 percent while the Berliners are at 25 percent). The latter reveals, in particular, a significant *type B* divergence between the two domestic elite groups (compare Table 4.4). What is interesting to see here when comparing the domestic elites' choices with those of the Brusselites is the *type A* divergence. This divergence is documented by both the comparison of the two German elite group samples in Berlin and Brussels *and* the comparison of the two British samples in London and Brussels. Thus, the German Brusselites' preference for accountability at 60 percent reveals a clear distinction from that of the Berliners (25 percent), while the British Brusselites' preference for responsibility (0 percent) indicates a drop from the Londoners (46.15 percent). The following two graphs provide an overview over substantive *preference swaps* with regard to the three types of divergence that were defined in chapter 4 (see Table 4.4), i.e. *type A* (domestic vs transnational), *type B* (domestic vs domestic) and *type C* (transnational vs transnational).

Note the relatively constant associative connotations with 'responsibility' along national identity lines depicted in Graph 7.1 with the Berliners scoring higher (70 percent) and the Londoners lower (46.15 percent). This outcome is consistent with the assumption that national identity options would inform politics beyond the state; however, there is a drop in reference to 'responsibility' when compared with the entries regarding the principle of accountability among the group of British Brusselites. In

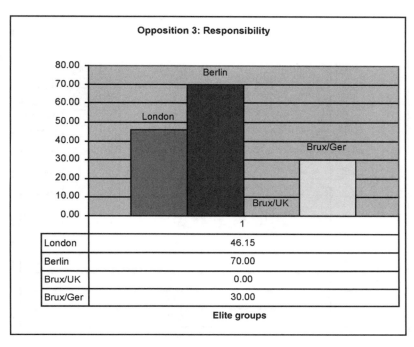

Graph 7.1 Responsibility.
Source: 'Text Corpus'; author's percentage calculation.

turn, there is a clear divergence between Londoners and Berliners and a convergence among both Brusselite elite groups as demonstrated in Graph 7.2, now with the Londoners scoring high (61.54 percent) and the Berliners low (25 percent) while the Brusselites both range between 60 and 70 percent. The associative connotations regarding attitude questions on responsibility and accountability hence confirm the rule-in-practice assumption which expects meanings to evolve and change in relation to *social practice in context* rather than *national identities*.

Conclusion

Similar to the situation more than a decade earlier, in 1993, when the concept of citizenship was formally included in the Maastricht Treaty,[55]

---

[55] The citizenship article at the time was Article 8e-f TEC (Maastricht Treaty); it was then renumbered under the Amsterdam Treaty changes to Articles 17–22 TEC.

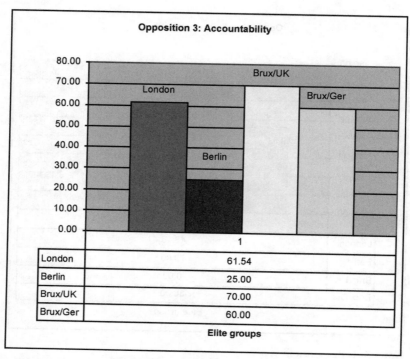

Graph 7.2 Accountability.
Source: 'Text Corpus'; author's percentage calculation.

inserting the reference to a 'constitution' into the European Union discourse has raised questions. It worried especially those who enjoyed relatively limited information and/or access to dialogue about the meaning of this term, and mobilised some (recall, e.g., the referendum debate and the 'no' votes in France and the Netherlands). The term has generated confusion among those who were European passport bearers as well as among those who were aspiring to obtain one in the near or mid-term future. After all, the language of 'things constitutional' is notably and meaningfully linked with EU citizens both as addressees of fundamental norms, rules and regulations following a constitutional settlement, and as voters who are to agree or disagree with the constitutional text during potential ratification processes. While the 'constitutional turn' has been noted and much commented upon in the academic literature, especially since the

Nice conference,[56] its role in a non-state context is yet to make a mark on constitutionalism as an academic artefact.

The comparison with the stipulation of citizenship in the 1993 Maastricht Treaty is particularly compelling as both innovations reflect the leading politicians' interest in strengthening the European Union's identity. This policy has been consistent despite the public political and academic oft-repeated emphasis on the need to improve the democratic quality of the EU as reported by the media. Thus, both citizenship rights and the constitution are presented to the public for their potential to carry symbolic expectation rather than for an interest in any actual procedural role they might entail. Despite this role, the constitution has been promoted as a practical innovation bearing the quality of 'tidying up' and as substantially entailing the promise of being 'more democratic' and therefore bringing more 'legitimacy' to the EU. However, it is notable with the benefit of hindsight, for example in the case of establishing European citizenship as the basis for a sustainable 'European' identity, that symbolic politics borrowed from modern nation-state experience is more likely to trigger conflict than enhance democratic legitimacy, since experience and expectations of symbolic meaning did not converge among the rather differently organised communities of modern states, on the one hand, and the EU's non-state polity, on the other.[57] In short, both concepts do not travel easily across cultural boundaries. In the process, they produce contested interpretations of fundamental norms. In sum, this final comparative chapter sustained the observation that experience forms expectation. In line with historical semantics, it confirms that experience has a notable – and potentially significant – impact on distinct ways in which norms are perceived by individuals.

Table 7.7 summarises the findings with regard to the fundamental norms of human rights and fundamental freedoms, sorted according to the core opposition (contract vs covenant) and two derived oppositions (finality vs single framework; identity vs participation). It displays two types of divergence: *type B* divergence among the domestic elites in London and Berlin, and *type A* divergence between elite

---

[56] For this literature, see among others Beaumont, Lyons and Walker 2002; De Burca and Scott 2003; Wiener and Shaw 2003; and Bogdandy and Bast 2006.

[57] See, for a comparative study, Brubaker 1992; for the specific reference to 'European' citizenship, see Wiener 2001.

Table 7.7 *Domestic arena and transnational arena: core and derived oppositions (1–2)*

Human rights and fundamental freedoms			
Domestic sample groups			
Divergence (either/or)			
Fundamental norm	Associative connotations	**London**	**Berlin**
Core opposition		Contract	Covenant
Derived opposition 1			
	Finality		[shaded]
	Single framework	[shaded]	
Derived opposition 2			
	Identity		[shaded]
	Participation	[shaded]	[a]

Transnational sample groups					
Diffusion (both/and)					
Transnational arena				*Transnational arena*	
UK/Brux				**Ger/Brux**	
Core opposition				*Core opposition*	
Contract	Covenant			Contract	Covenant
Derived opposition 1					
	[shaded]	Finality			[shaded]
[shaded]		Single framework		[shaded]	
Derived opposition 2					
	[shaded]	Identity			
[shaded]		Participation		[shaded]	

[a] This particular finding displays one deviation from the expected pattern of divergence between the Berliners and the Londoners.

Source: Tables 7.3 and 7.5 and Case Excerpt.

groups in domestic and transnational political arenas. This finding suggests that interaction in context matters. While the diverging inter- pretation of meanings of fundamental norms such as, for example, contract-oriented and functional expectations towards the fundamental norms of human rights and fundamental freedoms in London, and a covenant-oriented hence more emotional or identity-based expectation towards these norms in Berlin was to be expected, the innovative insight generated by the case study follows the closer examination of the two British and German samples in Brussels. Here, the layer-cake assumption would expect a relatively constant if not revolutionary process of harmonised (or in this case Europeanised) interpretation of meanings. Yet, the Brusselites of both nationalities confirm the pattern of diffused associative connotations of the previous two chapters. That is, they generate connotations with reference to a range of keywords as opposed to converging on a single keyword only, as the domestic samples did. Based on this diffused set of connotations generated by these groups, the findings hence suggest that transnationalisation – at least in the early stages which these interviews have been able to cover – is constitutive for an enhanced range of meanings and thus more flex- ibility. We can therefore conclude, at this point, that a wider repertoire of meanings has been identified by the empirical focus on cultural practices rather than organisational ones. What appear to be trivial differences over expectations of the constitution's role as functional and contract-oriented (London) (keyword: 'single framework') or as symbolic and covenant-oriented (Berlin) (keyword: 'finality') may turn out to be indicators for assessing political conflict or possibilities in the long term. The following two chapters elaborate on these empirical findings and discuss the potential political impact from a normative theoretical perspective.

Evaluation

8 | Comparative assessment and working hypothesis

The validity claimed for propositions and norms 'transcends spaces and times'; but in each case the claim 'is raised here and now, *in a specific context*, and accepted or rejected with concrete implications for social interaction'.

(Dallmayr 2001: 341; my emphasis)

Introduction

This chapter turns to the comparative assessment of the data obtained through empirical research and interview evaluation. To that end, it discusses the findings of the seven opposition-deriving exercises and the set of attitude questions revealed in the previous three case study chapters. The intention of this final assessment is to generate a working hypothesis for future research. Taken together, the findings demonstrate a notably distinctive outcome with regard to patterns of convergence, divergence or diffusion.[1] Both *type A* divergence (domestic vs transnationally derived meanings) and *type B* divergence (domestic vs domestically derived meanings) are recurring. By contrast, *type C* divergence was not a notable pattern. This finding indicates that, contrary to the literature which would expect enhanced harmonisation or Europeanisation, the convergence of associative connotations regarding the three sets of fundamental norms under investigation could not be confirmed. Convergence was found with reference to single domestic elite samples only. This pattern suggests that, notably, converging interpretations do not seem to depend on *nationality* but on *contextualised social practices* instead.

This conclusion has to be read with caution, to be sure. After all, the comparison involved a limited sample of four elite groups and fifty-three interviews only. Nonetheless, it does provide a valuable basis for generating a research hypothesis. That basis was substantiated by three

---

[1] For the guidelines for comparison, see Table 4.4.

crucial details in the conceptualisation of the empirical investigation. Firstly, the interviews comprised not only different domestic elite groups, i.e. in London and Berlin, but also groups of the same national background that operated in two different arenas. Thus, the research design allowed for a cross-check of interviewees of the same nationality, for example Germans in Berlin and in Brussels, as well as the British groups in London and Brussels, respectively. This research design also facilitated a cross-check of the impact generated by nationality vs that generated by social practices. Secondly, the reconstructive evaluation of the Case Excerpt based on the opposition-deriving technique was repeated seven times. This repetition allowed for double-checking emerging comparative patterns such as divergence vs diffusion. Thirdly, the findings were then submitted to another cross-check based on attitude questions. This final comparative exercise allowed for additional comparison based on two different interview strategies, i.e. explorative vs dichotomous responses. The data have been evaluated both qualitatively and quantitatively and presented in tables and graphs in the previous three chapters. This chapter conducts one more qualitative evaluation by reconstructing the normative structure of meaning-in-use with reference to each sample group's associative connotations. The following evaluation therefore prepares the ground for the normative theoretical discussion in chapter 9. The next section reconstructs the structures of meaning-in-use that emerged from the four elite groups interviewed in two types of political arenas. Subsequently, a section evaluates the empirical research results, and identifies the working hypothesis that follows from the empirical research. The final section summarises the findings.

Structures of meaning-in-use

The comparative evaluation with regard to understanding the way norms work proceeds with reference to the four main research assumptions and hypotheses which guided the empirical research. They include the liberal community hypothesis, the layer-cake assumption, the national identity-options assumption and the rule-in-practice assumption.[2] The structure of meaning-in-use which is reconstructed for each of the three arenas under investigation, including the domestic arenas in

---

[2] Compare chapter 3 Tables 3.4, 3.5, 3.6 and 3.7.

London and Berlin and the transnational arena in Brussels, should allow for the identification of patterns of contestation. The following reconstructs the three related structures of meaning-in-use for comparison. The general purpose of making meanings accountable is to provide an empirical basis for larger case studies and for normative theorising. Generally, a reconstruction of the respective normative structures of meaning-in-use is expected to offer pointers for answering three queries, including the range of contestedness of selected fundamental norms; the choice of organising principles that should be institutionalised to provide enhanced access to contestation; and the selection of standardised procedures that need to be implemented with a view to supporting the basic principles of democratic constitutionalism. These queries will be addressed in some more detail in the following chapter. For now, the reconstruction of the structure of meaning-in-use takes account of the three types of diversity which were central to the case study's opposition-deriving exercise.

Types of diversity

Once the relevant structures of meaning-in-use with reference to the contexts of London, Berlin and Brussels are established, it will be possible to discuss further steps towards improving the conditions of legitimacy and reducing the potential for political conflict in world politics. This process could, for example, focus on establishing new organising principles and standardised procedures that would enhance institutional options for dealing efficiently and democratically with the finding of increased diversity. The structure of meaning-in-use adds the set of normative meanings derived from the respective empirical findings to each sample group. Thus, the actual meaning-in-use that provides the framework of reference for each group will be revealed. Note that the design of the case study was intended to identify divergence, convergence or diffusion rather than elaborating on a specifically British, German or Brusselite interpretation of meaning. The reconstruction is therefore intended to assess conditions of contestation based on comparison rather than establishing generalised substantive meanings.

It is of key importance to establish whether or not there is a continuous tendency to swap associative connotations held, for example, by a domestic elite group towards the emergence of a transnational interface of shared interpretations of modern fundamental norms, or whether domestic associative connotations remain stable and are therefore likely to differ. The latter would suggest the rather significant finding of transnationalisation as an additional layer of interpretation implying an increase in diversity instead of a gradual harmonisation as the layer-cake assumption would expect. This would imply that pockets of Europeanisation rather than wholesale, albeit gradual, harmonisation following the layer-cake assumption and the liberal community hypothesis prevail. This section recalls the three contexts and the oppositions derived from discursive interventions on the fields of Schengen, Enlargement and Constitutional Politics.

The following four tables display the reconstructed structure of meaning-in-use with reference to the fundamental norms of citizenship, democracy and the rule of law as well as human rights and fundamental freedoms with regard to the four interviewed elite samples. The tables represent the third of three steps of an inductive qualitative text analysis. This analysis began with a text corpus of about 1,000 pages that entailed the full transcriptions of fifty-three interviews. It was then reduced in a second step to a Case Excerpt of 196 pages comprising interview excerpts that were organised according to policy fields, fundamental norms and keywords. This third step brings the results obtained through the technique of deriving oppositions together as the respective reconstructed normative structure of meaning-in-use. The tables thus allow for the comparative analysis of the interpretation of meaning based on nationality and context of interaction. For example, the London sample reveals an emphasis on the 'inside' of citizenship, on the 'society' dimension of governance and on the 'contract' aspect of treaties (see Table 8.1). The Berlin sample reveals an emphasis on the 'outside' of citizenship, on the 'community' dimension of governance and on the 'covenant' aspect of treaties (Table 8.2).

Both the German and British Brusselites' samples reveal no specific emphasis on oppositional pairs akin to those revealed by the interviews with the Londoners and the Berliners, respectively. No distinctive opposition was derived. Instead, the individual enacting of meaning-in-use reveals the predominant pattern of 'both/and' association (see Tables 8.3 and 8.4, respectively). That is, instead of one shared associative connotation among one group, a diversity of associations was revealed. This pattern suggests that transnational interaction diffuses nation-based associations. Whether or not the transnational context will

Table 8.1 *Meaning-in-use: London*

Norm	Core opposition	Derived opposition 1	Derived opposition 2	Derived opposition 3
Citizenship	*Inside*	Travel	Civil rights	
Democracy and the rule of law	*Society*	Fairness	Value-export	Stability
Human rights and fundamental freedoms	*Contract*	Single framework	Citizen participation	Accountability
Attitude question	Accountability			

Source: Tables 6.3, 6.5, 7.3, 7.5, 7.7.

Table 8.2 *Meaning-in-use: Berlin*

Norm	Core opposition	Derived opposition 1	Derived opposition 2	Derived opposition 3
Citizenship	*Outside*	Security	External borders	
Democracy and the rule of law	*Community*	Compliance	Participation (of candidates)	Finality
Human rights and fundamental freedoms	*Covenant*	Finality	Identity	
Attitude question	Responsibility			

Source: Tables 6.3, 6.5, 7.3, 7.5, 7.7.

ultimately lead to a convergence of similar consistence as suggested by each domestic sample remains to be demonstrated based on data that are more sociologically specific, i.e, obtained through interviews with individuals who have spent e.g. a period of a generation or more conducting social practices within a transnational context.

The lack of harmonisation reflects the input of cultural validation. For example, while at face value the debate about the European constitution appeared to be 'a *debate about terminology*', at a deeper level it reflects a fundamental 'background concern about issues of *legitimacy*

Table 8.3 *Meaning-in-use: German Brusselites*

Norm	Core opposition	Derived opposition 1	Derived opposition 2	Derived opposition 3
Citizenship	*Outside and inside*	Security, travel, community formation, cooperation	External borders, civil rights, border control obsolete, cooperation	
Democracy and the rule of law	*Society and community*	Compliance, fairness	Inclusion	Finality, stability
Human rights and fundamental freedoms	*Contract and covenant*	Finality, single framework	Participation	
Attitude question	Accountability and responsibility			

Source: Tables 6.3, 6.5, 7.3, 7.5, 7.7.

and finality of European jurisdiction' (Peters 2001: 31; my emphasis). That is, no matter where it may take place, the debate is generally spurred by 'deeply rooted and *sub-consciously* derived imaginations' (*ibid.*; my emphasis). This observation suggests that deeper concerns about 'things constitutional' might not have been acknowledged by those who were actually involved in drafting the treaty. The distinction between terminology and hidden background concerns as noted by Peters, raises the issue of how the latter might be conceptualised and, perhaps even more challenging for political scientists, how these could be studied. As this book proposes, the empirical dimension of such politically powerful, albeit predominantly invisible, aspects of politics entails making interpretations of fundamental norms accountable.

The central role of contestedness with a view to understanding the role of norms in politics points to two types of conflict which are empirically distinct. Each represents a politicising factor that can be exemplified with reference to the European constitutional process.

Table 8.4 *Meaning-in-use: British Brusselites*

Norm	Core opposition	Derived opposition 1	Derived opposition 2	Derived opposition 3
Citizenship	*Outside and inside*	Security, travel, border control obsolete, community formation	External borders, civil rights, border control obsolete, community formation, fortress Europe, cooperation	
Democracy and the rule of law	*Society and community*	Compliance, fairness, finality	Inclusion, value-export	Finality[a]
Human rights and fundamental freedoms	*Contract and covenant*	Finality, single framework	Participation	
Attitude question	Accountability			

[a] For a single deviation from the general pattern, compare Table 6.9
Source: Tables 6.3, 6.5, 7.3, 7.5, 7.7.

Thus, the first type of conflict identifies the functions of a constitution designated by the formal constitutional framework as a point of contestation. The second type of conflict sees the contingent development of constitutional interpretations as the cause for contestation. Both perspectives offer access points for an understanding (or explanation) of the conflict brought to the fore by the finality debate and the referendum process in Europe. That is, if a constitution is to organise the political successfully, its rules, norms and procedures need to be recognised as legitimate within a particular community. The successful implementation of fundamental norms hence depends on the availability of cultural interpretations of fundamental norms to all addressees. That availability is expected to decrease once the constitutional framework transgresses domestic political arenas.

Evaluation of empirical research results

The book's main research interest was to address conflictive interpretations of international agreements. It was argued that, to do this, a better understanding of how normative meanings were constructed was necessary. Considering growing notions of constitutional quality in contexts beyond the boundaries of modern states and an increase in transnationalisation based on moving social practices across national boundaries, it was therefore proposed to proceed with an empirical case study that would allow for the reconstruction of the structure of meaning-in-use in relation to specific norms and how they were interpreted by individuals belonging to two different nationalities, yet four different groups. The outcome of this empirical research is revealed in the four tables above.

The case study in the three political arenas of London, Berlin and Brussels showed that individuals operating for an extended period of time – in this case an average of about five years or more – within an area that is different from their national context of origin are likely to mobilise associative connotations that do not overlap with those of their national root arena. Recalling the most general research propositions formulated in chapter 2 and building on approaches to constitutionalism (compare Table 2.2), it is now possible to identify the case study's contribution to research on constitutionalism, as one of three propositions confirmed. That is, *proposition one* which holds that 'converging interpretations of the meaning of fundamental norms is more likely within one single political arena than in many different arenas' is sustained. *Proposition two* which states that 'converging interpretations of the meaning of fundamental norms in different political arenas are likely to increase with repeated interaction across community boundaries' is challenged. And, *proposition three* which expects that 'interaction across community boundaries is more likely to involve elites than other social groups' and that 'elites are therefore most likely to enhance cultural harmonisation' has been challenged as well.

The British and German Brusselites' associative connotations did not match those of the Londoners and Berliners, respectively. In addition, the Brusselites' discourse displays a diffused set of associative connotations. At the same time, two types of divergence are evident based on the series of seven opposition-deriving exercises. They are displayed by the two domestic elite groups' respective reference to different core oppositions (*type A* divergence). In addition, each domestic elite group differs from the transnational group of Brusselites (*type B* divergence). The third type of divergence (*type C* divergence), i.e. maintaining national identity options among the transnational group in Brussels, could not be confirmed.

With reference to the three issue areas of Schengen, Enlargement and Constitutional Politics which were addressed in the micro-events that generated discursive interventions on fundamental norms, distinctive associations were identified. For example, with reference to the policy field of constitutional politics, the Londoners understood the Constitutional Treaty as a text 'with a mission to provide simplicity and clarity and put an end to further deepening'; the Berliners expected the treaty 'to bring together an identifiable community of values and see it as the beginning of a process of further deepening'; and finally interviews in the Brussels transnational political arena suggest that both German and British Brusselites see the treaty as a text with a mission to provide a simple framework, though not without symbolic meaning. Most importantly, the case study's results suggest that an on-going divergence between the UK and the German domestic political arenas (London and Berlin samples) goes hand in hand with a clear divergence from any national identity options in the transnational political arena in Brussels (British and German Brusselites, respectively).

While this diverging pattern between transnational and domestic political arenas does not lead to an emerging pattern of convergence within the transnational arena, it does indicate a significant pattern of diffused associative connotations. The findings thus underline the observation that emerging transnational arenas *coexist* with domestic and supranational political arenas. In this respect, it is important to recall that the definition of transnationalisation applied in this book refers to type of activity rather than type of actors.[3] It is therefore not dependent on a fixed – politically delimited – unit, but rather it is constitutive for a flexible space instead. Its emergence is based on the frequency and type of activity which is constitutive for the context and

---

[3] Compare the section on modern and contextualised constitutionalism in chapter 2.

vice versa. The implications of this finding will be addressed in some more detail in chapter 9.

Divergence and diffusion, conflict and contestation

Two central findings were generated by the empirical case study's reconstruction of the normative structure of meaning-in-use in three political arenas (London, Berlin and Brussels) and with reference to four elite groups (Londoners, Berliners, British Brusselites and German Brusselites). They include firstly, *divergence* between different domestic arenas. This finding indicates a significantly lacking margin for flexible interpretations of normative meaning when individuals meet on the basis of individual international relations, i.e. outside their respective domestic contexts in which their respective day-to-day cultural practices are influential for individually transported associative connotations. The divergence has been identified as *type B* divergence between domestic arenas (see Table 4.4). Secondly, the case study established *diffusion* in the transnational arena. This finding demonstrates a range of associated meanings which are at the fingertips of the elites operating in this area. Since no specific opposition could be established, this finding implies a considerable degree of flexibility regarding the available meanings to elites operating within the transnational arena. Such a diffused pattern of meanings is likely to facilitate a fruitful reservoir of potential resources for compromise should elites, for example, feel pressed for quick reactions under conditions of crisis (see Table 4.1).

In sum, based on inductive evaluation, this research found two different patterns of oppositions. These have been used towards the reconstruction of the structure of meaning-in-use which provided the reference frame for individuals' day-to-day operations in the two domestic arenas of Berlin and London, as well as in the transnational arena of Brussels. A notable finding revealed by this comparative assessment points to the potential conflict that is expected once these individuals travel and hence carry their respective – domestically constituted – normative baggage along when engaging in international interaction elsewhere. In the absence of a sense of appropriateness in that context, they are likely to resort instinctively to applying the cultural validation available to them, but which is invisible to others. From the knowledge of the respective structures of meaning-in-use which display a pattern of core oppositions among these groups, and considering an international meeting between, say, individuals who have been predominantly interacting within the domestic contexts of London and Berlin, respectively, interpretations of meaning 'out of context' imply contestation at best and conflict at worst. By contrast, individuals who are positioned within the transnational arena of Brussels are unlikely to face conflict since their normative reference frame is a pattern of diffused meanings. That is, while for the former, the frame of reference creates an 'either/or' basis when engaging in international negotiation; for the latter, the frame of reference is one of 'both/and'. It is hence constitutive for contestation over a choice of possible options.

The working hypothesis

Even though the case study cannot be considered as representative, given the limited size of the sample, the findings do raise doubts about the project of reconstituting modern institutions of democracy in beyond-the-state contexts (Habermas 2004; Eriksen 2005a, 2006; Fossum and Eriksen 2006; critically Tully 2002b and Walker 2007). This scepticism is grounded in the observation that, so far, the European integration process has not achieved the level of harmonisation previously anticipated. Instead of finding the layer-cake assumption of more Europeanisation following European regional integration sustained, we encounter a phenomenon that is better described as pockets of Europeanisation.[4] The question is, therefore, whether these pockets consolidate into nodes that can be accessed by privileged citizens only, or whether they are likely to expand. In case of the latter, it is important to consider, both normatively and in terms of real-world policies, whether this expansion could be enhanced through specific institutional and/or policy changes. Ultimately, strategic constitutional politics, in the European Union and elsewhere, would want to begin here. After all, the pockets of Europeanisation may enable only an exclusive number of Europeans to enjoy full access to participation as citizens with fully fledged access to all institutions, duties and benefits provided by a political community. This finding would suggest that the basic condition for democratic legitimacy, i.e. potential access to contestation of the norms that rule a community, is not given.

---

[4] See also Eder's critical assessment of wholesale Europeanisation processes. He argues that based on different processes of social and cultural integration, the result is more likely to be 'two faces' of Europeanisation (Eder 2004).

While the case study was not intended to reconstruct patterns and possibilities of participation, it did aim to conduct an investigation of normative meanings as an inherent element of the structure of meaning-in-use to establish whether, and if so how, diversity might become a key factor for enhancing democratic constitutionalism in Europe and elsewhere. While this specific research project focused on Europe, it is possible to draw some general conclusions. For example, if elites within a relatively small and integrated social, legal and political space, such as the EU, are less likely to share interpretations of normative meanings, then other comparisons, e.g. among elites from different regions such as Europe, Africa and Asia, are expected to reveal even stronger divergence. It is from this perspective that the case study has produced significant findings for international political relations.

The case study assessed diversity based on the cultural rather than the organisational dimension of constitutionalism. In addition, it derived empirical data based on practices rather than on religious or other types of group-differentiated claims (e.g. Young 1990; Kymlicka 1995). Curiously, the case study identified a type of diversity which suggests that, in fact, the majority of Europeans – both residents and citizens – are likely to consider themselves as outsiders to the process of political integration. That is, a lack of shared associative connotations prevails despite the fact that the effects of economic integration are all-pervasive in EU member states. This feeling of exclusion reflects a general process of detachment and alienation between state- and society-based institutions. It is accompanied by an 'identity awakening' which sees a diverse set of groups engaging in 'contemporary struggles for recognition' (Taylor 2001: xiv–xv). It could therefore be argued that it contributes to the general observation of 'constitutive tensions' in contemporary democratic societies (*ibid.*; Gagnon and Tully 2001: 2). These tensions are then one likely explanation of the 'no' vote in the European referenda on the Constitutional Treaty. The working hypothesis following from the case study, therefore, holds that in the absence of an all-encompassing process of transnationalisation which could warrant equal access to both the organisational practices and the cultural practices of a transnationalised *nomos*, divergent interpretations of fundamental norms will prevail in beyond-the-state contexts (see Table 8.5).

That is, in the absence of all-encompassing transnationalisation, divergence according to national, local or other root contexts of

Table 8.5 *Working hypothesis*

In the absence of all-encompassing transnationalisation, international politics
  is constitutive for more rather than less diversity. International encounters are
  therefore expected to generate conflict and contestation.

individual cultural practices will undermine the notion of a shared sense
of recognition. If this notion can be maintained by further empirical
research, we can conclude that diversity, rather than a shared identity
based on a 'glue' of sorts,[5] would be the more likely and consistent
dimension in politics beyond the state which needs to be dealt with in
constitutional terms.

Conclusion

The present research insights sustain the rule-in-practice assumption
underlying this case study. That is, contrary to the liberal community
hypothesis and the layer-cake assumption, this book remained sceptical
about the emergence of a wholesale Europeanisation to the extent that a
'European' sense of appropriateness could be identified. It suggests that
interaction in the transnational arena generates a pattern best described
as diffusion rather than convergence. In the transnational arena individually transported and enacted associative connotations generate a
pattern of diffused options (rather than a selection of two oppositions)
in the interpretation of meaning. Such diffusion allows for a wider range
of potential negotiation outcomes. The advantage of transnationalisation is thus one of more flexibility.[6]

---

[5] On the recurring theme of 'glue' with reference to European integration, see Friese
and Wagner's (2002) review of the literature. On the effort to forge a European
identity, see for example the strategic discursive intervention by Habermas and
Derrida in *Le Monde* and *Frankfurter Allgemeine Zeitung* titled 'Unsere
Erneuerung. Nach dem Krieg: Die Wiedergeburt Europas' (translated as 'Our
Renewal after the War: The Rebirth of Europe'), published in Paris and Frankfurt/
Main, 31 May 2003. Note the action's critical reception by Iris Marion Young in
her article titled 'Europa leerer Mittelpunkt: Widerstand gegen die US-Politik kann
nur eine Dezentrierung der Demokratie leisten' (translated as 'Europe Empty Core:
Resistance Against US Politics Can Only be Achieved by a Decentralised
Democracy'), published in *Frankfurter Rundschau*, 22 July 2003, 9.

[6] I thank Raingard Esser for raising the point of diffused positions of transnational
elite groups in a discussion on 10 February 2006.

The consequence of finding a stable pattern of divergence among domestic groups as well as among domestic and transnational groups, on the one hand, and flexibility among the transnational group for politics in beyond-the-state contexts, on the other, is twofold. Firstly, divergence with regard to the domestic arenas is likely to generate conflict in international negotiations, and this is likely to increase in situations of crisis, as these enhance the decline of the social feedback factor (see Table 4.1). It follows that if divergence is not dealt with on an institutional basis, i.e. by introducing a set of organising principles and standardised procedures, conflict will be the most likely outcome. Secondly, diffusion in relation to the transnational arena suggests flexibility. Subsequently, we could hypothesise that encouraging transnationalisation on a broader scope would offer an access point to deal with conflicts resulting from contested interpretations of norms.

It is important to compare the correlation between convergence on one single keyword in each of the domestic political arenas and divergence between both domestic arenas. At the same time, the associative connotations uttered by elites of different nationalities operating within the Brussels transnational political arena do not reveal convergence on a single keyword according to nationality. They do, however, converge in their respective associative connotations with various keywords. While the Brusselites – whether British or German – did not share the reference to one single keyword, they tended to cover a rather broad range of associative connotations. In comparison with the domestic rather stable patterns of cultural validation, then, this finding suggests that a new flexibility might be emerging within the transnational space. Rather than insisting that only one interpretation is available with regard to the interpretation of normative meaning, now various meanings become possible. It could be argued then that the notion of flexibility has an enabling effect, in so far as it allows for a range of possible meanings to be taken into consideration. Whether this is the case and how to deal with this emerging transnational 'space',[7] its role and impact on governance and democratic constitutionalism beyond the state remains to be explored in the following chapter.

---

[7] See especially Edward Soja's (1989) work for bringing the notion of 'space' to the attention of the wider social science community.

9 | *Incorporating access to contestation*

As the result of two hundred years of constitution-making and remaking and of discussions of rival and changing theories of democratic-constitutional justice, we have a better understanding of how the two principles of legitimation work together in this open-ended and non-definitive manner. *Democratic constitutionalism is an activity rather than an end-state.*

(Tully 2002a: 209; my emphasis)

Introduction

As social constructs, norms are contested by default. They evolve through interaction in context and are hence considered as evolving and flexible except for limited periods of normative stability;[1] however, if their importance 'lies not in being true or false but in *being shared*' (Katzenstein 1993: 268; my emphasis), then the sense of appreciation of norms is likely to change according to time and place. This normative flexibility needs to be accounted for both conceptually and empirically. The research project presented in this book turned to examining the role of fundamental norms in world politics based on such a bifocal approach, i.e. engaging the interrelation between empirical and normative research. Three issues matter in this regard. Firstly, an empirically observable reaction suggests the existence of a norm. Secondly, an empirically observable and analytically expected reaction to an appropriate norm can be established. Thirdly, the conditions for normative legitimacy in the absence of both a constitutionally (no shared formal validity) and socially (no social recognition) limited modern context of governance need to be defined.

To that end, the research project sought to develop an approach to studying cultural validation that is constituted through individual

---

[1] See Reus-Smit 2001a: 526. For seminal studies on a relational approach to institution building, see Tilly 1975; Giddens 1979; Habermas 1985; Somers 1994.

day-to-day practices as a third dimension that matters for our understanding of contested norms. The book began with the observation that
apart from a shared sense of scepticism towards the emergence of constitutional quality beyond the modern contexts that are most familiar to
constitutionalists, there is little academic agreement on how to tackle
conflicting interpretations of fundamental norms. The case study was
conducted to explore ways of understanding the origin and impact of
normative conflict for international politics. To that end, it proposed an
approach which would allow us to highlight systematically heretofore
invisible causes of conflict about norms. As the literature on constitutionalism suggests, less common conceptualisations of the *nomos* do actually
work on the assumption of a Janus-faced *nomos* comprising both organisational (read: regulatory) and cultural (read: customary) practices.[2]
Following this insight as well as the literature on norms in international
relations, I assumed that the intangible dimension of norms might be
rather influential: it could turn into an unintended potential spanner in
the works of international politics, or adopt the function of an indicator
for a more democratic constitutionalism.

While the previous chapters have focused on empirical research with
a view to highlighting and reconstructing the invisible cultural validation of norms, this final chapter returns to the normative concern raised
at the beginning of the book. It recalls the problematic move of fundamental norms from domestic contexts into internationally negotiated
agreements, and the related argument that, unless flanking measures are
taken, the social practice of moving norms into the beyond-the-state
context is more likely to cause conflict than convergence (compare
chapter 1).[3] Accordingly, this chapter discusses the findings of the
case study from a normative theoretical perspective. The next section
addresses the shifting conditions of access to participation under conditions of transnationalisation. A further section juxtaposes reasoned
and dialogical perspectives[4] on how to tackle the challenge of contemporary constitutionalism. The final section provides an outlook for
future research on norms in international politics.

---

[2] Compare chapter 2.
[3] For other more recent work that shares this concern, if from different theoretical
  perspectives, see, e.g., Slaughter and Burke-White 2002; Slaughter 2004; Cohen
  2004; and Zürn, Binder, Ecker-Ehrhardt and Radtke 2007.
[4] Compare the 'logic of arguing', chapter 3 Table 3.2 and the 'principle of
  contestedness', chapter 3 Table 3.3.

Transnationalisation and diversity

That transnationalisation matters is a relatively uncontested observation among students of International Relations and International Law. More interesting and, indeed, puzzling in the light of hypotheses generated by the behaviourist literature on compliance with norms is the finding that variation in the interpretation of fundamental norms is more clearly related to contextualised social practices than national identity options or liberal community formation. This finding sustains the importance of an activity-based as opposed to an actor-based definition of transnationalisation. Based on the examination of four groups that share only two different nationalities between them, it was possible to demonstrate that social interaction in context has an impact on the way norms are interpreted. Table 9.1 details the findings and their respective correlation with the four research assumptions that were derived from the relevant literature prior to conducting the empirical research.

In global contexts beyond modern political, constitutional and social boundaries, legitimacy and conflict resolution depend increasingly on transnational arenas. Analyses of modern communities can relate to the constitutional framework of modern nation-states which provides the

Table 9.1 *Assumptions and findings*

Findings / Assumption	*Transnationalisation reveals the impact of contextualised social practices*	*In the absence of transnationalisation, domestic core oppositions remain stable*	*Transnationalisation diffuses core oppositions and increases diversity*
Liberal community	Sustained	Challenged	Challenged
Layer-cake	Sustained	Challenged	Challenged
National identity options	Challenged	Sustained	Challenged
Rule-in-practice	Sustained	Sustained	Sustained

fundamental norms, organising principles and standardised procedures that regulate, maintain and enforce politics. By contrast, analyses of beyond-the-state settings require a unit of analysis that differs from the modern state. The general research outcome points to the transnational arena as achieving new importance as a potential new 'unit of analysis' in research on democratic constitutionalism beyond the state.[5] As an interface where social and organisational practices converge, transnational spaces enable (and force) us to think outside the oft-lamented constraints of methodological nationalism. The conditions for such interfaces remain to be specified, however. So far, the changing quality of norms has been studied with a particular focus on how transnational arenas compare to domestic arenas, and based on a distinction of formal validity, social recognition and cultural validation. It thus opens up a new empirical angle on detailing the cultural validation of norms based on empirical studies of associative connotations that make meanings accountable. As the previous three empirical chapters have demonstrated, this dimension offers crucial insights towards an understanding of how norms work in contexts beyond modern states. It completes the jigsaw of the invisible constitution of politics.

Three observations matter in this regard. Firstly, formal validity is established through the stipulation of norms within a constitutional text or treaty. That is, the norms' legitimacy is based on an albeit abstract and mythical yet widely acknowledged social contract between the governors and the governed of a particular community. The social recognition of norms follows from the familiarity with, and habitual appreciation of institutional settings in particular societies, where a society is defined as 'the legitimate order through which communicating individuals organise their respective belongingness to social groups and secure solidarity' (Habermas 1988: 209). Finally, the cultural validation of norms is based on cultural practices and expressed as individually transported associative connotations of a particular norm that is derived from and constituted by individual access to cultural practices.

---

[5] For example, Ulrich Beck emphasises the search for a new 'unit of analysis' which is able to reflect cosmopolitan – read 'non nation-state' – societal conditions (Beck 2005; Beck and Grande 2005; see also Zürn 2000; 2005: 6). Note that the emergence of 'families of shared meanings', for example, including groups of countries similar to Scharpf's finding on welfare state families in Europe (Scharpf 2000), may be conducive to creating such interfaces.

Interfaces

Any stock-taking regarding the feasibility of constitutionalism for trans-national or international politics needs to begin by acknowledging that various types of domestic constitutional frameworks such as, for example, the Canadian, the French, the German, the British, on the one hand, and internationally negotiated frameworks such as the European Union and the United Nations, on the other, coexist. Among these coexisting yet context-specific constitutional frameworks, occasional interfaces emerge; however, these will develop fully only once formal validity, social recognition and cultural validation overlap. The slim likelihood of coincidental overlap indicates an equally slim chance for legitimate and democratic politics in beyond-the-state contexts. Yet the conditions for such interfaces to achieve stability are not evident from existing research on the structural power of norms (compare chapter 3). To fill that gap, this book engaged in the empirical endeavour of making meanings accountable. The research on the invisible constitution of politics showed that meanings are contested by individuals when such an interface does not exist.

To assess particular conditions under which the possibility of inter-faces increases, I have addressed the meaning and reach of funda-mental norms along three dimensions. These include formal validity based on facts established by a treaty, agreement or convention; social recognition with reference to social institutions in a given environ-ment; and cultural validation based on associative connotations shared by individuals. The last perspective validates each element in the process of norm appreciation and hence is equipped to reach beyond state boundaries. Formal validity, social recognition and cultural validation are therefore considered the three constitutive dimensions for legitimate governance which range on a scale from a more visible to a more invisible stage of evolving normative meaning (see Table 9.2).

That is, fundamental norms acquire formal validity through their stipu-lation in a community's constitution. With decreasing direct political access to formal institutions, social recognition and eventually cultural validation based on day-to-day practices gain in importance. Cultural validation is the most flexible condition among the three steps towards establishing normative meaning. Therefore, it is the condition which tra-vels most easily. In turn, social recognition is less flexible and moves more

Table 9.2 *Three dimensions of norm implementation*

Evaluation ╲ Institutions	Formal validity	Social recognition	Cultural validation
visible ▲ ▼ invisible			
Democratic legitimacy	less ◄		► more

slowly if at all. Both are required for generating interpretations of norms that are understood as legitimate in international encounters.

Reconstituting democracy beyond the state?

With regard to the discussion about the concept of constitutionalism, it is important to note that this study's findings sustain the claim that a constitution 'must be difference-aware or diversity-aware: that is, it must accord equal due recognition and respect, in some way, to the respectworthy cultural differences of all citizens' (Tully 2002b: 350). The theoretical question which remains to be discussed is whether the dialectical tension between facts and norms can be meaningfully applied as a *Grundnorm* of democratic constitutionalism in the absence of fully reconstituted institutions of modern constitutionalism. Can it be a guarantor for democratic dialogue in contexts which do not conform with a Hegelian perspective on 'state and society as one' (Gordon 1999: 77)? A contextual perspective cannot but remain sceptical about the project of reconstituting democracy beyond the state. While not opposed to defending modern fundamental norms in practice, a critical perspective cautions against the universalism of modern constitutionalism (see chapter 2).

Access to critical dialogue about the rules that govern a polity is rightly and importantly considered as the cornerstone of democratic politics – if and when it not only follows but also precedes constitution building. The timing, conditions and quality of such debate are critical. The case study suggests mapping the realm of international politics as a context in which differentiated bases of access to participation present a *general condition*. This finding should stand, especially when considering that it was derived from interviews with elites as that social group which is, according to the layer-cake assumption, most likely to interact internationally. Hence there is little reason to assume that by extending the empirical examination to other groups of European citizens (and residents) the access rate was to be improved. The general question derived from the democratic literature then is that of who enjoys equal and full access to the organisational and cultural practices of the *nomos*, respectively? According to the bifocal approach that underlies this research and following from the working hypothesis formulated in the previous chapter (see Table 8.5), two normative questions need to be raised.

The more general question addresses the issue of how to deal with diversity. Is diversity a mere issue of conflict, or does this finding open a new perspective on democratic international politics (Cohen 2004)? The more specific question turns to the communication gap between formal validity and social recognition. As the case study has demonstrated, in the absence of a communicative link between the two dimensions of normative interpretation, cultural validation (identified by research on individually transported associative connotations) is likely to turn out as influential for international decisions taken in environments beyond modern contexts. Since this dimension is usually invisible to others, it will come to the fore only in situations of enhanced contestation (see Table 4.1). At issue is therefore whether and how, in light of the documented diversity, the gap could be addressed so that diversity can be dealt with prior to the moment of expected conflict. I elaborate on this question by discussing the role of the *principle of contestedness* in democratic international politics below. One promising comparative angle in this respect is Tully's distinction between a 'civil' and a 'civic tradition of citizenship' (Tully 2007). The distinction is crucial because it allows for an analytical perspective on the otherwise invisible cultural practices. The following first addresses the issue of access to transnational cultural practices before the next section turns to the more general aspect of how to incorporate the principle of contestedness as a potential meta-norm of democratic constitutionalism beyond the state.

The working hypothesis derived from the case study implies that in a partially transnationalised world the concept of membership in a community needs to be scrutinised so as to include the coexistence of different types of arenas in which norms emerge and/or where they are interpreted. Thus the concept of citizenship as a 'developing institution' which involves the gradual expansion of citizenship rights towards 'full membership in a community'[6] stands to be revised, so as to reflect the new element of transnational spaces in addition to a multiplicity of communities. The basic assumption would remain, however, the condition of access to participation in dialogue and contestation as proposed by democratic constitutionalism (Tully 2002a). If we take Marshall's concept of citizenship as access to full membership in a community as a yardstick[7] and reformulate it according to the key condition of access to contestation, 'membership in a community' needs to be replaced with 'access to transnational cultural practices'.

Modern constitutionalism's main focus on organisational practices has resulted in reduced attention to cultural practices making them invisible to the analytical eye. By highlighting the impact of cultural validation as one of three dimensions that matter with regard to the interpretation of normative meaning, this book set out to examine the invisible constitution of politics. The case study demonstrates that, even among elites, differentiated access to participation prevails. That is, access to transnational cultural practices is available exclusively to those who operate in transnational arenas on a day-to-day basis over an extended period of time. This reduces the group with access to the process of contesting the values, norms and rules that govern all Union citizens considerably. While the number of citizens voting in European elections is increasing, the number of those who actually participate in the necessary process of contestation prior to voting appears to be declining.[8] The logical conclusion of this research suggests that as long as exclusively organisational practices such as voting are transferred to the transnational realm while cultural practices are not transnationalised in equal measure, the voting procedure will be perceived not only as distant, but also actually lacking the democratic

---

[6] See Marshall 1950: 28 and 8, respectively and Riesenberg 1992.
[7] An increasing number of comparative policy analysts in both political science and law have been drawing on Marshall to scrutinise the political theory of citizenship; for many contributions, see the work of Shaw 1997; Kostakopoulou 2005; and Jenson 2007.
[8] See Shaw 2007 on the progress of EU citizens' electoral behaviour.

legitimation that would have been constituted through full access to contestation.

Dealing with diversity: Kantian reconstitution or dialogical contestation?

In keeping with the concern about how to counter the invisible constitution of politics with a view to the development of democratic legitimacy in international relations, the following probes two distinct perspectives for their respective approach to diversity. The background for this discussion is provided by a contextualised approach which builds on Brandom's helpful juxtaposition of Kantian regulism and Wittgensteinian pragmatism (Brandom 1998). It will bring to bear Tully's call for the equiprimordiality of the principle of constitutionalism and the principle of democracy (Tully 2002a). The two perspectives can be distinguished as being definite and based on universal principles in the first case, and as taking a view of constitutional practices as indefinite and proceeding in an agonistic fashion which leaves room for a constitutional multiverse to unfold, in the second case. Each addresses ways of dealing with diversity within a constitutional framework. The first option has been elaborated by a growing number of scholars with an interest in theorising the reconstitution of democracy within a global context.[9] These scholars propose to focus on Habermas's theory of communicative action. The assumption is that deliberation generates legitimacy based on agreement about universal values. The policy-relevant action is to warrant access to participation in such processes of deliberation so as to provide the procedural means to question norms and procedures that govern politics by all those affected by them. The second option focuses on establishing contingent agreements about institutions based on the condition of the constitution's role allowing for peaceful coexistence.[10] In the following, each approach is briefly recalled.

[9] See, e.g., the work of Fossum and Eriksen (2007) and Eriksen (2007) who draw on Habermas; for a summary, see also Habermas's more recent work (2005).

[10] Compare Foucault's critical question: 'In what is given to us as universal, necessary, obligatory, what place is occupied by whatever is singular, contingent, and the product of arbitrary constraints?' (Tully 2002b, 334–5, citing Foucault 1997: 124–5).

The power of deliberation?

International Relations theorists who build on Habermas's communicative action theory are aware of the dilemmatic interrelation between the speech-act and the *'unlimited community of interpretation* to which the negotiated positions must appear reasonable in order to be justified, and in other words, acceptable' (Habermas 1992: 35; my emphasis). As Habermas points out, while 'the universality of the assumed rational acceptability pushes beyond all contexts', it is 'only the binding acceptance of validity in a particular situation which prepares the ground for smooth performance of *everyday practice'* (*ibid.*: 37; my emphasis). This everyday practice is embedded in the sociocultural context of the predominantly domestic arena of the life-world; the lack of this life-world presents a problematic absence in beyond-the-state contexts (Müller 2001, 2004; Deitelhoff 2007).

Since the integrative function of the law between individuals and systems (Habermas 1992, 2004) cuts too short in beyond-the-state contexts, the additional focus on the socially derived means of interpreting the law offers a crucial access point in addressing the gaps in compliance with norms in contexts which exceed the environment of modern western societies.[11] After all, in contexts beyond the modern state no full-blown constitutionalised setting supports and sustains the interpretation of the law. Nonetheless, norms do assume a role within these proto-constitutional settings. These contexts are governed by a set of less stable and more contested norms than fully constitutionalised modern nation-states. They lack the possibility to refer to a set of social institutions for recognition and appropriateness of legal institutions.[12] The importance of these factors varies according to the type of negotiation context, i.e. its degree of institutionalisation or constitutionalisation.

Comparing transnational and domestic social practices offers an opportunity to elaborate on the conceptual dilemma inherent in the Habermasian approach, i.e. the validity of legal norms cannot exclusively be deduced from the social acceptance of norms by the involved elites. Instead, formal validity requires inductive demonstration

---

[11] See Habermas 1992: 15; see critically Schluchter 2003: 548 and Beck and Grande 2005.

[12] See Curtin and Dekker 1999; Finnemore and Toope 2001; and Brunnée and Toope 2001.

through discursive procedures that alone can establish legitimacy through communication (Habermas 1992: 47). Accepting the tension between facticity and validity as a *Grundnorm*, then, implies that deliberations about norms should not be limited to identifying and validating one norm amongst a choice of others. Instead, it also includes assessing the meaning of a norm by taking into account sociocultural trajectories. That meaning is a necessary condition for identifying the norm's perception by involved (individual) actors.

While the facticity–validity tension offers a principled approach to the contested and constitutive role of norms, the question about the role of norms in the absence of modern communities that provide the context for both life-world and system world, a situation which Habermas calls the 'postnational constellation' (1998: 494), remains on two grounds. Firstly, the validity claims of norms are exclusively based on norm choices not norm meanings. Secondly, and following from the first observation, if norms are dealt with as ontologically primitive units, their contested substance – a precondition for legitimate norms – is not acknowledged. In other words, validity claims sustain the legitimacy of a norm within a specific context, say a negotiation situation; however, they cannot account for the assessment of sustained norm legitimacy once norms are transferred into another context, or, once they are considered over an extended period of time. In turn, the societal perspective considers norm contestation as a condition for establishing the shared validity of norms. It conceptualises contestation 'all the way down' with a view to transcending (and possibly challenging) the meaning of norms between contexts (Johnston 2001: 494). As Habermas points out, 'If contexts of interaction, as I assume with Durkheim and Parsons, cannot be transformed into stable orders on the basis of mutually interacting success-oriented actors, then society must be integrated through communicative interaction, *in the end*' (Habermas 1992: 43; emphasis in original). The literature that displays a notable enthusiasm for Habermas-inspired approaches to communication encourages deliberation, pointing to different types of conversation and dialogue which are, according to some observers, central to the on-going constitutionalisation in the European Union.[13] Yet the manifold dialogues which have been observed must be scrutinised according to their openness and reflection of both

---

[13] Compare the newly established 6th Framework Programme's integrated project RECON (Reconstituting Democracy in Europe) which is directed by

organisational and cultural practices. Such dialogues include, for instance, 'judicial conversations' or 'constitutional dialogues' between the European Court of Justice and the national constitutional courts of the member states, as well as 'political conversations' among heads of state and government which take place at Intergovernmental Conferences. These are more broadly conceived as 'constitutional conversations' and include the input of a range of actors throughout some five decades of constitution-making in the EU (Witte 2002: 40, cited in Walker 2000: 21; Stone Sweet 1998: 305). For example, as Bruno de Witte observes quite correctly and importantly: 'This stretches the metaphorical capacity of the term "dialogue" very far. The members of these courts hardly know each other, and certainly never sit together formally to examine a particular case or abstract question' (2002: 40). Those who actually enter into dialogue in the EU's beyond-the-state context are more likely to be the elites involved in interactions interrelated with politics and policy-making on a day-to-day basis. By operating within the same context over extended periods of time, they are therefore more likely to develop shared or, at least, significantly overlapping associative connotations than others. The lack of overlap and the absence of an interface will therefore continue to generate a new level of diversity which needs to be addressed; however, as the case study demonstrated, not even elites can be taken to enjoy equal access to emerging transnational spaces.

The need for dialogue and contestation

Dialogical approaches assume that, if and when conducted according to the meta-norm of democratic constitutionalism, politics and policy-making in any arena would need to be conducted following two principles or norms. These norms involve the 'principle of constitutionalism (or the rule of law) and the principle of democracy (or popular sovereignty)' respectively (Tully 2002a: 205). While the principle of constitutionalism refers to a particular institutional context, that context may be defined in either a narrow sense including only fundamental norms, or a broader sense including all three types of norms. In any case, it is assumed that the type of political arena where the rule of law applies is characterised by albeit varying degrees of constitutionalisation qualified

Erik O. Eriksen at the University of Oslo, details at www.reconproject.eu/ (accessed 20 August 2007).

by the interplay of its legal, social and cultural spheres. In turn, the principle of democracy or popular sovereignty requires the rules to be imposed on all addressees of these fundamental norms including the representatives of that very constitutional system. Efforts to make democratic constitutionalism and constitutional democracy co-equal thus face the challenge of conceptualising the condition of being constitutionally legitimate and democratically legitimate at the same time.

In order for a constitutional framework to be able to reflect both leading norms in equal measure, a constitutional order must be either 'negotiated' or continuously 'conciliated' (*ibid.*: 208). However, for these principles to be translated into an open dialogue, the additional principle of equal access to participation in the transnational arena must be entrenched in the constitutional order. Next to sovereignty and the rule of law as the two principles of democratic constitutionalism, equal access to contestation must be established for all citizens. Once these structural components of democratic constitutionalism are established and agreed among those affected by them, justification of day-to-day matters can proceed. Further to contextualising diversity, this approach works with a concept of continuous yet contingent diversity which holds that, 'the entire exercise of democratic freedom in relation to the existing rule of law must be intersubjective and open-ended practical reasoning' (Tully 2002a: 217).

Conflicting interpretations of norms or contested norm implementation are not necessarily due to a lack of agreement about a norm's meaning. Instead, it may be due to a lack of understanding of that meaning (Taylor 1993: 47, 50). It follows that with the declining homogeneity of social environments the need for explanations increases. This observation suggests an enhanced role for individual social practice as a key contribution in the process of norm recognition. Two challenges for International Relations theory and democratic constitutionalism follow. Firstly, it is necessary to explore the validity and variation of normative meaning with reference to specific types of norms in selected contexts. Differences are expected when the boundaries of interactive contexts are transgressed such as, for example, in different member states or in different transnational arenas.[14] This

---

[14] For the coordination of research in this field, see, for example, the Network of Excellence Team working on *Establishing Diversity (and Commonality) in Interpreting the Meaning of Democratic Principles and Procedures*; www.mzes. uni-mannheim.de/projekte/typo3/site/index.php?id=64 (accessed 29 June 2006).

research limits potential political contestation points based on cultural reference frames. So far, this issue has mainly been tackled by comparative theoretical debates, for example on the extension of transnational public spheres or on the Europeanisation of specific policy sectors (Eder, Kantner and Trenz 2000; Peters 2005). Secondly, the observation about the key role of practice in processes of norm interpretation raises the normative question of how different expectations about constitutional substance ought to be integrated in constitutional debates, or in environments which produce constitutional quality.

This latter aspect addresses the democratic legitimacy of constitutional substance on a more general level. It has been discussed along two different dimensions. The first dominates in the European discussion. It is based on universal values which are rooted in the constitution and are guarded by it. This debate is marked by the discussion about European norms and values as a condition of a European community. By contrast, a second debate, which has been formulated more distinctively if not exclusively outside Europe, suggests that universality might be a misleading assumption considering that '*the world of constitutionalism is not a universe, but a multiverse*: it cannot be represented in universal principles or its citizens in universal institutions' (Tully 1995: 131; my emphasis). This position would suggest that the accommodation of diversity be considered a value in itself. Diversity would therefore be conceptualised as a goal rather than a problem of democratic constitutionalism. This perspective brings the issue of institutional conditions for maintaining diversity as opposed to the substantial definition of particular 'European' values to the fore. It means that a constitutional framework must be able to accommodate diversity without overcoming it, and reflect shared principles, norms and values in institutions that are recognised by those affected by them.

Maintaining diversity

The first approach stresses a reasoned view of norms. It works with the principal assumption of establishing the preferred constitutional setting which had been agreed to by the negotiators and which is expected to entail validity for all signatories of the constitutional text and, by definition, the citizens linked to the respective heads of state. In turn, the second approach stresses a dialogical perspective on norms. It works with the principal assumption of an on-going diversity of preferred constitutional settings that will always exist and therefore must be considered. While the former approach works only on the basis of a reasoned consensus that surpasses the stage of diversity, the second seeks to accommodate diversity. The distinction between the two approaches can therefore be pinpointed as one of keeping diversity at bay vs maintaining and encouraging it.

While both the reasoned and the dialogical approaches stress inter-action as a core element of legitimate constitutional rule, they differ significantly in their respective universal and multiversal position. Both address the validity of fundamental norms and values in different ways. For example, the universal approach works with the assumption of general values which are to be identified through communicative inter-action (Habermas 1988a and 1988b). Appropriate institutions towards this end are procedures which facilitate space for deliberation. In turn, an 'agonistic' approach seeks to accommodate institutions which allow for the establishment of the three conventions of mutual recognition, consent and cultural continuity in order to ensure on-going dialogue and infinite negotiation of fundamental norms and subordinate procedures (Tully 2002a; Bader 2005). The aim of this approach is 'not to overturn but to amend the institutions of constitutional democracy, so they will express the cultural plurality of the sovereign people, or peoples, rather than impose the dominant culture's identity' (Tully 2002b: 339). In the light of the working hypothesis derived from the empirical findings of the case study, the dialogical approach offers more promise than the Kantian model which always ultimately depends on a stable reservoir of shared cultural 'glue' in the end. It can therefore be argued that the

contestable character of constitutional democracy should not be seen as a flaw that has to be overcome. The democratic freedom to disagree and enter into agonistic negotiations over the prevailing constitutional arrangements (or some subset of them) and the dominant theory of justice that justifies them … is precisely the practice of thought and action that keeps them from becoming sedimented – either taken for granted or taken as *the* universal, necessary and obligatory arrangements. (Tully 2002a: 218)

The implementation of the principle of contestedness is particularly crucial with a view to implementing international treaties and main-taining diversity in the global realm. In international contexts, the expectation of diversity based on social difference is reflected by the tradition of maintaining treaty language on a considerably general level.

That is, while recognition of internationally negotiated norms is expected from all signatories, such treaties rarely entail detailed instructions as to the procedures of implementation (Chayes and Chayes 1993: 189). The interpretation of treaty substance is thus transferred into contexts of interaction which are subordinate to the international arena such as, for example, domestic political arenas. It is precisely this type of subordinated arena of implementation which bears potential for conflicting interpretations of norms which have been transposed from the international arena into the domestic, since normative meanings require continuous mechanisms for exploration and updating.

Conclusion: implications for follow-up research

Governance beyond the state involves an understanding of norms as working outside the familiar modern context. In practice, the interpretation of norms occurs at a distance from the root-contexts in which they originated through interaction. That is, norm interpretation requires the additional and relatively new step of establishing a relationship between the formal validity of a norm according to treaty language, on the one hand, and the social recognition of a norm according to its appropriateness within a given community, on the other. To establish this link when social practices have moved outside modern contexts, each travelling individual will face the task of setting up the link by themselves. To do so, they will tap into their individual normative baggage as the cultural validation available to them on location. In the absence of interfaces between political arenas such as e.g. the London, Berlin and Brussels arenas examined by this book's case study, norms are likely to be contested. To avoid misunderstandings based on such spontaneous conflict, and to achieve more legitimate understandings of norms, future research would want to focus on the potential of institutional and/or procedural innovation, including, for example, additional space for interaction to generate contestation or a mechanism to involve transnational groups for advising international decision-makers.[15] Such tools could offer the access point for normative and policy-oriented proposals with a view to optimising contestation and minimising unwanted conflict.

Further research needs to assess the conditions and possibilities of divergence, convergence and diffusion of normative meanings based on

---

[15] For steps in that direction, see, e.g., Puetter 2006 and Puetter and Wiener 2007.

larger more comprehensive research samples. Such samples would want to explore the contested meaning of norms along four angles of comparative expansion. These angles include: (i) a different set or combination of fundamental norms such as non-intervention, sovereignty and the abstention from torture; (ii) a different choice of social groups such as students, workers or others; (iii) a numerically larger sample of interviewees; and (iv) a smaller sample of interviewees where the method of evaluation stresses the qualitative aspect, for example based on interpretative or 'metaphor' analysis. All would contribute in different yet important ways to offer a better understanding of how transnational spaces enhance the possibilities of sustained constitutional quality in beyond-the-state contexts.

Whilst the thrust of normative research in world politics has stressed the structuring quality of norms, the additional dimensions of context and time cast light on a more complex approach that appreciates the dual quality of norms as structuring, and constructed through, social interaction. As a new unit of analysis, transnational space provides a reference for comparative research across different spaces because it allows for an approach that captures not only the stable but also the flexible aspect of norms. For example, adding the comparison with elite groups operating in transnational arenas to that of domestic arenas provides distinct insights for both the empirical identification of conflictive interpretations of meaning as well as the normative discussion of mediating contested normative meanings. Working with this new unit of analysis involves an analytical move from systems and societies towards individual interaction and the cultural representations created therein.

Since conflicting interpretation of norms occurring in the absence of transnationalised interaction patterns are expected in situations of norm transfer between different types of political arenas, we can expect an increasing diversity in the interpretation of normative meanings. In the absence of institutional innovations (possibly of constitutional quality) that would allow for the accommodation of increased diversity in the interpretation of norms, more – rather than less – political conflict is to be expected in the aftermath of international negotiations. As all individuals carry normative baggage, only those groups of individuals who engage in continuous day-to-day interactions within a transnational arena are likely to share a perception of formal validity, social recognition and cultural validation. This implies that actors who engage only temporarily in international interaction will display expectations that are informed by diverging cultural experiences. Hence, they enter international negotiations based on different patterns of recognition. It follows that even if the formal validity of constitutional texts is accepted and a social environment, such as in an international organisation, exists to provide reference frames for interpretation, cultural validation is likely to generate divergence. Subsequently, expectations of the role of any particular norm are likely to differ as long as transnationalisation remains exclusive, partial and underestimated analytically.

Annex

List of interviewees[1]

Name	Institution
Dr Mads Andenas	The British Institute of International and Comparative Law
Cornelia Bolesch	*Süddeutsche Zeitung*
Stephen Castle	*The Independent*
Damian Chalmers	London School of Economics, Law
Nicholas Clegg	Member of the European Parliament (Liberal Democrats)
Prof Sir Bernard Crick	Home Office
Dr Eckart Cuntz	Foreign Office
Kim Darroch	Foreign and Commonwealth Office
Dr Manfred Degen	Regional Representation, North-Rhine Westphalia
Robert Dixon	Foreign and Commonwealth Office
Dr Gernot Erler	Member of Parliament (SPD)
Jane Ferrier	Permanent Representation to the EU
Kim Feus	Federal Trust
Joachim Fritz-Vannahme	*Die ZEIT*
David Galloway	Council of Ministers, Secretariat
Leigh Gibson	Foreign and Commonwealth Office
Dr Heather Grabbe	Centre for European Reform
Prof Dr Dieter Grimm	Humboldt University Berlin, Law
Dr Ulrike Guérot	Deutsche Gesellschaft für Auswärtige Politik
Ted Hallet	Foreign and Commonwealth Office
Dr Klaus Hänsch	Member of the European Parliament (Social Democrats)

[1] All interviewees – except one who is entered as 'NN' – have agreed to be listed as long as anonymous reference to their respective discursive interventions is provided. The listings document the position, appointment and title given at the time of the interview.

Name	Institution
Prof Robert Hazell	University College London, Politics
Folker Hellmund	Regional Office (Hanse)
Dr Alan Hick	Economic and Social Committee
Dr Kirsty Hughes	Centre for Policy Studies
Eckart von Klaeden	Member of Parliament (CDU/CSU)
Dr Claas Knoop	Permanent Representation to the EU
Anja Köhne	Heinrich Böll Foundation
Prof Dr Michael Kreile	Humboldt University Berlin, Politics
Dr Sabine Leutheusser-Schnarrenberger	Member of Parliament (FDP)
Dr Klaus Linsenmeier	Heinrich Böll Foundation
Dr Friedrich Löper	Home Office
Dr Caroline Lucas	Member of the European Parliament, Greens
Tim McNamara	European Commission, Representation London
Dr Hartmut Offele	European Commission
Thomas Ossowski	Foreign Office
Prof Dr Ingolf Pernice	Humboldt University Berlin, Law
Dr Wolfgang Petzold	European Commission
Dr Melanie Piepenschneider	Konrad Adenauer Foundation
Michael Roth	Member of Parliament (SPD)
Joscha Schmierer	Foreign Office
Andreas Schultz	Home Office
Victor Smart	Project Floyd (formerly: The European)
Dr Julie Smith	The Royal Institute of International Affairs
Christian Sterzing	Member of Parliament (Bündnis 90/GREENS)
Dr Eiko Thielemann	London School of Economics, Politics
Tony Venables	European Citizen Action Service, ECAS
Christoph Verenkotte	Home Office
Karsten D. Voigt	Foreign Office
Dr Martina Weber	Home Office
Caroline Wilson	Permanent Representation to the EU
Ulrike Wisser	BBJ Consult
NN	European Commission

References

Abbott, Kenneth W., Keohane, Robert O., Moravcsik, Andrew, Slaughter, Anne-Marie and Snidal, Duncan 2000. 'The Concept of Legalization', *International Organization* 54(3): 401–19

Ackerman, Bruce 1993 [1991]. *We the People I: Foundations*. Cambridge, MA and London: Belknap Press of Harvard University Press

Adler, Emanuel 1997. 'Seizing the Middle Ground: Constructivism in World Politics', *European Journal of International Relations* 3(3): 319–63
2005. *Communitarian International Relations: The Epistemic Foundations of International Relations*. London and New York: Routledge

Anderson, Benedict 1991 [1st edn 1983]. *Imagined Communities*. London: Verso

Aziz, Miriam and Millns, Susan (eds.) 2007. *Values in the Constitution of Europe*. London: Ashgate

Bader, Veit 2005. 'Against Monism: Pluralist Critical Comments on Danielle Allen and Philip Pettit', in M. Williams and S. Macedo (eds.), *Political Exclusion and Domination*. New York: New York University Press, pp. 164–78

Barnett, Michael 1999. 'Culture, Strategy and Foreign Policy Change: Israel's Road to Oslo', *European Journal of International Relations* 5(1): 5–36

Barnett, Michael and Finnemore, Martha 2004. *Rules for the World. International Organizations in Global Politics*. Ithaca, NY: Cornell University Press

Beaumont, Paul, Lyons, Carol and Walker, Neil (eds.) 2002. *Convergence and Divergence in European Public Law*. Oxford and Portland, OR: Hart Publishing

Beck, Ulrich 1993. *Die Erfindung des Politischen*. Frankfurt/Main: Suhrkamp
2005. 'Contribution to the Controversial Debate: Competing Conceptions Regarding the Societal Foundation of the EU', keynote presented at the CONNEX, Mid-Term Conference, Mannheim MZES, 3–5 November 2005

Beck, Ulrich and Grande, Edgar 2005. *Das kosmopolitische Europa*. Frankfurt/Main: Suhrkamp

Begg, Iain 2007. 'Contested Meanings of Transparency in Central Banking', *Comparative European Politics* 5(1): 36–52

Beiner, Ronald 1995. 'Introduction: Why Citizenship Constitutes a Theoretical Problem in the Last Decade of the Twentieth Century', in Ronald Beiner (ed.), *Theorizing Citizenship*. New York: SUNY Press, pp. 1–28

Beljin, Saja 2006. 'Rights in European Union Law', paper presented at the workshop 'Binding Unity and Diverging Concepts in EU Law', 12–13 January 2006; www.uvt.nl/faculteiten/frw/departementen/europeesrecht/budc-conference/papers/ [accessed 19 January 2006]

Bellamy, Richard 2003. 'Legitimizing the Euro-"Polity" and its "Regime"', *European Journal of Political Theory* 2(1): 7–34.

  2005. 'Still in Deficit: Rights, Regulation and the Democracy in the EU', paper presented at the annual conference of the Consortium of Democratic Constitutionalism of the University of Victoria, DEMCON, 30 September to 2 October 2005; www.law.uvic.ca/demcon/2005_presenters.htm [accessed 23 June 2006]

Bendix, Reinhard 1963. 'Concepts and Generalizations in Comparative Sociological Studies', *American Sociological Review* 28(4): 532–9

  1964. *Nation Building and Citizenship*. New York: John Wiley

Benhabib, Seyla 2004. *The Rights of Others: Aliens, Residents and Citizens*. Cambridge: Cambridge University Press

Berger, Peter and Luckmann, Thomas 1991 [1966]. *The Social Construction of Reality*. London: Penguin Books

Böckenförde, Ernst-Wolfgang 1992. 'Geschichtliche Entwicklung und Bedeutungswandel der Verfassung', in Ernst-Wolfgang Böckenförde *Staat, Verfassung, Demokratie*. 2nd edn. Frankfurt/Main: Suhrkamp, pp. 29–52

Bogdandy, Armin von 1999. 'The Legal Case for Unity: The European Union as a Single Organization with a Single Legal System', *Common Market Law Review*, 36(5), 887–910

Bogdandy, Armin von, and Bast, Juergen (eds.) 2006. *Principles of European Constitutional Law*. Oxford: Hart Publishing

Bohman, James and Rehg, W. (eds.) 1997. *Deliberative Democracy. Essays on Reason and Politics*. Cambridge, MA: MIT Press

Bohnsack, Ralf 2000. *Rekonstruktive Sozialforschung – Einführung in die Methodologie und Praxis*. Opladen: Leske and Budrich

Bonham, G. Matthew and Shapiro, Michael J. 1977 [1973]. *Thought and Action in Foreign Policy*. Center for Advanced Study in the Behavioral Sciences, Stanford, CA, Proceedings of the London Conference on Cognitive Process Models of Foreign Policy, March 1973. Basel and Stuttgart: Birkhauser

Börzel, Tanja A. and Risse, Thomas 2000. 'When Europe Hits Home: Europeanization and Domestic Change', *European Integration Online Papers* 4(15); http://eiop.or.at/eiop/texte/2000-015a.htm [accessed 17 September 2007]

Bös, Matthias 2000. 'Zur Kongruenz sozialer Grenzen. Das Spannungsfeld von Territorien, Bevölkerungen und Kulturen in Europa', Kölner *Zeitschrift für Soziologie und Sozialpsychologie* 40 (Special issue 52): 429–55

Bourdieu, Pierre 1982 [1977]. *Outline of a Theory of Practice.* Cambridge: Cambridge University Press

  1993. *The Field of Cultural Production.* Cambridge: Polity Press

Bovens, Mark 2007. 'New Forms of Accountability and EU-Governance', *Comparative European Politics* 5(1): 104–20

Brandom, Robert B. 1998. *Making it Explicit. Reasoning, Representing, and Discursive Commitment.* Cambridge, MA: Harvard University Press

Brandt, Richard B. 1950. 'Stevenson's Defense of the Emotive Theory', *Philosophical Review* 59(4): 535–40

Breda, Vito 2006. 'A European Constitution in a Multinational Europe or a Multinational Constitution for Europe?', *European Law Journal* 12(3): 330–44

Brubaker, Rogers 1989. *Immigration and the Politics of Citizenship in Europe and North America.* Lanham: University Press of America

  1992. *Citizenship and Nationhood in France and Germany.* Cambridge, MA: Harvard University Press

Brücker, Herbert 2005. 'EU-Osterweiterung: Übergangsfristen führen zur Umlenkung der Migration nach Großbritannien und Irland. *Wochenbericht des DIW*', Deutsches Institut für Wirtschaftsforschung, Berlin, 353–9

Brunnée, Jutta and Toope, Stephen J. 2001. 'International Law and Constructivism: Elements of an Interactional Theory of International Law', *Columbia Journal of Transnational Law* 39(1): 19–74

  2008. *Legitimacy and Persuasion: The Hard Work of International Law.* Cambridge: Cambridge University Press

Bublitz, Hannelore (ed.) 1999. *Das Wuchern der Diskurse. Perspektiven der Diskursanalyse.* Frankfurt/Main: Campus

Bulmer, Simon and Burch, Martin 2001. 'The "Europeanisation" of Central Government: The UK and Germany in Historical Institutionalist Perspective', in Mark Aspinwall and Gerald Schneider (eds.), *The Rules of Integration: Institutionalist Approaches to the Study of Europe.* Manchester: Manchester University Press, pp. 73–96

Buzan, Barry 1993. 'From International System to International Society: Structural Realism and Regime Theory Meet the English School', *International Organization* 47: 327–52

Cairns, Alan 1989. 'The Living Canadian Constitution', in R.S. Blair and J.T. McLeod (eds.), *The Canadian Political Tradition*. Scarborough: Nelson, pp. 3–16

Cass, Deborah Z. 2001. 'The "Constitutionalization" of International Trade Law: Judicial Norm-Generation as the Engine of Constitutional Development in International Trade', *European Journal of International Law* 12(1): 39–75

Cassirer, Ernst 1946. *The Myth of the State*, New Haven, CT: Yale University Press

Chayes, Abram and Chayes, Antonia Handler 1993. 'On Compliance', *International Organization* 47(2): 175–205

1995. *The New Sovereignty. Compliance with International Regulatory Regimes*. Cambridge and London: Harvard University Press

Checkel, Jeffrey T. 2001a. 'Why Comply? Social Norms Learning and European Identity Change', *International Organization* 55(3): 553–88

2001b. 'The Europeanization of Citizenship?', in Maria Green Cowles, James Caporaso and Thomas Risse (eds.), *Transforming Europe. Europeanization and Domestic Change*. Ithaca, NY: Cornell University Press, pp. 180–97

2005. 'International Institutions and Socialization in Europe: Introduction', *International Organization* 59(4): 801–26

Chyrssouchoou, Dimitris N. 2002 'Europe, in the Republican Imagination', ConWEB Webpapers on Constitutionalism and Governance Beyond the State, 3, 2002

Cini, Michelle (ed.) 2003. *European Union Politics*. Oxford: Oxford University Press

Cohen, Jean L. 2004. 'Whose Sovereignty? Empire Versus International Law', *Ethics and International Affairs* 18(3): 1–24

Colombo, Monica 2003. 'Reflexivity and Narratives in Action Research: A Discursive Approach', *Forum Qualitative Sozialforschung / Forum: Qualitative Social Research* 4(2); www.qualitative-research.net/fqs-texte/2-03/2-03colombo-e.htm [accessed 25 July 2007]

Copi, Irving M. 1998 [1961]. *Introduction to Logic*. Upper Saddle River, NJ: Prentice-Hall

Cowles, Maria Green, Caporaso, James A. and Risse-Kappen, Thomas 2001. *Transforming Europe: Europeanization and domestic change*. Ithaca, NY: Cornell University Press

Craig, Paul 2001. 'Constitutions, Constitutionalism, and the European Union', *European Law Journal* 7(2): 125–50

Crawford, Neta 2004. 'Understanding Discourse: A Method of Ethical Argument Analysis', *Qualitative Methods Symposium: Discourse and Content Analysis* (2): 22–5

Curtin, Deirdre 1996. 'Betwixt and Between: Democracy and Transparency in the Governance of the European Union', in J. A. Winter, D. M. Curtin, A. E. Kellerman and B. de Witte (eds.), *Reforming the Treaty on European Union: The Legal Debate*. The Hague/Boston/London: Kluwer Law International, pp. 95–121

Curtin, Deirdre and Dekker, Ige 1999. 'The EU as a "Layered" International Organization: Institutional Unity in Disguise', in Paul Craig and Grainne De Burca (eds.), *The Evolution of EU Law*. Oxford: Oxford University Press, pp. 83–136

Daase, Christopher 2005. Zeitschrift für Internationale Beziehungen **12**(2), editor's introduction to the *Symposium on the Constitutional Debate*

Dahl, Robert A. 1971. *Polyarchy. Participation and Opposition*. New Haven and London: Yale University Press

Dallmayr, Fred 2001. 'Conversation Across Boundaries: Political Theory and Global Diversity', *Millennium: Journal of International Studies* **30**(2): 331–47

De Burca, Grainne, Beaumont, Paul, Lyons, Carole and Walker, Neil (eds.) 2002. *Convergence and Divergence in European Public Law*. Oxford: Hart Publishing

De Burca, Grainne and Scott, Joanne (eds.) 2000. *Constitutional Change in the EU: From Uniformity to Flexibility?* Oxford: Hart Publishing
    (eds.) 2003. *The EU and the WTO: Legal and Constitutional Issues*. Oxford: Hart Publishing

De Burca, Grainne and Walker, Neil 2003. 'Law and Transnational Civil Society: Upsetting the Agenda?' *European Law Journal* **4**(9): 387–400

Deitelhoff, Nicole 2007. 'Was vom Tage übrigblieb – Inseln der Überzeugung im vermachteten Alltagsgeschäft internationalen Regierens', in Niesen and Herborth (eds.), pp. 26–56

Deitelhoff, Nicole and Müller, Harald 2005. 'Theoretical Paradise – Empirically Lost? Arguing with Habermas', *Review of International Studies* **31**(1): 167–80

Della Salla, Vincent 2001. 'Constitutionalising Governance: Democratic Dead End or Dead on Democracy?', ConWEB Webpapers on Constitutionalism and Governance Beyond the State, **6**, 2001

Den Boer, Monica (ed.) 1997. *The Implementation of Schengen: First the Widening, Now the Deepening*. Maastricht: European Institute of Public Administration

Deutsch, Karl W. 1953. 'The Growth of Nations: Some Recurrent Patterns of Political and Social Integration', *World Politics* **5**(2): 168–95

Diez, Thomas and Wiener Antje 2003. 'Introducing the Mosaic of Integration Theory', in Antje Wiener and Thomas Diez (eds.), *European Integration Theory*. Oxford: Oxford University Press, pp. 1–21

Di Fabio, Udo 2001. 'A European Constitutional Treaty: The Blueprint to the European Union', *German Law Journal* 2(14): 8; www.germanlawjournal.com/article.php?id=77 [accessed 17 September 2007]

Dimitrova, Antoaneta 2005. 'The Power of Norms in Transposition: Norms and Conditionality in Slovakia', paper presented at the workshop 'Contested Compliance in International Policy Coordination – Bridging Research on Norms and Policy Analysis', 17–18 December 2005, Portaferry, County Down, Northern Ireland

Doty, Roxanne Lynn 1993. 'Foreign Policy as Social Construction: A Post-Positivist Analysis of US Counterinsurgency Policy in the Philippines', *International Studies Quarterly* 37: 297–320.

Dunn, John 1978. 'Practising History and Social Science on "Realist" Assumptions', in Christopher Hookway and Philip Pettit (eds.), *Action and Interpretation: Studies in the Philosophy of the Social Sciences.* Cambridge: Cambridge University Press, pp. 145–75

Dworkin, Ronald M. 1978. *Taking Rights Seriously.* Cambridge, MA: Harvard University Press

Eder, Klaus 2004. 'The Two Faces of Europeanization. Synchronizing a Europe Moving at Varying Speeds', *Time and Society* 13(1): 89–107

Eder, Klaus, Kantner, Cathleen and Trenz, Hans-Jörg 1993 [1988]. 'Introduction', in Jon Elster and Rune Slagstad (eds.), *Constitutionalism and Democracy.* Cambridge: Cambridge University Press, pp. 1–17

2000. 'Transnationale Öffentlichkeit und die Strukturierung politischer Kommunikation in Europa', *Antrag auf Förderung eines Forschungsvorhabens im Rahmen des DFG Schwerpunkts Regieren in Europa.* Unpublished manuscript, Humboldt University, Berlin

Eriksen, Erik Oddvar (ed.) 2005. *Making the European Polity.* London: Routledge

2006. 'Reconstituting Democracy in Europe (RECON)', EU Sixth Framework Programme, Integrated Project, Oslo, ARENA; www.arena.uio.no/news/News2006/recon_jan06.xml [accessed 22 June 2006]

2007. 'Introduction: How to Reconstitute Democracy in Europe', in Erik O. Eriksen (ed.), *How to Reconstitute Democracy in Europe.* Proceedings from the Opening Conference, Oslo, 26 January 2007. Arena Working Report No. 8/09 & RECON Report No. 3, pp. 1–6

Everson, Michelle 2004. 'Review Article: Accountability and Law in Europe: Towards a New Public Legal Order?', *Modern Law Review* 67 (1): 124–38

Fairclough, Norman 1992. 'Discourse and Text: Linguistic and Intertextual Analysis Within Discourse Analysis', *Discourse and Society* 3, 193–217

Fierke, K.M. 1998. *Changing Games, Changing Strategies.* Manchester: Manchester University Press

2006. 'Consistent Constructivism', in Tim Dunne, Milja Kurki and Steve Smith (eds.), *International Relations Theory: Discipline and Diversity*. Oxford: Oxford University Press, pp. 166–84

Fierke, K.M. and Jørgensen, Knud Erik (eds.) 2001. *Constructing International Relations: The Next Generation*. Armonk, NY: M. E. Sharpe

Fierke, K.M. and Wiener, Antje 1999. 'Constructing Institutional Interests: EU and NATO Enlargement', *Journal of European Public Policy* 6(5): 721–42

Finnemore, Martha 1996. 'Norms, Culture and World Politics: Insights from Sociology's Institutionalism', *International Organization* 50(2): 325–347
2000. 'Are Legal Norms Distinctive?' *Journal of International Law and Politics* 32: 699–705

Finnemore, Martha and Sikkink, Kathryn 1998. 'International Norm Dynamics and Political Change', *International Organization* 52(4): 887–917

Finnemore, Martha and Toope, Stephen J. 2001. 'Alternatives to "Legalization": Richer Views of Law and Politics', *International Organization* 55(3): 743–58

Fischer-Lescano, Andreas 2005. *Globalverfassung. Die Geltungsbegründung der Menschenrechte*. Weilerswist: Velbrueck Wissenschaft

Fiske, John 1987. *Television Culture*. London: Routledge

Fiske, Susan T. and Taylor, Shelley E. 1991. *Social Cognition*. New York: McGraw-Hill

Florini, Ann 1996. 'The Evolution of International Norms', *International Studies Quarterly* 40: 363–89

Fossum, John Erik and Eriksen, Erik O. 2007. 'Reconstituting Democracy in Europe', in Erik O. Eriksen (ed.), *How to Reconstitute Democracy in Europe*. Proceedings from the Opening Conference, Oslo, 26 January 2007. Arena Working Report No. 8/09 & RECON Report No. 3, pp. 7–47

Foucault, Michel 1997. 'What Is Enlightenment?', in Sylvere Lotriner (ed.), *The Politics of Truth*. New York: Columbia University Press, pp. 101–34

Franck, Thomas 1990. *The Power of Legitimacy*. Oxford: Oxford University Press

Fraser, Nancy 2005. 'Re-Framing Justice in a Globalizing World', paper presented at the conference 'Intersubjectivity and International Politics: Motives from the Work of Jürgen Habermas in International Relations and Political Theory', Johann Wolfgang Goethe-University Frankfurt/Main, Campus Westend, 16–18 June 2005; www.gesellschaftswissenschaften. uni-frankfurt.de/index.pl/konferenz_intersubjektivitaet_programm [accessed 22 June 2006]

Friese, Heidrun and Wagner, Peter 2002. 'Survey Article: The Nascent Political Philosophy of the European Polity', *Journal of Political Philosophy* 10(3): 342–64

Gagnon, Alain-G. and Tully, James (eds.) 2001. *Multinational Democracies.* Cambridge: Cambridge University Press

Gallie, Walter Bryce 1956. 'Art as an Essentially Contested Concept', *Philosophical Quarterly* 6(23): 97–114

Galloway, Donald 1998. 'Citizenship – A Jurisprudential Paradox', in Massimo La Torre (ed.), *European Citizenship*. Dordrecht: Kluwer, pp. 65–83

Garfinkel, Harold 1967. *Studies in Ethnomethodology*. Englewood Cliffs, NJ: Prentice-Hall

Geddes, Andrew 2000. *Immigration and European Integration: Towards Fortress Europe?* Manchester: Manchester University Press

Gerhards, Jürgen 1992. 'Dimensionen und Strategien öffentlicher Diskurse', *Journal für Sozialforschung* 32(3/4): 307–18

Gerth, H.H. and Mills, C. Wright (eds.) 1972 [1946]. *From Max Weber: Essays in Sociology*. New York: Oxford University Press

Giddens, Anthony 1979. *Central Problems in Social Theory*. Berkeley and Los Angeles: University of California Press

 1984. *The Constitution of Society*. Berkeley and Los Angeles: University of California Press

Gordon, Scott 1999. *Controlling the State: Constitutionalism from Ancient Athens to Today*. Cambridge, MA, and London: Harvard University Press

Grawert, Rolf 1973. *Staat und Staatsangehörigkeit*. Berlin: Duncker and Humblot

Green, Philip 1993. '"Democracy" as a Contested Idea', in Philip Green, *Democracy*. Atlantic Highlands, NJ: Humanities Press, pp. 2–18

Haas, Peter M. 1992. 'Epistemic Communities and International Policy Coordination', *International Organization* 46(1): 187–224

Habermas, Jürgen 1985 [1982]. *Zur Logik der Sozialwissenschaften*. Frankfurt/Main: Suhrkamp

 1988a. *Theorie des kommunikativen Handelns*, vol. I. Frankfurt/Main: Suhrkamp

 1988b. *Theorie des kommunikativen Handelns*, vol. II. Frankfurt/Main: Suhrkamp

 1992. *Faktizität und Geltung*. Frankfurt/Main: Suhrkamp

 1994. 'Über den internen Zusammenhang von Rechtsstaat und Demokratie', in Ulrich K. Preuss (ed.), *Zum Begriff der Verfassung: Die Ordnung des Politischen*. Frankfurt/Main: Fischer, pp. 83–94

 1998. *Die postnationale Konstellation. Politische Essays*. Frankfurt/Main: Suhrkamp

2004. 'Hat die Konstitutionalisierung des Völkerrechts noch eine Chance?', in Jürgen Habermas, *Der gespaltene Westen*. Frankfurt/Main: Suhrkamp, pp. 113–93

2005. 'Zur Konstitutionalisierung des Völkerrechts', paper presented at the conference 'Intersubjectivity and International Politics: Motives from the Work of Jürgen Habermas in International Relations and Political Theory', Johann Wolfgang Goethe-University Frankfurt/Main, Campus Westend, 16–18 June 2005; www.gesellschaftswissenschaften. uni-frankfurt.de/index.pl/konferenz_intersubjektivitaet_programm [accessed 22 June 2006]

Hall, Peter 1989. *The Political Power of Economic Ideas*. Princeton, NJ: Princeton University Press

Hall, Peter and Taylor, Rosemary 1996. 'Political Science and the Three New Institutionalisms', *Political Studies* 44(4): 936–57

Harlow, Carol 2002. *Accountability in the European Union*. Oxford: Hart Publishing.

Hart, Vivien 2001. 'Constitution-Making and the Transformation of Conflict', *Peace and Change* 26(2): 153–76

Hauck, Gerhard 1984. *Geschichte der soziologischen Theorie. Eine ideologiekritische Einführung*. Reinbeck bei Hamburg: Rowohlt

Hix, Simon 1999. *The Political System of the European Union*. Houndmills and London: Macmillan

Hoffmann-Lange, Ursula 1990. 'Eliten in der modernen Demokratie', in Ursula Hoffmann-Lange, *Eliten in der Bundesrepublik Deutschland*. Stuttgart: Kohlhammer, pp. 11–27

Holbrook, Allyson L., Krosnick, Jon A., Carson, Richard T. and Mitchell, Robert Cameron 2000. 'Violating Conversational Conventions Disrupts Cognitive Processing of Attitude Questions', *Journal of Experimental Social Psychology* 36: 465–94

Huffschmid, Anne 2004. *Diskursgerilla: Wortergreifung und Widersinn. Die Zapatistas im Spiegel der mexikanischen und internationalen Öffentlichkeit*. Heidelberg: Synchron Publishers

Hüllsse, Rainer 2003. *Metaphern der EU-Erweiterung als Konstruktionen europäischer Identität*. Baden-Baden: Nomos

Ikenberry, G. John and Slaughter, Anne-Marie 2006. *Forging a World of Liberty under Law: US National Security in the 21st Century*. Princeton: Woodrow Wilson School of Public and International Affairs, Princeton University

Ireland, Patrick 2004. *Becoming Europe: Immigration, Integration and the Welfare State*. Pittsburgh: Pittsburgh University Press

Jachtenfuchs, Markus, Diez, Thomas and Jung, Sabine 1998. 'Which Europe? Conflicting Models of a Legitimate European Political Order', *European Journal of International Relations* 4(4): 409–45

Jackson, Robert 2005 [2000]. *The Global Covenant. Human Conduct in a World of States*. Cambridge: Cambridge University Press

Jacobson, David 1996. *Rights Across Borders: Immigration and the Decline of Citizenship*. Baltimore: Johns Hopkins University Press

Jenson, Jane 2007. 'The European Union's Citizenship Regime: Creating Norms and Building Practices', *Comparative European Politics* 5(1): 53–69

Jenson, Jane and Phillips, Susan 1996. 'Staatsbürgerschaftsregime im Wandel – oder: Die Gleichberechtigung wird zu Markte getragen. Das Beispiel Kanada', *Prokla. Zeitschrift für kritische Sozialwissenschaft* 26 (4): 515–42

Joerges, Christian 2002. '"Deliberative Supranationalism" – Two Defences', *European Law Journal* 8: 133–51

Johnston, Alastair Iain 2001. 'Treating International Institutions as Social Environments', *International Studies Quarterly* 45(4): 487–515

Kahn, Paul W. 1999. *The Cultural Study of Law. Reconstructing Legal Scholarship*. Chicago: Chicago University Press

Kalish, Donald 1964. 'Review of "Introduction to Logic" by Irving M Copi', *Journal of Symbolic Logic* 29(2): 92–3

Kaplan, William 1993. 'Who Belongs? Changing Concepts of Citizenship and Nationality', in William Kaplan (ed.), *Belonging: The Meaning and Future of Canadian Citizenship*. Montreal and Kingston: McGill-Queen's University Press, pp. 245–64

Katzenstein, Peter J. 1993. 'Coping with Terrorism: Norms and Internal Security in Germany and Japan', in Judith Goldstein and Robert O. Keohane, (eds.), *Ideas and Foreign Policy: Beliefs, Institutions, and Political Change*. Ithaca, NY: Cornell University Press, pp. 265–95

(ed.) 1996. *Cultural Norms and National Security: Police and Military in Post War Japan*. Ithaca, NY: Cornell University Press

Katzenstein, Peter J., Keohane, Robert O. and Krasner, Stephen D. 1998. 'International Organization and the Study of World Politics', *International Organization* 52(4): 645–85

Katzenstein, Peter J. and Okawara, Nobuo 1993. 'Japan's National Security: Structures, Norms, and Policies', *International Security* 17(4): 84–118

Keck, Margaret E. and Sikkink, Kathryn 1998. *Activities Beyond Borders*. Ithaca, NY, and London: Cornell University Press

Kelsen, Hans 1968. 'The Essence of International Law', in Karl W. Deutsch and Stanley Hoffmann (eds.), *The Relevance of International Law*. Cambridge, MA: Schenkmann, pp. 85–92

Kemmerling, Garth 2002. *Philosophy and Logic*; www.philosophypages.com/lg/e04.htm [accessed 23 June 2006]

King, Gary, Keohane, Robert O. and Verba, Sidney 1994. *Designing Social Inquiry*. Princeton: Princeton University Press

Klotz, Audie 1995. 'Norms Reconstituting Interests: Global Racial Equality and US Sanctions Against South Africa', *International Organization* 49(3): 451–78

2001. 'Can We Speak a Common Constructivist Language?', in Fierke and Jørgensen (eds.), pp. 223–35

Knill, Christoph and Lenschow, Andrea (eds.) 2000. *Implementing EU Environmental Policy. New Directions and Old Problems*. Manchester: Manchester University Press

Kommers, Donald P. and Thompson, W.J. 1995. 'Fundamentals in the Liberal Constitutional Tradition', in Joachim Jens Hesse and Nevil Johnson (eds.), *Constitutional Policy and Change in Europe*. Oxford: Oxford University Press, pp. 23–45

Koskenniemi, Martti 2002. '"The Lady Doth Protest Too Much" Kosovo, and the Turn to Ethics in International Law', *Modern Law Review* 65(2), 159–75

2007. 'The Fate of Public International Law: Between Technique and Politics', *Modern Law Review* 70(1): 1–30

Koslowski, Rey and Kratochwil, Friedrich 1994. 'Understanding Change in International Politics: The Soviet Empire's Demise and the International System', *International Organization* 48(2): 215–47

Kostakopoulou, Dora 2005. 'Ideas, Norms and European Citizenship: Explaining Institutional Change', *Modern Law Review* 68(2): 233–67

Kowert, Paul and Legro, Jeffrey 1996. 'Norms, Identity, and Their Limits: A Theoretical Reprise', in Katzenstein (ed.), pp. 451–97

Kratochwil, Friedrich 1984. 'The Force of Prescriptions', *International Organization* 38(4): 685–708

1989. *Rules, Norms, and Decisions: On the Conditions of Practical and Legal Reasoning in International Relations and Domestic Affairs*. Cambridge: Cambridge University Press

1994. 'Citizenship: The Border of Order', *Alternatives* 19: 485–506.

Kratochwil, Friedrich and Ruggie, John G. 1986. 'International Organization: A State of the Art on an Art of the State', *International Organization* 40(4): 753–75

Kruse, Jan 2007. 'Seminar-Reader "Introduction to Qualitative Interview Research"', unpublished manuscript, University of Freiburg

Kymlicka, Will 1995. *The Rights of Minority Cultures*. Oxford: Oxford University Press

Lasswell, Harold Dwight 1946. 'Describing the Contents of Communication', in Bruce Lannes Smith, Harold Dwight Laswell and Ralph Droz Casey (eds.), *Propaganda, Communication, and Public Opinion: A Comprehensive Reference Guide*. Princeton: Princeton University Press, pp. 74–94

Leibfried, Stephan and Zürn, Michael 2005. *Transformations of the State?* Cambridge: Cambridge University Press

Lenschow, Andrea 1997. 'Variation in EC Environmental Policy Integration: Agency Push Within Complex Institutional Structures', *Journal of European Public Policy* 4: 109–27

Lessig, Lawrence 1996. 'Post Constitutionalism. Review of "Constitutional Domains: Democracy, Community, Management" by Robert C Post. Cambridge: Harvard University Press. 1995', *Michigan Law Review* 94 (May): 1422–70

Liebold, Renate and Trinczek, Rainer 2003. 'Experteninterview – Qualitative Methoden in der Organisationsforschung', *Forum Qualitative Research Net*; www.qualitative-research.net/organizations/or-exp-d.htm [accessed 23 June 2006]

Liese, Andrea 2001. 'Staaten am Pranger. Zur Wirkung internationaler Regime auf die innerstaatliche Menschenrechtspolitik', unpublished dissertation, Department of Political Science, University of Bremen

Lister, Ruth 2003. *Citizenship: Feminist Perspectives*. New York: New York University Press

Locher, Birgit 2002. 'Trafficking in Women in the European Union. A Norm-Based Constructivist Approach', unpublished dissertation, Department of Political Science, University of Bremen

Loewenstein, Karl 1965. *Political Power and the Governmental Process*. Chicago: University of Chicago Press

Lustick, Ian S. 1996. 'History, Historiography, and Political Science: Multiple Historical Records and the Problem of Selection Bias', *American Political Science Review* 90(3): 605–18

Maddox, Graham 1982. 'A Note on the Meaning of "Constitution"', *American Political Science Review* 76(4): 805–9

Maduro, Miguel Poiares 2003. 'Europe and the Constitution: What if This Is as Good as it Gets?', in Weiler and Wind (eds.), pp. 74–102

Manners, Ian 2002. 'Normative Power Europe: A Contradiction in Terms?' *Journal of Common Market Studies* 40(2): 235–58

  2006. 'Normative Power Europe Reconsidered: Beyond the Crossroads', *Journal of European Public Policy* 13(2): 182–99

March, James G. and Olsen, Johan P. 1989. *Rediscovering Institutions: The Organizational Basis of Politics*. New York: Free Press

  1998. 'The Institutional Dynamics of International Political Orders', *International Organization* 52(4): 943–69

Marcussen, Martin, Risse, Thomas, Engelmann-Martin, Daniela, Knopf, Hans-Jochen and Roscher, Klaus 1999. 'Constructing Europe? The Evolution of French, British and German Nation-State Identities', *Journal of European Public Policy* 6(3), Special Issue: 614–33

Marshall, T. H. 1947 [1958]. *Constitutionalism: Ancient and Modern*. Ithaca, NY: Cornell University Press

1950. *Citizenship and Social Class*. Cambridge: Cambridge University Press

McIlwain, Charles H. 1958 [1947]. *Constitutionalism: Ancient and Modern.* Ithaca, NY: Cornell University Press.

McKenna, Marian C. 1993. 'Introduction: A Legacy of Questions', in Marian C. McKenna, *The Canadian and American Constitutions in Comparative Perspective*. Calgary: University of Calgary Press, pp. ix–xlvi

Melucci, Alberto 1988. 'Getting Involved: Identity and Mobilization in Social Movements', *International Social Movement Research* 1: 329–48

1989. *Nomads of the Present: Social Movements and Individual Needs in Contemporary Society*. London: Hutchinson Radius

Merton, Robert K. 1948. 'The Bearing of Empirical Research upon the Development of Social Theory', *American Sociological Review* 13(5): 505–15

Miller, Fred 2002. *Aristotle's Political Theory, The Stanford Encyclopedia of Philosophy [Fall 2002 Edition]*, ed. Edward N. Zalta; http://plato.stanford.edu/archives/fall2002/entries/aristotle-politics/ [accessed 7 January 2006]

Milliken, Jennifer 1999. 'The Study of Discourse in International Relations: A Critique of Research and Methods', *European Journal of International Relations* 5(2): 225–54

Moellers, Christoph 2003. 'Begriffe der Verfassung in Europa', in Armin von Bogdandy (ed.), *Europäisches Verfassungsrecht. Theoretische und dogmatische Grundzüge*. Heidelberg: Springer, pp. 1–57

Morgan, Glyn 2006. 'Public Justification and European Integration', paper prepared for the conference on 'The Political Theory of the European Union', the German Political Science Association at Johann Wolfgang Goethe-University, Frankfurt/Main, 15–17 June; www.gesellschafts wissenschaften.uni-frankfurt.de/index.pl/konferenz_theorie_der_eu [accessed 26 June 2006]

Morris, Richard T. 1956. 'A Typology of Norms', *American Sociological Review* 21(5): 610–13

Müller, Harald 2001. 'International Relations as Communicative Action', in Fierke and Jørgensen (eds.), pp. 160–78

2004. 'Arguing, Bargaining, and All That: Reflections on the Relationship of Communicative Action and Rationalist Theory in Analysing International Negotiation', *European Journal of International Relations* 10(3): 395–495

Murphy, Walter 1993. 'Constitutions, Constitutionalism and Democracy', in Douglas Greenberg, Stanley N. Katz, Melanie Beth Oliviero and Steven G. Wheatley (eds.), *Constitutionalism and Democracy: Transitions in the Contemporary World*. New York and Oxford: Open University Press, pp. 3–25

Mwihaki, Alice 2004. 'Meaning as Use: A Functional View of Semantics and Pragmatics', *Swahili Forum* **11**: 127–39

Nastri, Jacqueline, Pena, Jorge and Hancock, Jeffrey T. 2006. 'The Construction of Away Messages: A Speech Act Analysis', *Journal of Computer-Mediated Communication* **11**: 1025–45

Nettl, Peter 1968. 'The State as a Conceptual Variable', *World Politics* **20**: 559–92

Neunreither, Karlheinz and Wiener, Antje 2000. *European Integration after Amsterdam: Institutional Dynamics and Prospects for Democracy*. Oxford: Oxford University Press

Niesen, Peter and Herborth, Benjamin (eds.) 2007. *Anarchie der kommunikativen Freiheit. Jürgen Habermas und die Theorie der internationalen Politik*. Frankfurt/Main: Suhrkamp

Olsen, Johan P. 2004. 'Survey Article: Unity, Diversity and Democratic Institutions: Lessons from the European Union', *Journal of Political Philosophy* **12**(4): 261–95

Onuf, Nicholas 2002. 'Institutions, Intentions and International Relations', *Review of International Studies* **28**: 211–28

Pateman, Carol 1970. *Participation and Democratic Theory*. Cambridge: Cambridge University Press

Peters, Anne 2001. *Elemente einer Theorie der Verfassung Europas*. Berlin: Duncker and Humblot

Peters, Bernhard 2005. 'Public Discourse, Identity and the Problem of Democratic Legitimacy', in Eriksen (ed.), pp. 84–123

Petite, Michel 1998. *The Treaty of Amsterdam*, Jean Monnet Papers, Harvard Law School; www.jeanmonnetprogram.org/papers/98/98-2-.html [accessed 19 September 2007]

Pettit, Philip 1999. *Republicanism: A Theory of Freedom and Government*. Oxford: Oxford University Press

Pfister, Thomas 2007. 'The Changing Nature of Citizenship in the European Union: Implementing Gender Equality in Germany, Hungary and the United Kingdom', unpublished doctoral dissertation, Queen's University, Belfast

Preuss, Ulrich K. 1994. 'Der Begriff der Verfassung und ihre Beziehung zur Politik', in Ulrich K. Preuss, *Zum Begriff der Verfassung: Die Ordnung des Politischen*. Frankfurt/Main: Fischer, pp. 7–33

Price, Richard and Reus-Smit, Christian 1998. 'Dangerous Liaisons? Critical Internatioanl Theory and Constructivism', *European Journal of International Relations* **4**(3): 259–94

Puetter, Uwe 2006. *The Eurogroup as a Forum for Informal Deliberation Among Ministers*. Manchester: Manchester University Press

Puetter, Uwe and Wiener, Antje 2007. 'Accommodating Normative Divergence in World Politics: European Foreign Policy Coordination', *Journal of Common Market Studies* 45(5): 1063–86

Puntscher-Riekmann, Sonja 2007. 'In Search of Lost Norms: Is Accountability the Solution to the Legitimacy Problems of the European Union?', *Comparative European Politics* 5(1): 121–37

Radaelli, Claudio M. 2000. 'Policy Transfer in the European Union: Institutional Isomorphism as a Source of Legitimacy', *Governance: An International Journal of Policy and Administration* 13(1): 25–43

Rawls, John 1971. *A Theory of Justice*. Cambridge, MA: Belknap Press of Harvard University Press

Reus-Smit, Christian 1997. 'The Constitutional Structure of International Society and the Nature of Fundamental Institutions', *International Organization* 51(4): 555–89

2001a. 'Human Rights and the Social Construction of Sovereignty', *Review of International Studies* 27: 519–38

2001b. 'The Strange Death of Liberal International Theory', *European Journal of International Law* 12(3): 573–93

2003. 'Constructivism', in Scott Burchill, Andrew Linklater, Richard Devetak *et al.* (eds.), *Theories of International Relations*. Houndsmills, Basingstoke: Palgrave Macmillan, pp. 209–30

Riesenberg, Peter N. 1992. *Citizenship in the Western Tradition: Plato to Rousseau*. Chapel Hill: University of North Carolina Press

Risse, Thomas 2000. '"Let's Argue!" Communicative Action in World Politics', *International Organization* 54(1): 1–39

Risse, Thomas and Ropp, Stephen C. 1999. 'International Human Rights Norms and Domestic Change: Conclusions', in Risse, Ropp and Sikkink (eds.), pp. 234–78

Risse, Thomas, Ropp, Stephen C. and Sikkink, Kathryn (eds.) 1999. *The Power of Human Rights: International Norms and Domestic Change*. Cambridge: Cambridge University Press

Risse-Kappen, Thomas (ed.) 1995. *Bringing Transnational Relations Back In: Non-State Actors, Domestic Structures and International Institutions*. Cambridge: Cambridge University Press

Rittberger, Berthold and Schimmelfennig, Frank (eds.) 2007. 'Constitutio-nalisation in the European Union', *Journal of European Public Policy* 14, Special Issue

Rosamond, Ben and Wincott, Daniel 2006. 'Constitutionalism, European Integration and British Political Economy', *British Journal of Politics and International Relations* 8(1): 1–14

Rosenfeld, Michel 1994. 'Modern Constitutionalism as Interplay Between Identity and Diversity', in Michel Rosenfeld (ed.), *Constitutionalism,*

Identity, Difference and Legitimacy: Theoretical Perspectives. Durham and London: Duke University Press, pp. 3–38

1997. 'Review: Constitutional Policy and Change in Europe', *American Political Science Review* 91(1): 215–16

Rosert, Elvira and Schirmbeck, Sonja 2006. 'Zur Erosion internationaler Normen: Nukleares Tabu und Folterverbot', Nachwuchstagung der Sektion Internationale Politik der DVPW, 26–28 May 2006, Arnoldshain

Ruggie, John Gerard 1998a. *Constructing the World Polity*. London: Routledge

1998b. 'What Makes the World Hang Together? Neo-Utilitarianism and the Social Constructivist Challenge', *International Organization* 52(4): 855–85

Ruiter, D.W.P. 1993. *Institutional Legal Facts, Legal Powers and their Effects*. London: Kluwer

Sajó, András 1995. 'Reading the Invisible Constitution: Judicial Review in Hungary', *Oxford Journal of Legal Studies* 15: 253–67

Sartori, Giovanni 1962. 'Constitutionalism: A Preliminary Discussion', *American Political Science Review* 56(4): 853–64

Scharpf, Fritz W. 1995. *Demokratische Politik in Europa*, Europäisches Zentrum für Staatswissenschaften und Staatspraxis, Discussion Paper, No. 4

2000. 'The Viability of Advanced Welfare States in the International Economy: Vulnerabilities and Options', *Journal of European Public Policy* 7(2): 190–228

Schimmelfennig, Frank 2001. 'The Community Trap: Liberal Norms, Rhetorical Action, and the Eastern Enlargement of the European Union', *International Organization* 55(1): 47–80

2003. 'Liberal Intergovernmentalism', in Antje Wiener and Thomas Diez (eds.), *European Integration Theory*. Oxford: Oxford University Press, pp. 75–94

Schimmelfennig, Frank and Sedelmeier, Ulrich 2002. 'Theorizing EU Enlargement: Research Focus, Hypotheses, and the State of Research', *Journal of European Public Policy* 9(4): 500–28

(eds.) 2005. *The Politics of European Union Enlargement: Theoretical Approaches*. London: Routledge

Schluchter, Wolfgang 2003. 'The Sociology of Law as an Empirical Theory of Validity', *European Sociological Review* 19(5): 537–49

Schmitter, Philippe C. 2000. *How to Democratize the EU ... And Why Bother?* New York: Rowman and Littlefield

Schneider, Jens 2001. *Deutsch Sein – Das Eigene, das Fremde und die Vergangenheit im Selbstbild des vereinten Deutschland*. Frankfurt/Main: Campus

Schutz, Alfred 1932. *Der sinnhafte Aufbau der sozialen Welt; eine Einleitung in die verstehende Soziologie*. Vienna: J. Springer

Schwellnus, Guido 2005. 'The Adoption of Non-Discrimination and Minority Protection Rules in Romania, Hungary and Poland', in Frank Schimmelfennig and Ulrich Sedelmeier (eds.), *The Europeanization of Central and Eastern Europe*. Ithaca, NY: Cornell University Press, pp. 51–70

  2007. 'Dynamics of Norm-Construction and Norm- Resonance in the Context of EU Enlargement: Minority Rights in Poland', unpublished doctoral dissertation, Queen's University, Belfast

Scott, Shirley V. 2004. *International Law in World Politics: An Introduction*. Boulder, CO, and London: Lynn Rienner Publishers

Searle, John 1995. *The Construction of Social Reality*. New York: Free Press

Shaw, Jo 1997. 'The Many Pasts and Futures of Citizenship in the European Union', *European Law Review* 22(6): 554–72

  2001. 'Process, Responsibility and Inclusion in EU Constitutionalism', ConWEB Webpapers on Constitutionalism and Governance Beyond the State, 4, 2001; www.bath.ac.uk/esml/conWEB/conweb_archive.htm [accessed 22 August 2007]

  2007. *Transforming Citizenship? The European Union, Electoral Rights and the Restructuration of European Public Space*. Cambridge: Cambridge University Press

Sikkink, Kathryn 1993. 'The Power of Principled Ideas: Human Rights Policies in the United States and Western Europe', in Judith Goldstein and Robert O. Keohane (eds.), *Ideas and Foreign Policy: Beliefs, Institutions, and Political Change*. Ithaca, NY: Cornell University Press, pp. 139–70

Sjursen, Helene (ed.) 2006. 'What New Kind of Power?', *Journal of European Public Policy* 13(2), Special Issue: 169–81

Skinner, Quentin 1988. 'Meaning and Understanding in the History of Ideas', in James Tully (ed.), *Meaning and Context: Quentin Skinner and his Critics*. Princeton: Princeton University Press, pp. 29–67

Skocpol, Theda 1986. 'Bringing the State Back In: Strategies of Analysis in Current Research', in Peter Evans, Dietrich Rueschemeyer and Theda Skocpol (eds.), *Bringing the State Back In*. Cambridge: Cambridge University Press, pp. 3–34

Slaughter, Anne-Marie 2004. *A New World Order*. Princeton: Princeton University Press

Slaughter, Anne-Marie and Burke-White, William 2002. 'An International Constitutional Moment', *Harvard International Law Journal* 43(1): 1–21

Smith, Karen E. 2003. 'EU External Relations', in Cini (ed.), pp. 229–45

Snyder, Francis 1990. *New Directions in European Community Law*. London: Weidenfeld and Nicholson

Soja, Edward W. 1989. *Postmodern Geographies: The Reassertion of Space in Critical Social Theory*. London: Verso

Somers, Margaret 1994. 'Rights, Relationality, and Membership: Rethinking the Making and Meaning of Citizenship', *Law and Social Inquiry* **19**: 63–112

Soysal, Yasemin N. 1994. *The Limits of Citizenship: Migrants and Postnational Membership in France*. Chicago: University of Chicago Press

Stone, Alec 1994. 'What Is a Supranational Constitution? An Essay in International Relations Theory', *Review of Politics* **55**: 444–71

Stone Sweet, Alec 1998. 'Constitutional Dialogues in the European Community', in Anne-Marie Slaughter, Alec Stone Sweet and J.H.H. Weiler (eds.), *The European Court and the National Courts: Legal Change in its Social, Political and Economic Context*. Oxford: Hart Publishing, pp. 303–28

   2002. 'Constitutional Courts and Parliamentary Democracy', *West European Politics* **25**(1): 77–100

Tamanaha, Brian Z. 2004. *On the Rule of Law. History, Politics, Theory*. Cambridge: Cambridge University Press

Tarrow, Sidney 1995. 'Review: Bridging the Quantitative-Qualitative Divide in Political Science', *American Political Science Review* **89**(2): 471–4

Taylor, Charles 1993. 'To Follow a Rule ...', in Craig Calhoun, Edward LiPuma and Moishe Postone (eds.), *Bourdieu: Critical Perspectives*. Cambridge: Polity Press, pp. 45–60

   1994. *Multiculturalism: Examining the Politics of Recognition*. Princeton: Princeton University Press

   2001. 'Foreword', in Gagnon and Tully (eds.), pp. xiii–xv

Tilly, Charles 1975. 'Reflections on the History of State-Making', in Charles Tilly (ed.), *The Formation of National States in Western Europe*. Princeton: Princeton University Press, pp. 3–83

   1980. 'Two Callings of Social History', *Theory and Society* **9**(5), Special Issue: 679–81

Titscher, Stefan, Meyer, Michael, Wodak, Ruth and Vetter, Eva 2005 [2000]. *Methods of Text and Discourse Analysis*. London: Sage Publishing

Toennies, Ferdinand 1988. *Gemeinschaft und Gesellschaft*. New Brunswick, NJ: Transaction Publishers

Tully, James 1995. *Strange Multiplicity: Constitutionalism in an Age of Diversity*. Cambridge: Cambridge University Press

   2000. 'Struggles over Recognition and Distribution', *Constellations* **7**(4): 469–82

   2001. 'Multinational Democracies: Introduction', in Gagnon and Tully (eds.), pp. 1–35

2002a. 'The Unfreedom of the Moderns in Comparison to their Ideals of Constitutionalism and Democracy', *Modern Law Review* 65(2): 204–28

2002b. 'The Kantian Idea of Europe: Critical and Cosmopolitan Perspectives', in Anthony Pagden (ed.), *The Idea of Europe: From Antiquity to the European Union*. Washington, DC, and Cambridge: Woodrow Wilson Center Press and Cambridge University Press, pp. 331–58

2007. 'Two Modes of Global Citizenship: An Apprenticeship Manual', unpublished manuscript, University of Victoria, Canada

Ulbert, Cornelia and Risse, Thomas 2005. 'Deliberately Changing the Discourse: What Does Make Arguing Effective?', *Acta Politica* 40(3): 351–67

Vipond, Robert C. 1996. 'Citizenship and the Charter of Rights: The Two Sides of Pierre Trudeau', *International Journal of Canadian Studies* 14 (Fall): 181

Walker, Neil 2000. 'Flexibility Within a Metaconstitutional Frame: Reflections on the Future of Legal Authority in Europe', in De Burca and Scott (eds.), pp. 9–30

2002. 'The Idea of Constitutional Pluralism', *Modern Law Review* 65(3): 317–59

2003. 'Constitutionalising Enlargement, Enlarging Constitutionalism', *European Law Journal* 9(3): 365–85

forthcoming. 'Making a World of Difference? Habermas, Cosmopolitanism and the Constitutionalization of International Law', in O.P. Shabani (ed.), *Multiculturalism and the Law: Critical Debates*. Cardiff: University of Wales Press

Weber, Max 1972 [1946]. 'Politics as Vocation', in Gerth and Mills (eds.), pp. 77–128

1978. *Economy and Society: An Outline of Interpretive Sociology* (2 vols.), ed. Guenther Roth and Claus Wittich. Berkeley: University of California Press

1984 [1921]. *Soziologische Grundbegriffe*. Tübingen: J. C. B. Mohr (Paul Siebeck).

1988. 'Die "Objektivität" sozialwissenschaftlicher und sozialpolitischer Erkenntnis. 1904', in Max Weber, *Gesammelte Aufsätze zur Wissenschaftslehre*. Tübingen: J. C. B. Mohr (Paul Siebeck), pp. 146–214

Weiler, J.H.H. 1986. 'Eurocracy and Distrust: Some Questions Concerning the Role of the European Court of Justice in the Protection of Fundamental Human Rights within the Legal Order of the European Communities', *Washington Law Review* 101: 1103–42

1999. *The Constitution of Europe: 'Do the New Clothes Have an Emperor?' and Other Essays on European Integration*. Cambridge and New York: Cambridge University Press

2003. 'In Defence of the Status Quo: Europe's Constitutional Sonderweg', in Weiler and Wind (eds.), pp. 7–26

Weiler, J.H.H. and Wind, Marlene (eds.) 2003. *European Constitutionalism Beyond the State*. Cambridge: Cambridge University Press

Weinberger, O. 1991. *Law, Institution and Legal Practice: Fundamental Problems of Legal Theory and Social Philosophy*. Dordrecht: Kluwer Academic Publishers

Weldes, Jutta 1998. 'Bureaucratic Politics: A Critical Constructivist Assessment', *Mershon International Studies Review* 42: 2216–25

Weldes, Jutta and Saco, Diana 1996. 'Making State Action Possible: The United States and the Discursive Construction of "The Cuban Problem", 1960–1994', *Millennium* 25(2): 361–95

Wendt, Alexander E. 1987. 'The Agent-Structure Problem in International Relations Theory', *International Organization* 41(3): 335–70

Whitman, Richard G. and Manners, Ian 2000. *The Foreign Policies of European Union Member States*. Manchester: Manchester University Press

Wiener, Antje 1997. 'Making Sense of the New Geography of Citizenship: Fragmented Citizenship in the European Union', *Theory and Society* 26 (4): 529–60

1998. *'European' Citizenship Practice: Building Institutions of a Non-State*. Boulder, CO: Westview Press

1999. 'Forging Flexibility – The British "No"' to Schengen', *European Journal of Migration and Law* 4(1): 441–63

2001. 'Zur Verfassungspolitik jenseits des Staates: Die Vermittlung von Bedeutung am Beispiel der Unionsbürgerschaft', *Zeitschrift für internationale Beziehungen* 8(1): 73–104

2003a. 'Constructivism: The Limits of Bridging Gaps', *Journal of International Relations and Development* 6(3): 253–76

2003b. 'Citizenship', in Cini (ed.), pp. 394–414

2004. 'Contested Compliance: Interventions on the Normative Structure in World Politics', *European Journal of International Relations* 10(2): 189–234

2006. 'Soft Institutions', in Bogdandy and Bast (eds.), pp. 419–49

2007a. 'The Dual Quality of Norms and Governance Beyond the State: Sociological and Normative Approaches to "Interaction"', *Critical Review of International Social and Political Philosophy* 10(1): 47–69

2007b. 'Contested Meanings of Norms: A Research Framework', *Comparative European Politics* 5(1), Special Issue: 1–17

Wiener, Antje and Della Sala, Vincent 1997. 'Constitution-Making and Citizenship Practice – Bridging the Democracy Gap in the EU?', *Journal of Common Market Studies* 35(4): 595–614

Wiener, Antje and Schwellnus, Guido 2004. 'Contested Norms of European Enlargement', in George Bermann and Katharina Pistor (eds.), *Law and Governance in an Enlarged Europe*. Oxford: Hart Publishing, pp. 455–88

Wiener, Antje and Shaw, Jo 2003. 'Evolving Norms of Constitutionalism', *European Law Journal* 9(1), Special Issue

Williamson, Andrew 2000. 'Enlargement of the Union and Human Rights Conditionality: A Policy of Destination?', *European Law Review* 25: 601–17

Witte, Bruno de 2000. 'Politics Versus Law in the EU's Approach to Ethnic Minorities', European University Institute, EUI Working Paper No. RSC 2000/4

2002. 'The Closest Thing to a Constitutional Conversation in Europe: The Semi-Permanent Treaty Revision Process', in Beaumout, Lyons and Walker (eds.), pp. 39–57

Wittgenstein, Ludwig 1984. *Tractatus logico-philosophicus. Tagebücher 1914–1916, Philosophische Untersuchungen*. Frankfurt/Main: Suhrkamp

2003 [1977]. *Philosophische Untersuchungen*. Frankfurt/Main: Suhrkamp

Wodak, Ruth 1996. *Disorders of Discourse*. London: Longman

Wolf, Klaus Dieter (ed.) 2007. *Staat und Gesellschaft – Fähig zur Reform?* Baden-Baden: Nomos.

Young, Iris M. 1990. 'Polity and Group Difference: A Critique of the Ideal of Universal Citizenship', in Cass Sunstein (ed.), *Feminism and Political Theory*. Chicago: Chicago University Press, pp. 117–42

Zürn, Michael 2000. 'Democratic Governance Beyond the Nation-State: The EU and Other International Institutions', *European Journal of International Relations* 6(2): 183–221

2005. 'Introduction: Law and Compliance at Different Levels', in Michael Zürn and Christian Joerges (eds.), *Law and Governance in Postnational Europe*. Cambridge: Cambridge University Press, pp. 1–39

Zürn, Michael, Binder, Martin, Ecker-Ehrhardt, Matthias and Radtke, Katrin 2007. 'Politische Ordnungsbildung wider Willen', *Zeitschrift für Internationale Beziehungen* 14(1): 129–64

Zürn, Michael and Checkel, Jeffrey T. 2005. 'Getting Socialized to Build Bridges: Constructivism and Rationalism, Europe and the Nation State', *International Organization* 59(4): 1065–76

Index